Grace
The Glorious Theme

Books by Lewis Sperry Chafer

He That Is Spiritual
A classic on the Christian's relation to the Holy Spirit.

Salvation
A handbook on the cross, salvation, and security.

Grace
An enlightening study of the heart of Christianity.

Satan
Expositions of his origin, purpose, and program.

True Evangelism
Sane, Scriptural methods for the church's great task.

Systematic Theology
An 8-volume comprehensive and unabridged study of the
teachings of Holy Scripture.

Major Bible Themes
a manual of Christian doctrine.

Grace
The Glorious Theme

By
Lewis Sperry Chafer, D.D., Litt.D.
Founder and first president,
Dallas Theological Seminary, Dallas, Texas

ZONDERVAN
PUBLISHING HOUSE
OF THE ZONDERVAN CORPORATION | GRAND RAPIDS, MICHIGAN 49506

ISBN 0-310-22331-8

Printed in the United States of America

83   84   85   86   87   88 — 30   29   28   27

THIS BOOK IS
AFFECTIONATELY DEDICATED TO THE LATE

CYRUS INGERSON SCOFIELD, D.D.,

FOR MANY YEARS MY
FRIEND, COUNSELOR, TEACHER,
WHO IN HIS GENERATION EXCELLED AS
CHAMPION AND EXPONENT OF GRACE

AUTHOR'S PREFACE

THROUGH false emphasis by many religious leaders, Christianity has become in the estimation of a large part of the public no more than an ethical system. The revealed fact, however, is that the supreme feature of the Christian faith is that supernatural, saving, transforming work of God, which is made possible through the infinite sacrifice of Christ and which, in sovereign grace, is freely bestowed on all who believe. God has given instruction to those who are saved, it is true, as to the manner of life which is consistent with their new heavenly calling and standing in Christ; but in its spiritual blindness, the world, led by its blind leaders, sees in Christianity only the rule of life which is secondary. The blindness of the world at this point, with the consequent neglect of all that is vital in the Christian faith, is both anticipated and explained in the Word of God.

The two foundation truths which determine all spiritual perception are that, by divine arrangement, (1) the Spirit is given only to those who are saved, and (2) spiritual understanding is made to depend exclusively on the presence of the Spirit of God in the heart.

The precise body of truth which may be understood only through the ministry of the indwelling Spirit is described as, *"things"* related to the Fa-

ther, *"things"* related to the Son, *"things"* related
to the Spirit, *"things"* to come, and *"the kingdom of
God."* We read:

"But the natural man receiveth not the things of
the Spirit of God: for they are foolishness unto him:
neither can he know them, because they are
spiritually [by the Spirit] discerned" (1 Cor. 2:14).

"Except a man be born again, he cannot see the
kingdom of God" (John 3:3).

"Even the Spirit of truth; whom the world cannot
receive, because it seeth him not, neither knoweth
him" (John 14:17).

"But if our gospel be hid, it is hid to them that
are lost: in whom the god of this world hath blinded
the minds of them which believe not, lest the light of
the glorious gospel of Christ . . . should shine unto
them" (2 Cor. 4:3, 4).

"The world by wisdom knew not God" (1 Cor.
1:21).

"He that is spiritual judgeth [discerneth] all
things, yet he himself is judged of no man"
(1 Cor. 2:15).

"Now we have received . . . the spirit which is of
God; that we might know the things that are freely
given to us of God" (1 Cor. 2:12).

"Howbeit when he, the Spirit of truth, is come, he
will guide you into all truth: for he shall not speak
of himself; but whatsoever he shall hear, that shall
he speak: and he will shew you things to come. He
shall glorify me: for he shall receive of mine, and
shall shew it unto you. All things that the Father
hath are mine: therefore said I, that he shall take of
mine, and shall shew it unto you" (John 16:13-15).

"But the anointing which ye have received of him abideth in you, and ye need not that any man teach you: but as the same anointing teacheth you of all things, and is truth, and is no lie, and even as it hath taught you, ye shall abide in him" (1 John 2:27).

"Eye hath not seen, nor ear heard, neither have entered into the heart of man, the things which God hath prepared for them that love him. But God hath revealed them unto us by his Spirit: for the Spirit searcheth all things, yea, the deep things of God" (I Cor. 2:9, 10).

"Through faith we understand" (Heb. 11:3).

Spiritual understanding is not, therefore, dependent upon human sagacity or learning; it depends only on the teaching of the indwelling Spirit. Possessing this Biblical testimony, misunderstanding at this point is without excuse.

Likewise, the terms upon which men may now be saved and thus receive the Spirit are as clearly defined in the Scripture. Salvation is by grace through faith. It is the result of the transforming work of God for man, and not the result of the work of man for God. It is that which God does for the one who trusts the Saviourhood of Christ. By that trust, Christ is personally received as the divine Redeemer who shed His blood as a sufficient ransom for the guilt and penalty of sin, as the One who reconciles by having taken away the sin of the world, and as the divine Propitiation who, as Substitute, met every indictment brought against the sinner under the holy government of God.

Since the Spirit is given only to those who are saved through faith in Christ, they alone are able to receive the particular body of truth which the Spirit teaches. Neglect of this fundamental, unalterable fact is the key-error of all modernism.

It is assumed by the modernist that any person whose education has qualified him to be an authority in matters of human learning, regardless of the new birth and the indwelling Spirit, is also qualified, because of that learning, to speak with authority concerning the things of God.

That the leaders of modernism are unregenerate men and therefore themselves spiritually blind is self-revealed by their attitude toward that truth which forms the only basis upon which, according to the Scriptures, a soul may be saved. When men avowedly disbelieve that the death of Christ was vicarious and substitutionary, they have rejected the only grounds upon which, according to the Word of God, the saving work of God righteously can be wrought for the sinner. Rejecting the saving truth of the Gospel, these men could *not* be saved upon any promise or provision of God. Though educated, religious, and sympathetic to the ethical ideals of the Bible, such men, being unregenerate, are of necessity totally blind to all that body of truth which is said to be imparted by the indwelling Spirit. Preaching and teaching under these limitations, Christianity is represented by these men as a system of ethics only.

The first step in spiritual understanding is the knowledge of God as Father. "Neither knoweth any man the Father, save the Son, and he to whomsoever the Son will reveal him" (Mt. 11:27). "And this is life eternal, that they might know thee the only true God, and Jesus Christ, whom thou hast sent'' (John 17:3).

Until God becomes real to the heart by the direct ministry of Christ as Saviour, all His ways and works are unreal. Not knowing God, the unregenerate mind is not satisfied with the explanation of the origin of things which declares that God directly created things as they are. To such a mind, it is actually easier to believe in a supposed natural development from nothing to something, and to hide all attending problems resulting from this theory behind the mists of a measureless past. If God is not real, there could be no inerrant Book; the Bible must be fallible as man; nor could God be manifest in the flesh; the Son of God must be of illegitimate birth, and though the greatest of all teachers, to them, He is really no more divine than ordinary mortals. These blind guides are forced to give some explanation to the meaning of the death of Christ. They therefore contend that He died as an heroic martyr, a loyal patriot, as a wonderful moral example of fortitude, or to show the wickedness of sin. They utterly reject the only reason given in the Word of God for the death of Christ—He died that others might not die. They brand this saving truth as ''immoral,'' and ''unworthy of the goodness of God.'' They understand little of the resurrection of Christ, His present ministry in heaven, and nothing of the revelation that He is coming again. To these religious leaders, there is no supernatural; for God is not real. There could be no immediate salvation through the Spirit. The salvation in which they believe is assumed to be the result of a self-created character, and the life to be lived is represented only as an heroic struggle of the flesh. If unregenerate men could understand anything better than this, the Word of God would be proven untrue.

It is equally true, that, those who are spiritually blind are unconscious of their blindness until they are saved by the grace and power of God through Christ. Coming thus into the light, they testify, as all who have ever been saved have testified: "Whereas I was blind, now I see." They, like all the unsaved, could be aware of their blindness if they would receive the testimony of God concerning their own limitations; but this is precisely what they will *not* do. Therefore, a notable neglect of the most vital truths of Scripture and the denial of the essential glories of divine grace is to be expected from these religious leaders who reject the only grounds of salvation through the substitutionary death of Christ.

Modernists content themselves with borrowing some ideals from the Bible while reserving the right to reject whatever is not desired. Those portions which are acceptable to the unregenerate mind are received and taught as being authorative on the basis of the fact that these ideals are in the *Bible*. Here, indeed, is strange inconsistency on the part of men who pride themselves on their scientific reasonings.

The unsaved preacher or teacher, being able to comprehend only the ethical teachings of the Scriptures, is a living proof of the truthfulness of the divine Testimony. He cannot *see* the kingdom of God. He sees nothing of the glories of divine grace —the things of the Father, the things of Christ, the things of the Spirit, and things to come. He blindly ignores every dispensational division of the Word of God and is, therefore, free within himself to draw material from the kingdom teachings of Christ and from the law of Moses while constructing his world-improvement, sociological theories which he imposes on a Christ-rejecting world.

Men of this character are sufficiently numerous in this day of apostacy to be responsible for the present-day impression that the sole objective of Christianity is the improvement of human conduct. Being blind to the real principles and purposes of saving grace, they teach that it makes little difference what is believed, it is the life that counts. Against this is the overwhelming testimony of the Word of God that every aspect of salvation and every blessing of divine grace in time and eternity is conditioned only on what is *believed.*

Influenced by these misunderstandings concerning the Truth, few serious-minded young men will choose to enter the ministerial profession; for it would mean the assumption of the role of a mere *moralist.* Common modesty generally precludes such an assumption. On the other hand, when the essential message of Christianity is seen to be the measureless, transforming grace of God with all of its eternal glories in the new creation in Christ, it is a challenge to the deepest impulses of the heart, and offers a ministry for which one may well sacrifice all.

Christians are ambassadors for Christ and are commissioned to preach the Gospel to every creature. This ministry does not consist in either the education or the moral improvement of lost men while they are on their way to hell; it is the proclamation of the mighty, redeeming, transforming grace of God which offers eternal life and eternal glory to all who will *believe*.

If it shall please God to use this exposition in any measure to the unfolding of the riches of His grace, the labor expended in its preparation will not have been in vain. This very inadequate treatment concerning the grace of God is committed to Him that He may in some way use its message to the glory of the Lord Jesus Christ.

LEWIS SPERRY CHAFER.

March, 1922.

AUTHOR'S PREFACE TO THE SECOND EDITION

The kind reception accorded to the first edition of this book is cause for thanksgiving to God. Appreciation has been general and far exceeding the merit. If there has been any blessing gained from the reading of these pages, praise should be given to Him to whom it alone belongs. As in the days of the Apostle Paul, the great issues of pure grace are sure to call out sincere question from those who, perchance, through a legalistic training do not comprehend its infinite glories. Such has been the kindly criticism of a very few out of the many.

After reviewing the book more carefully, could I recast it at all, I should perhaps give still greater emphasis to the exposition of the second of the two fundamental facts concerning the life under grace. The first being that, under grace, a separate, complete, and wholly independent rule of life is purposed for the child of God. Of that enough has been written. The second truth which might profitably be more fully developed is that of the new manner of life which is first wrought as a purpose in the heart by the Spirit and is then lived out in the power of the same Spirit, accompanied by that heavenly joy which always attends the realization of heavenly desires. Everything in the walk under grace contemplates an overflowing, Spirit-filled life, and there is no provision for any other. The carnal Christian is not urged to *try* to live a spiritual life; he is rather besought to *yield* himself to God, apart from which there can be no Spirit-filling with its realization of power.

The divine provision and plan for a life under grace is a perfect system in itself and rightfully cannot be combined or even compared with any other. The successive steps in this system are: (1) The age-characterizing fact of the Spirit indwelling every believer; (2) The filling with the Spirit resulting in a joyous, abounding delight in the whole will of God; And, (3), the imparted, enabling power of the Spirit which is sufficient for a complete realization of that will.

Is this grace-system a success? Is it really practical? Does the impelling love of a mother's heart provide a better care for her child than would be provided by a heartless obedience to a statute of the State requiring such care? The true answer is obvious. If it is practical and if it be true that the power of inwrought grace is the one and only divine program for the life of the children of God in this age, how important is this body of truth! Under this relationship all human responsibility centers in that adjustment of heart by which alone the divine power may be realized.

If this great theme is new its careful and prayerful study with an open mind may lead to the discovery of the only way by which the divine glory may be realized through a human life.

May the blessing of God rest increasingly upon this testimony to His infinite grace.

LEWIS SPERRY CHAFER.

December 1922

CONTENTS

SYNOPSIS

Contents

Contents

Contents

Contents

Contents

Contents

Grace
The Glorious Theme

CHAPTER 1

THE exact and discriminate meaning of the word *grace* should be crystal clear to every child of God. With such insight only can he feed his own soul on the inexhaustible riches which it unfolds, and with such understanding only can he be enabled clearly to pass on to others its marvelous, transforming theme. Here is a striking illustration of the fact that very much may be represented by one word. When used in the Bible to set forth the grace of God in the salvation of sinners, the word *grace* discloses not only the boundless goodness and kindness of God toward man, but reaches far beyond and indicates the supreme motive which actuated God in the creation, preservation and consummation of the universe. What greater fact could be expressed by one word?

The meaning of the word *grace,* as used in the New Testament, is not unlike its meaning as employed in common speech,—but for one important exception, namely, in the Bible the word often represents that which is limitless, since it represents realities which are infinite and eternal. It is nothing less than the unlimited love of God expressing itself in measureless grace.

The word *favor* is the nearest Biblical synonym

3

for the word *grace*. In this connection it may be observed that the one thought which is almost exclusively expressed in the New Testament by the word *grace,* is, in the Old Testament, almost exclusively expressed by the word *favor*. Grace is favor, and favor is grace. Thus, in considering the Bible teaching on this great theme, equal attention should be given to all passages wherein either the word *grace* is used or *favor* is found. *Grace* means pure unrecompensed kindness and favor. What is done in grace is done graciously. From this exact meaning there can be no departure; otherwise grace ceases to be grace. To arrive at the scope and force of the Bible doctrine of salvation by grace alone we need to follow consistently the path indicated by the exact meaning of the word.

SEVEN FUNDAMENTAL FACTS ABOUT GRACE.

First.   *Grace is not Withheld Because of Demerit.*

This fact about grace is more evident, perhaps, than any other. It is the sense of demerit more than anything else which impels a soul to cry out for the kindness and benefits of grace. So, also, grace finds its greatest triumph and glory in the sphere of human helpessness. Grace ceases to be grace if God is compelled to withdraw it in the presence of human failure and sin. In fact, grace cannot be exercised where there is the slightest degree of human merit to be recognized. On the other hand the issue of human sin must be disposed of forever. Christ the Lamb of God, having taken away the sin of the world, has by His cross forever disposed of the condemnation of sin. He has by the cross created an entirely new relation between God and man. Consequently, men are now either accepting or rejecting Christ who has borne their sins. "He that believeth on him is not condemned: but he that believeth not is condemned already, because he hath not believed in the name of the only begotten Son of God" (John 3:18). There is no middle ground. All questions of demerit have been banished. Thus God is righteously free to exercise grace in *every* case. Salvation is by grace alone.

Second. *Grace Cannot be Lessened Because of Demerit.*

God cannot propose to do less in grace for one who is sinful than He would have done had that one been less sinful. Grace is never exercised by Him in making up what may be lacking in the life and character of a sinner. In such a case, much sinfulness would call for much grace, and little sinfulness would call for little grace. The sin question has been set aside forever, and equal exercise of grace is extended to all who believe. It never falls short of being the measureless saving grace of God. Thus grace could not be increased; for it is the expression of His infinite love: it could not be diminished; for every limitation that human sin might impose on the action of a righteous God has, through the propitiation of the cross, been dismissed forever.

God does not ignore or slight the fact of human guilt and sin; for He has met these issues perfectly and finally for all men in the death of His Son. There remains no demerit, nor degrees of demerit, to be considered or recognized. By grace there is now offered alike to *all* men *all* the infinite resources of the saving power of God. The grace of God is, therefore, exercised in perfect independence of human sin, or any degree of human sin.

Third. *Grace Cannot Incur a Debt.*

An act is in no sense gracious if under any conditions a debt is incurred. Grace, being unrecompensed favor, is necessarily unrecompensed as to obligations which are past, unrecompensed as to obligations which are present, and unrecompensed as to obligations which are future. Grace must always remain unadulterated in its generosity and benefit. How emphatically this is true of the grace of God towards sinners! Yet how often this aspect of divine salvation is perverted! Infinite and eternal transformations are wrought by the power of God when He exercises His grace. He is thereby glorified and sinners are saved. Such far-reaching results cannot fail to satisfy and delight Him eternally; but He remains *unrecompensed* for His salvation through grace. What He does He bestows as a *gift*. Rightfully a benefit cannot be called a gift if it is paid for before, at the time, or after. This is a fundamental truth of the Word of God, and it is imperative that it be kept free from all confusing complications.

When a recompense for the gift of God is proposed, every element of salvation is obscured, and the true motive for Christian service is sacrificed as well. The Scriptures everywhere guard these two truths from such perversion; for, in the Bible, salvation is always presented as a *gift,* an unrecompensed *favor,* a pure *benefit* from God (John 10:28; Rom. 6:23). And, in like manner, no service is to be wrought, and no offering is to be given, with a view to *repaying* God for His gift. Any attempt to compensate God for His gift is an act so utterly out of harmony with the revealed Truth, and exhibits such a lack of appreciation of His loving bounty, that it cannot be other than distressing to the Giver. All attempts to repay His gift, be they ever so sincere, serve only to frustrate His grace and to lower the marvelous kindness of God to the sordid level of barter and trade. How faithfully we should serve Him, but never to repay Him! Service is the Christian's means of expressing his love and devotion to God, as God has expressed His love to those whom He saves by the gracious thing He has done. Christian service for God should be equally gracious.

It therefore becomes those who have received His gifts in grace to be jealous for the purity of their motives in service for Him. Unwittingly the grace of God is too often denied by well-meaning attempts to compensate God for His benefits. No semblance of the most vital facts about divine grace can be retained unless salvation is, in its every aspect, treated as a *gift* from God, and Christian service and faithfulness is deemed to be only the expression of love and gratitude to God.

According to the Scriptures, salvation is never conditioned on human faithfulness, or on the promise of human faithfulness. There is no payment required, past, present, or future. God saves unmeriting sinners in unrelated, unrecompensed, unconditioned, sovereign *grace.* Good works should follow; but with no thought of compensation. Christians are "created in Christ Jesus unto good works" (Eph. 2:10); they are to be a "peculiar people, zealous of good works" (Tit. 2:14); and "they which have believed in God might be careful to maintain good works" (Tit. 3:8). Thus, and only thus, are "good works" related to the gracious salvation from God through Christ Jesus. Grace is out of question when recompense is in question.

Fourth. *Grace is not Exercised in the Just Payment of a Debt.*

The fact is self-evident that the payment of an honest debt could never be an act of grace. In no circumstances, however, is the recognition of this truth more important than when grace is declared to be the present divine plan for the salvation of sinners. If God should discover the least degree of merit in the sinner, this, in strict righteousness, He must recognize and duly acknowledge. By such a recognition of human merit, He would be discharging an obligation toward the sinner and the discharge of that obligation toward the sinner would be the payment, or recognition, of a debt. "Now to him that worketh is the reward not reckoned of grace, but of debt" (Rom. 4:4).

It is therefore imperative that every vestige of human merit shall be set aside completely if an opportunity is provided whereby pure grace may be exercised in the salvation of men. For the sole purpose that pure grace might be exercised toward men, the human family has been placed under the divine judicial sentence of sin. It is obviously true that all men are sinners both by nature and by practice; but the present divine decree goes far beyond this evident state of sinfulness wherein one man might be deemed to be more, or less, sinful than another; for God, in this dispensation, which began with the cross, has pronounced an equal and absolute sentence of judgment against all, both Jew and Gentile. Men are now "already condemned" (John 3:18); they are "children of disobedience" (Eph. 2:2); not on the ground of their own sinfulness, but on the ground of their federal headship in fallen Adam. Men are now judicially reckoned to be "in unbelief" (Rom. 11:32); they are "under sin" (Rom. 3:9; Gal. 3:22); and they are "guilty" (Rom. 3:19). Thus all human merit has been disposed of absolutely and forever, and there is no longer the slightest possibility that, because of personal merit, a divine obligation may now exist toward any individual. The sole divine object in thus universally and judicially disposing of all human merit is clearly revealed: "For God hath concluded them all in unbelief, that he might have mercy upon all" (Rom. 11:32). Also, "But the scripture hath concluded all under sin, that the promise by faith of Jesus Christ might be given to them that believe" (Gal. 3:22).

That God now saves sinners by grace alone and apart from every human merit is the teaching of His Word: "For by grace are ye saved though faith; and that not of yourselves: it is the gift of God: not of works, lest any man should boast. For we are his workmanship, created in Christ Jesus unto good works, which God hath before ordained that we should walk in them" (Eph. 2:8-10).

In this passage the only order which can exist between divine grace and human merit is made clear. Man is permitted to *do* nothing until God has *done all* that His grace designs. "Good works" grow out of, and are made possible by, the gracious work of God. To this exact order all revelation concerning divine grace is in agreement.

A striking emphasis is given to the fact that God now saves by grace alone when the Biblical doctrines of salvation by grace and the believer's rewards for service are contrasted. Salvation, being always and only a work of God for man, is always and only by *grace* alone; while rewards, being always and only that which is merited by the faithful service of the Christian, are always and only based on *works*. Human merit is always in view in the divine bestowment of rewards; and the grace of God is never mentioned in connection with His bestowment of rewards (1 Cor. 3:9-15; 9:18-27; 2 Cor. 5:10). So, also, human works are never included as forming any part of the divine plan of salvation by grace.

An act ceases to be gracious, therefore, when it is a recognition of merit, or the payment of a just debt. "Being justified freely [without cause] by his grace through the redemption that is in Christ Jesus" (Rom. 3:24).

Fifth. *Grace is Never the Over-payment of a Debt.*

Grace is no longer grace if it is complicated in the slightest degree with the payment of a just debt. It can never be that which is added to, or a part

of, a righteous transaction. A bounty may be added
to the payment of a debt,—an extra amount above
the full measure due; but in no case should this
extra amount be considered a matter of pure grace.
The character of the bounty thus added would, of
necessity, be qualified to some extent by the relation
of the bounty to the debt. The bounty will be either
more, or less, than it would have been had it stood
alone. Inevitably it will be affected to some degree
by the righteous transaction with which it is combined. In the Word of God, as in common usage, the
word *grace*, in its exact meaning, precludes any complications with other acts or issues however righteous
and just. Grace speaks of a gift, not of barter or
trade however unequal. It is pure kindness, not
the fulfilling of an obligation. An act in order to
be gracious must stand disassociated and alone.
Divine salvation is, therefore, the *kindness* of God
toward sinners. It is not less than it would be had
they sinned less. It is not more than it would be
had they sinned more. It is wholly *unrelated* to
every question of human merit. Grace is neither
treating a person *as* he deserves, nor treating a
person *better* than he deserves. It is treating a
person *graciously* without the slightest reference to
his deserts. Grace is infinite love expressing itself
in infinite goodness.

Through the death of Christ by which He took
away the sin of the world, and through the divine
decree which has constituted all to be "under sin,"
grace is free to save in *every* case, and only grace
can save in *any* case. Divine grace is never decreased

or increased. It offers a standardized, unvarying blessing to every individual alike. The blessing is measureless since it represents in every case no less than *all* that God, being actuated by infinite love, can do.

Sixth. *Grace does not Appear in the Immediate Divine Dealings with the Sins of the Unsaved.*

It is probable that no point in the Gospel of God's saving grace is so misunderstood, and, consequently, so misstated as the revealed truth concerning the immediate divine dealings with the sins of the unsaved. It seems most difficult for the mind to grasp the fact that, as revealed in God's Word, God does not deal with any sin in mercy, or leniency. The sinner is never forgiven because God is big-hearted enough to remit the penalty, or to waive the righteous judgments. Any presentation of divine forgiveness which represents God as directly exercising clemency toward a sinner is a fatal detraction from the meaning of the cross of Christ, and is a disastrous misrepresentation of the truth contained in the Gospel of His saving grace. Those who dare to preach the Gospel should give to the cross its true place of vital importance as given to it in the Word of God. How can God utter a more alarming warning on this point than is disclosed in the revelation of the unrevoked anathema upon all who pervert the Gospel of grace? "But though we, or an angel from heaven, preach any other gospel unto you than that which we have preached unto you, let him be accursed. As we said before, so say I now again, If any man preach any other gospel unto you than that ye have received, let him be accursed'' (Gal. 1:8, 9).

Turning from human speculation to the Scriptures of Truth, we discover one basic fact: The Lamb of God has already ''taken away'' the sin of the world (John 1:29). The fact that Christ, as Substitute, has *already* borne the undiminished righteous judgments of God against sin, is the sole ground upon which divine forgiveness is now exercised. The forgiveness of God toward sinners, therefore, is not an immediate act of grace; it is rather a judicial pardon of a debtor in view of the fact that his debt has been fully paid by Another. We could not know how *much* He paid; yet, though unable to measure redemption, we may rejoice in the fact that *all*, even to the measure of the righteous reckoning of God, is absolutely and eternally paid by Christ. It is not a question of the relative benefits which might possibly accrue to the sinner under one form of forgiveness or another,—were he forgiven graciously, or in strict justice; it is a question of the *basis* upon which *any* divine forgivness can be extended righteously. This righteous basis has been provided in the cross. By Gospel preaching, sinners are to be told that they may now stand forever pardoned before God: not because God is gracious enough to excuse their sins; but because there is plentiful redemption through the blood that has been shed (Rom. 3:24; Eph. 1:7). Being free to forgive at all, God is free to forgive *perfectly*. On no other ground can the marvelous statement,—''having forgiven you all trespasses'' (Col. 2:13), be understood. This Scripture is addressed to Christians and it exactly defines the scope of divine forgiveness which is theirs. It likewise indicates the measure of forgiveness which is offered to the unsaved.

When God thus forgives, absolutely and eternally, through the cross of Christ He is acting as Judge. By this judicial decree, He sets aside forever all condemnation. Such judicial forgiveness, which guarantees an unchangeable standing and position in sonship, should not be confused with the Father's forgiveness toward His sinning child, which is wholly within the family relationship, and which restores lost fellowship and joy to the child of God.

Every unsaved person is under the three-fold sentence of sin. He is a sinner by practice, a sinner by nature, and a sinner by divine decree. God deals with this three-fold aspect of sin by a three-fold achievement in grace. There is forgiveness for man in view of the fact that he is a sinner by practice; there is imputed righteousness for man in view of the fact that he is a sinner by nature; and there is the divine decree of justification for man in view of the fact that he is a sinner who, by divine decree, is "under sin."

Judical forgiveness itself is not an act of grace, nor is judicial forgiveness a mere act of divine clemency for some particular sins of present moment to the sinner: judicial forgiveness covers *all* sin, and by it the sinner is, as to possible condemnation, pardoned *forever*. This pardon covers *all* sins past, present, or future. God the Righteous Father will, in infinite faithfulness, correct and chasten His sinning child, and the sinning child will need to confess his sin in order to be restored into fellowship with his Father; but the Father will never *condemn* His child (John 3:18; 5:24; Rom. 8:1 R. V.; I Cor. 11:31, 32). The forgiveness of God toward the sinner is, then, made possible only through the cross and is never an act of immediate grace, and, when it is free to be extended at all, it is *boundless*. It contemplates and includes *all* sin. It forever absolves and acquits the sinner.

Though divine forgiveness results in a position for the sinner wherein there is no condemnation, this fact should in no wise be confused with the deeper aspect of God's saving grace wherein He justifies the sinner. Forgiveness cancels every debt before God, but justification declares the sinner to be forever judicially righteous in the eyes of God. One is subtraction, the other is addition; and both are righteously made possible through the cross.

Of the various divine undertakings in the salvation of a sinner, some are acts of divine justice, and some are acts of the immediate, super-abounding grace of God. Those acts which deal with human unworthiness and sin are acts of justice. These include forgiveness, justification, death to the law, freedom from the law, and the whole new creation. All this is made possible through the cross of Christ and, therefore, is not accomplished by an act of immediate grace. On the other hand, those aspects of salvation wherein God is revealed as imparting and bestowing His benefits are said to be immediate acts of grace. These include the gift of eternal life, the imputed righteousness of God, and every spiritual blessing. Limitless grace is seen in the love of God which provided the cross; but when that cross *is* provided, every saving act that is based upon it becomes an act of *justice,* rather than an act of immediate *grace.* "That he might be just, and the justifier of him which believeth in Jesus" (Rom. 3:26).[1]

Seventh. *Grace does not Appear in the Immediate Divine Dealings with the Sins of the Saved.*

The divine dealings with the sins of the saved are similar to the divine dealings with the sins of the unsaved in one particular, namely, what God does in either case is done on the ground of the cross of Christ. By that cross *all* sin, whether it be that of saint or sinner, has been righteously judged, and the ransom price, which satisfies every demand of infinite holiness, has been paid. By His death, Christ provided the sufficient ground for both the salvation of the unsaved, and the restoration of the saved. It is because of what has already been accomplished in the cross concerning the sin of the world, that the

[1] Under grace, the salvation of a sinner is declared in about 115 passages to depend only on *believing,* and in about 35 passages to depend on faith, which is but a synonym of believing. The Scripture everywhere harmonizes with this overwhelming body of truth. Without due consideration of the precise bearing of this revelation on the doctrine of grace, zealous workers have proposed to add certain conditions to the plan of salvation other than *believing.* (1) It is not, "believe and pray." In view of His grace, it is in no wise necessary, or fitting, to implore God to save. (2) It is not "believe and confess sin." Confession of sin, which is the one condition upon which a saint may be restored to fellowship, is *never* imposed on the unsaved. Confession is foreign to the ground on which they stand. (3) It is not "believe and confess Christ before men." This condition, though imposed in the kingdom teachings of Christ (Mt. 10:32), is not, and could not be, a condition of salvation under grace. Romans 10:9 is given its final order

unregenerate are freely forgiven and justified. This is a part of God's saving grace, and is wrought on the sole condition that they *believe;* while the regenerate are forgiven and cleansed on the sole condition that they *confess.* These two requirements indicated by these two words, it will be noted, are wholly different. The human obligation as represented by each word is exactly adapted in each case to the precise relationships which, on the one hand, exist between God and the unsaved, and, on the other hand, exist between God and the saved. The salvation of the sinner is unto *union* with God: the restoration of the saint is unto *communion* with God. *Believing* and *confessing* are two widely differing human conditions, or obligations, and should never be confused or interchanged. The lost are never saved by *confessing,* and the saved are never restored by *believing.*

That there is no greater demand imposed upon

and force in verse 10. There confession is seen to be the the expression of salvation which has been received by *believing.* It is primarily the voice of the new-born babe in Christ speaking to its Father,—"*Abba Father.*" Multitudes have been saved who were deprived of any opportunity of a public confession. (4) It is not "believe and be baptized." Mark 16: 16 is the one instance in Scripture where these two conditions are linked together. Not only is the context—Mark 16: 9-20—omitted in the oldest manuscripts, the omission of the word *baptized* from the negative statement, "he that believeth not shall be damned," is evidence that baptism is not the essential condition in the positive statement. (5) It is not "believe and repent." About six times these two conditions are thus joined in the Scriptures which are addressed to the unsaved in this dispensation, and for obvious reasons. Over against this, it should be considered that *believe,* or *faith,* is used, apart from the word *repentance,* no less than 150 times; the Gospel by John

the unsaved than that he *believe,* and no greater
demand imposed upon the saved than that he *confess,* is due to that which Christ accomplished on
the cross. He wrought in behalf of sinner and
saint in bearing the sin of the world, and every requirement of infinite justice is met for all in the
finished work of Christ. In the one case, there is
nothing left to be done but to *believe;* while in the
other case, there is nothing left to be done but to
confess.

The revealed attitude of God toward all men is
that of *grace* alone. Therefore He does not need to
be coaxed or persuaded. With His hand out-
stretched to bestow *all* that His grace can offer, it is
highly inconsistent to plead with Him to be gracious,

which was written that men might be saved, does not use
repentance in any form of the word; and the Book of Romans,
which was written to unfold the whole doctrine of salvation,
like the Gospel by John, does not once condition salvation on
repentance, or anything other than *believing. Repentance,*
which means "a change of mind," is never *excluded* from the
terms of salvation; it is *included* as an essential part of believing. There is no Scriptural warrant for the grace-con-
fusing practice of some who insist that repentance and believing are separate obligations to be imposed on the unsaved.
It is impossible for a person to believe who does not repent.
In believing, he will experience that change of mind which
turns from all else unto Christ as the Object of trust. Measureless harm has been done to souls when it has been taught
that a self-imposed repentance must *precede* faith in Christ.
Such insistence ignores every vital aspect of saving grace.

Saving faith is more than a belief in historical facts
concerning Christ; it is to *rely* on Christ, to *depend* on His
saving grace, and to *receive* Him; it is to *believe* the record
God has given concerning His *Son.* In preaching the Gospel,
emphasis should not fall on the mere human act of believing;
it should fall, rather, on the precise message which is to be
believed.

or to coax Him to be good. By the unvarying teaching of God's Word, and by the inexorable logic of the accomplished value of the cross, the forgiveness and blessing of God to the unsaved is conditioned upon *believing*, and to the saved it is conditioned upon *confessing*.

1 John 1:1 to 2:2 is the central passage in the Bible wherein the divine method of dealing with the sins of Christians is stated. A portion of this most important passage is as follows: "If we confess our sins, he is faithful and just to forgive us our sins, and to cleanse us from all unrighteousness. . . . My little children, these things write I unto you, that ye sin not [be not sinning]. And if any man sin, we have an advocate with the Father, Jesus Christ the righteous: and he is the propitiation for our sins: and not for ours only, but also for the sins of the whole world."

According to this Scripture, four vital elements enter into that divine forgiving and cleansing which constitutes the restoration of a sinning saint: (1) Confession is the one and only condition on the human side; (2) Absolute forgiveness and cleansing is promised on the divine side; (3) The Christian, while sinning, has been safe as to divine condemnation, because of his Advocate with the Father, Jesus Christ the righteous; and (4) Divine forgiveness and cleansing is exercised toward the believer in unchallenged faithfulness and justice because Christ is "the propitiation for our sins."

In this transaction, as it is thus disclosed, the believer makes no disposition of his own sin; that has been made for him. So, also, the Advocate makes no excuses for the sinning Christian, nor does He plead for the clemency of the Father in behalf of the believer who has sinned. The Advocate presents the sufficiency of His own blood to meet the condemnation of every sin. The Father does not act in gracious kindness when forgiving and cleansing the believer: He acts in strict *faithfulness* to His convenant and promise of eternal keeping, and in strict *justice* because of the shed-blood. Such is the unchanging value of the propitiation which Christ made in His blood.

It should also be noted that, according to this revelation, the sinning saint is never before any tribunal other than that of his own Father. The eternal relationship between the Father and His child can never be set aside. The Father may correct and chasten His erring child (1 Cor. 11:31, 32; Heb. 12:3-15), and through confession the child may be restored to the place of fellowship; but all of this is wholly within the inner circle of the family and household of God. Condemnation, which would expel the child from the place of a son, is forever past. Nor does the sinning Christian draw on the mercy and favor of God when he is restored to fellowship in the household of God. How easily mercy and favor might be exhausted and overdrawn! On the contrary, the Christian, sheltered under the blood of propitiation, and standing in the merit of his Advocate, is on a basis where no past offences have accumulated against him; for he is cleansed and forgiven under the legal justice of the Father. The justice of God is made possible and is righteously demanded in view of the shed-blood of His own Son.

Let it not be supposed that this divine plan of restoration of the child of God to the Father's fellowship will react in an attitude of carelessness on the part of the Christian. The sufficient answer to this challenge is three-fold: (1) True confession is the expression of a very real repentance, or change of mind, which turns from the sin. This is the exact opposite of becoming *accustomed* to the sin, or becoming *careless* with regard to it. (2) This very revelation is given, we are told, not to encourage, or license us to sin; but rather that "ye sin not" (be not sinning). According to the Scriptures and according to human experience, the believer's safety in the faithfulness and justice of the Father and the advocacy and propititation of the Son, is the greatest incentive for a holy life. It is clearly revealed that God has, by other and sufficient means, guarded against all careless sinning on the part of those whom He has eternally saved through the merit of His Son. And (3) God can righteously deal with sin in no other way than through the absolute value of the blood of His Son; but when sin has been laid on the Substitute, it can never be laid back on the sinner, or on any other. In the cross of Christ, the question of a possible condemnation because of sin is adjusted forever. Mercy and grace can never be co-mingled with divine justice. Boundless grace is disclosed in the provision of a perfect propitiation for the sins of the believer; but the application of the propitiation is never gracious; it is none other than the *faithfulness* and *justice* of the Father. Therefore grace does not appear in the forgiving and cleansing of the Christian's sins.

RESTATEMENT

It may be concluded that the word *grace,* as used in the Bible in relation to divine salvation, represents the uncompromised, unrestricted, unrecompensed, loving favor of God toward sinners. It is an unearned blessing. It is a gratuity. God is absolutely untrammeled and unshackled in expressing His infinite love by His infinite grace (1) through the death of His Lamb by whom every limitation which human sin could impose has been dispelled, (2) through the provision which offers salvation as a gift by which human obligation has been forever dismissed, and (3) through the divine decree by which human merit has been forever deposed. Grace is the limitless, unrestrained love of God for the lost, acting in full compliance with the exact and unchangeable demands of His own righteousness through the sacrificial death of Christ. Grace is more than love; it is love set absolutely free and made to be a triumphant victor over the righteous judgment of God against the sinner.

Having examined into the meaning of the word *grace,* the three-fold divine ministry and undertaking in grace should be considered. It will be observed that:

I. God *saves* sinners by grace,

II. God *keeps* through grace those who are saved, and,

III. God *teaches* in grace those who are saved and kept how they should live, and how they may live, to His eternal glory.

CHAPTER II

SCRIPTURE discloses the fact that the power and resources of God are more taxed by all that enters into the salvation of the soul than His power and resources were taxed in the creation of the material universe. In salvation God has wrought to the extreme limit of His might. He spared not His own Son, but delivered Him up for us all. He could do no more.

Four aspects of His saving grace are now to be examined: (1) Three divine motives in grace, (2) Three principles which cannot co-exist with grace, (3) The gracious work of God for man, and (4) Saving grace is sovereign grace.

I. THREE DIVINE MOTIVES IN GRACE.

In the Bible, three motives are assigned to God for the salvation of sinners. These motives are to be considered in what seems to be the order of their importance; beginning with that which seems to be the least and moving on to that which seems to be the greatest.

First. *Men are Said to be Saved that "Good Works" may Result.*

A statement of this truth is found in Eph. 2:10: "For we are his workmanship, created in Christ

23

Jesus unto good works, which God hath before ordained that we should walk in them." Few portions of the Scriptures present more of the essentials of salvation than this passage. It should be considered in its various revelations:

"We are his workmanship."

Whatever enters into the transformation of the individual at the time he is saved is wholly a work of God for man. It is in no wise related to any work which man might do for God. According to the Scriptures, God alone can save, and God alone can keep. *All* that will have been done when God's saving work is completed, will be seen to be "his workmanship."

"Created in Christ Jesus."

The divine work in behalf of a saved person is nothing less than a new creation. He has passed through the creative hand of God a second time and has become a new creature. The result is a new birth,—a regeneration by the Spirit. This new creation is organically related to Christ as a branch is *in* the vine, and as a member is *in* the human body. So the believer is *in* Christ. He is "created in Christ Jesus."

"Unto good works."

Never is the sinner created in Christ Jesus *by* good works. The divine purpose is here revealed. Good works are possible only to those who are "created in Christ Jesus." This truth is twice stated in the Epistle to Titus: "Who gave himself for us, that he, might redeem us from all iniquity, and purify unto himself a peculiar people, zealous of good works''; ''This is a faithful saying, and these things I will that thou affirm constantly, that they which have believed in God might be careful to maintain good works. These things are good and profitable unto men'' (2: 14; 3: 8). So, also, this is the order of truth in the great doctrinal Epistles. The work of God for man is first stated. After this, and growing out of this, is a new obligation which is the appeal for the faithful work of man for God. It is the reasonable demand for a life corresponding to the transformation which God hath already wrought in the believer through His saving grace.

"Which God hath before ordained that we should walk in them."

This phrase limits and qualifies the exact scope of the ''good works'' which form the new obligation of the one who is ''created in Christ Jesus.'' These works are particular and definite. They are none other than those good works which have been before ordained for each believer. Such ''good works'' can be discovered and realized only as the life is wholly yielded to the will of God.

Three revelations concerning the place and value of human works in relation to salvation should be distinguished:

1. *Works as required under the Law.*

In all this body of Truth, human works are set forth as being meritorious. It was because of human works that divine blessings were bestowed. This was an essential characteristic of law-relationships to God, and it is the exact opposite of grace-relationships. Under grace, it is because of divine blessings that human works are wrought. The law was exactly and appropriately applied by Christ to the lawyer when He said: "This do and thou shalt live" (Lk. 10:28. Cf Mt. 22:34-40; Mk. 12:28-34. See, also Mt. 19:16-26; Mk. 10:17-30; Lk. 18:18-30).

2. *Works as the proper test of saving faith.*

This aspect of truth is taught by James (2:14-26). In this Scripture it is declared that true salvation will be manifested outwardly by good works. This should be expected when salvation is said to be "unto good works." Such good works will serve to justify the saved one in the eyes of the world. This is but the counterpart of the more fundamental doctrine that justification before God is by faith alone (Rom. 5:1). An important exception to all this is the fact that a saint may, for a time, be walking "in darkness." At such a time there will be abnormal results in his life before God and before the world.

3. *Works as indicative of the attitude of heart toward the grace of God.*

Works which are impelled by the consciousness of a right relation to God through His grace, are treated as works of obedience and unto life eternal; while works of any character which are wrought apart from saving faith are treated as works of disobedience unto indignation and wrath (Rom. 2:1-16). One manner of life represents the obedience of faith; the other manner of life represents the disobedience of unbelief.

The first purpose of God in saving men to be mentioned, and which seems to be least, is, then, the good works which are made possible only through the salvation that is wrought by His power and grace. If this revelation concerning our salvation "unto good works" stood alone,—which, alas, it too often is supposed to do,—the work of God for man would be greatly limited and misrepresented. Under a solitary emphasis on this aspect of the divine purpose in the salvation of men, God is made to appear as a heartless taskmaster directing infinite undertakings and interested in humanity only to the extent of the service that He can derive from man. And, should their productiveness cease through age or weakness, they inevitably must be thrown into the refuse. Happily this divine motive in the salvation of men does not stand alone.

Second. *Men are Said to be Saved Because of the Benefits which Accrue to Them.*

This motive is stated in John 3:16: "For God so loved the world, that he gave his only begotten Son, that whosoever believeth in him should not perish, but have everlasting life." By this Scripture, God is said to be moved in man's salvation because of two priceless blessings which will thus be bestowed on the one who believes: (1) That he "should not perish" and (2) that he should "have everlasting life."

This divine motive would seem all-sufficient, and it is, again, and too often, the only motive which is considered by many. Individual salvation with its personal benefits is now challenged by some writers and teachers as being selfish and narrow. This challenge is both unwarranted and wicked. Salvation must be individual by its very nature, and the eternal benefits to the individual who receives the gift and grace of God are beyond comprehension. These personal benefits are the expression of the very essence of the love and favor of God. To challenge them is no less a sin than to discredit the wisdom and goodness of God. The Scriptural safeguard against an over-emphasis on the human advantage and benefit in salvation does not consist in discrediting the tremendous revelations regarding individual salvation; it consists rather, in the exposition of the just balance of truth which is gained from the added revelation concerning the third and far greater motive in the salvation of men, to wit:

Third. *Men are Said to be Saved for the Manifestation of Divine Grace.*

The final and supreme motive of God in the salvation of men is declared in Eph. 2:7: "That in the ages to come he might shew the exceeding riches of his grace in his kindness toward us through Christ Jesus."

Accompanying this declaration of the supreme purpose of God, a statement is made concerning the saving work of God for the individual. By this saving work, men are "made alive" who were "dead in trespasses and sins," and are "raised" and made to "sit together in heavenly places in Christ Jesus," who were "without Christ . . . having no hope, and without God in the world." By these two revelations regarding the present estate of the saved, two essential aspects of the divine undertaking in man's salvation are disclosed: (1) That which is wrought *in* man,—represented by the gift of eternal life, and (2) that which is wrought *for* man, even the eternal positions in Christ,—represented by the fact that an individual being saved, is now seated in the heavenly in Christ Jesus.

What, then, is the supreme motive in the salvation of men? The answer is clear: "That in the ages to come he might shew the exceeding riches of his grace in [by means of] his kindness [that gracious, saving thing he does] toward us through Christ Jesus." God's supreme motive is nothing less than His purpose to demonstrate before all intelligences,—principalities and powers, celestial beings, and terrestial beings,—the exceeding riches of His grace. This God will do by means of that gracious thing which He does through Christ Jesus. All intelligences will know the depth of sin and the hopeless estate of the lost. They will, in turn, behold men redeemed and saved from that estate appearing in the highest glory,—like Christ. This transformation will measure and demonstrate the "exceeding riches of his grace."

The supreme purpose of God is to be realized through the salvation of men by grace alone. So fully does that supreme purpose now dominate the divine undertakings in the universe that everything in heaven and in the earth is contributing solely to the one end. To gain the realization of this supreme purpose, this age, which continues from the death of Christ to His coming again, was ushered in. These long centuries of human struggle were decreed for this one purpose. No vision which is less than this will prove sufficient. Men with blinded eyes do not see afar off. To such the world is moving on by mere chance, or to the supposed consummation of some human glory in the earth. Eyes thus blinded see naught of the glory of heaven; minds thus darkened understand nothing of the supreme purpose of God in the demonstration of the exceeding riches of His grace. But, when this age is consummated it will be clearly seen by all beings in heaven and in the earth that these centuries of the on-moving universe have been designed for no other reason than the realization of the supreme purpose of God in the salvation of men by grace alone. The out-calling of the "church which is his body" from both Jews and Gentiles is the out-working of God's purpose to gather into one heavenly company all the redeemed of this age. The supreme purpose is realized in their salvation and this design was the "mystery," or sacred secret, which was hid in other ages, but which is now revealed to "holy apostles and prophets" of this dispensation. The ministry entrusted to the Apostle Paul was, "To make all men see what is the fellowship of the mystery, which from the beginning of the world hath been hid in God, who created all things by Jesus Christ: to the intent that now unto the principalities and powers in heavenly places might be known by the church the manifold wisdom of God, according to the eternal purpose which he purposed in Christ Jesus our Lord" (Eph. 3:9-11). Israel must remain blinded *until* this purpose is realized (Rom. 11:25), and the mystery of iniquity must work *until* this heavenly company is saved and taken away with the removal of the restraining Spirit of God (2 Thes. 2:7).

It may be added, as well, that the other divine motives in the salvation of men, already mentioned, only contribute to the realization of the one supreme motive. The "good works" of those who are saved are the "effectual working" of every part of the body making "increase of the body" (Eph. 4:16), and the results of that saving grace which is exercised toward the sinner—that he should not perish but have everlasting life—are only to the end that all of the saved ones together may demonstrate in the ages to come the exceeding riches of His grace.

And, again, the purpose of God, which is to shew the exceeding riches of His grace, reaches beyond the boundaries of this age and is the supreme divine purpose in the whole creation, preservation, and consummation of the universe. Christ is declared to be the cause, center, purpose and benefactor of all creation. "All things are created by him, and for him: and he is before all things, and by him all thing consist" (Col. 1: 16, 17), but the important aspect of all salvation centers in the fact that "through the blood of his cross" He is to reconcile all things unto Himself. "And you, that were sometimes alienated and enemies in your mind by wicked works, yet now hath he reconciled in the body of his flesh through death" (Col. 1:21, 22). Of all the aspects of His eternal Person, the emphasis falls on the fact that, He was a Lamb slain from the foundation of the world. Even those who are redeemed by His precious blood and who are the outshining manifestation of the grace of God, were chosen in Him "before the foundation of the world"; moreover, the "good works" of those who are saved, which are unto the proclamation of the Gospel of His saving grace, were "before ordained" that they should walk in them. So, likewise, sweeping on into the ages to come, we are told that of all the glories that will belong to the Lord of Glory, that glory which was given unto Him because of His redeeming love will be all-surpassing: "Who, being in the form of God, thought it not robbery to be equal with God: but made himself of no reputation, and took upon him the form of a servant, and was made in the likeness of men: and being found in fashion as a man, he humbled himself, and became obedient unto death, even the death of the cross. Wherefore God also hath highly exalted him, and given him a name which is above every name: that at the name of Jesus every knee should bow, of things in heaven, and things in earth, and things under the earth; and that every tongue should confess that Jesus Christ is Lord, to the glory of God the Father" (Phil. 2:6-11). It is declared of Him that He is "appointed heir of all things"; by Him the ages were programmed; He is the brightness of the Father's glory, and the express Image of His Person; and he upholdeth all things by the word of His power. But to what purpose is this marvelous unfolding of His eternal Being if it is not to relate His Deity to His present saving grace; to accomplish which, it is stated, He, having "by himself purged our sins, sat down on the right hand of the Majesty on high" (Heb. 1:2, 3)? Thus absolutely does the whole universe throughout the program of the ages center about the sacrificial death of the Son of God, by whom that heavenly company are to be redeemed, purified, transformed, and translated into the eternal manifestation of the riches of grace.

The complete manifestation of divine grace which is to be revealed in the glory will be by means of *all* that combines in Christ—the Glorious Head, together with His redeemed Body, every member of which will have been transformed into His very image. What a spectacle for angels and archangels, principalities and powers, mankind and demons! Yea, what a spectacle for God Himself; for He will then gaze on that surpassing manifestation of His grace to His own "exceeding joy" (Jude 24)!

Divine grace could have had no place in this universe until sin had entered. Through creation, the wisdom and power of God had been disclosed; but there had been no unveiling of God's love for the undeserving, since there had been no occasion for its manifestation. This statement does not imply that we are to sin that grace may abound. There is a wide difference between the fact that God permitted sin to enter the world, and the thought that thereby God licenses man to sin. Whether there have been greater motives which have actuated God in permitting sin to enter the world than He has revealed, none can say. It is certain, however, that the greatest motive that He has been pleased to reveal is to be inferred from the fact that grace cannot be exercised where there is no demerit, and that He designs above all else that His saving grace shall have an actual and adequate demonstration in all the ages to come. How could it be otherwise? What poverty of experience would

reign in a universe that had never dreamed of true
heart-compassion, the incomparable joy of forgiving
and being forgiven, or that never would have heard
the victory song of the redeemed! A universe which
otherwise would have been, with all its magnificence
of celestial glory, as cold, unyielding, and unapproachable as the law of infinite righteousness itself,
has been colored and warmed by the penitent's tears,
and by the unveiling of the unfathomable grace of
God toward the sinful. Highest of all revealed
glories,—and who can measure its relative import?—,
the boundless grace of God is being manifested
through the salvation of sinners. Such is the spectacle concerning which angelic hosts and human
throngs will marvel, and about which they will sing
throughout the ages of the ages to come.

Returning to Eph. 3: 8-11 we read that the Apostle
Paul was sent to preach the "unsearchable riches
of Christ." Such riches could be brought to light
only by means of the fact of sin and its cure through
the cross of Christ. The Apostle was also sent "to
make all men see what is the fellowship of the mystery
[sacred secret], which from the beginning of the
world hath been hid in God, who created all things
by Jesus Christ." This sacred secret is, according
to the preceding context, the calling out and saving
in this age of a company from both Jews and Gentiles,
which company is the true "church which is his
body." By the salvation of these, He purposes to
unveil before all heavenly hosts His greatest display of wisdom as it is seen in the manifestation
of His bosom of love through the coming of Christ

into the world to redeem the lost. For we read: "To the intent that now unto the principalities and powers in heavenly places might be known by the church the manifold wisdom of God, according to the eternal purpose which he purposed in Christ Jesus our Lord."

At no point can tolerance be given to the theory that the Innocent Man in the Garden of Eden was God's first and highest ideal, that sin entered in spite of God, and that redemption is an after-thought —the best available remedy in view of the wreckage of sin. It is a redeemed sinner who takes the highest place in glory. This redemption was in view before all creation. The finite mind is soon overwhelmed in the contemplation of the eternal facts and purposes of God; but there is much that we may understand when we read, first, concerning the coming of Christ into the world to redeem by His precious blood: "Who verily was foreordained before the foundation of the world, but was manifest in these last times for you" (1 Pet. 1:20); "The Lamb slain from the foundation of the world" (Rev. 13:8); and, "Him, being delivered by the determinate counsel and foreknowledge of God, ye have taken, and by wicked hands have crucified and slain" (Acts 2:23). And, second, when we read concerning the eternal purpose of God in the saved: "Elect according to the foreknowledge of God the Father" (1 Pet. 1:2), and, again, "For whom he did foreknow, he also did predestinate to be conformed to the image of his Son, that he might be the firstborn among many brethren. Moreover whom he did predestinate, them he also called: and whom he called, them he also justified: and whom he justified, them he also glorified" (Rom. 8:29, 30).

It is evident, therefore, that the supreme motive of God in the creation, preservation, and consummation of the universe, in the permission of evil to enter the world, and in the mighty undertakings of salvation as it is now offered to sinful men through the death and resurrection of Christ, is that His "riches of grace" may be disclosed to all intelligences within the whole scope of creation.

If the supreme motive of God is to reveal His grace, then salvation must be by grace alone, or the eternal purpose of God must fail. Hence we read: "For by grace are ye saved through faith; and that not of yourselves: it is the gift of God: not of works, lest any man should boast. For we are his workmanship, created in Christ Jesus unto good works, which God hath before ordained that we should walk in them" (Eph. 2:8-10); "Now to him that worketh is the reward not reckoned of grace, but of debt. But to him that worketh not, but believeth on him that justifieth the ungodly, his faith is counted for righteousness" (Rom. 4:4, 5); "And if by grace, then it is no more of works: otherwise grace is no more grace. But if it be of works, then is it no more grace: otherwise work is no more work" (Rom. 11:6); "But we believe that that through the grace of the Lord Jesus Christ we shall be saved" (Acts 15:11). On no other basis can grace be manifested than by salvation which is wholly unrelated to human merit or works.

II. THREE PRINCIPLES WHICH CANNOT CO-EXIST WITH GRACE.

It has been shown that the three essential principles which antagonize and if permitted would frustrate the principle of pure grace are set aside in this age for the sole purpose that grace may prevail uncomplicated and uncompromised. The divine annulling of every opposing principle to pure grace is not only natural, but necessary, if the supreme divine purpose of this age is the manifestation of grace and that purpose is to be realized. The three essential principles already mentioned and which can never co-exist with pure grace are:

First. *Any Recognition of Human Guilt.*

God must be free to exercise grace without the slightest limitation because of human demerit and sin; for grace would no longer be grace if its benefits are withheld from the sinner in the least degree because of sin. Grace can only be exercised where every question of unworthiness has been banished forever. This God has accomplished in the cross, and for the purpose that His supreme manifestation of grace may be realized unto infinite perfection. The Lamb of God *has* taken away the sin of the world, and God *has* laid on Him the iniquity of us all. By these and many other Scriptures it is revealed that the grace-opposing principle of sin and demerit has been removed from before the eyes of God for all men. Thus, and only thus, could divine grace be exercised toward all men. But since God through the death of Christ has, in the absolute sense, dealt with the sin of the whole world, He is now free by the exercise of grace, in the absolute sense, to lavish its riches upon the chief of sinners without reservation or diminution. Divine grace thus awaits on divine justice; for only as the last demand of infinite righteousness against sin has been paid can divine grace be exercised. There can be no admixture of these principles wherein divine justice is *partly* satisfied and to such an extent God is *partly* free to act in grace. Every vestige of demerit must be removed before God can exercise grace. This vital truth about grace cannot be too strongly emphasized. The operations of divine grace can never overlap or share in any aspect of the operations of divine justice; but when divine justice has *finished* its work and *abandoned* the field forever, divine grace is free to occupy the field alone in the full blaze of its infinite glory.

Thus grace now "reigns through righteousness"; but it is grace alone that reigns. A righteous throne of awful justice, wrath, and blasting judgments has become "a throne of grace." Such is the marvel of God's infinite favor. Such is the good news which is to be proclaimed to a ruined world; for it is grace alone that is now offered to hell-deserving sinners. Only by the *absolute* removal of the condemnation of all sin could the way be made clear for the *absolute* manifestation of the grace of God.

Second. *Any Recognition of Human Obligation.*

No more can grace remain grace, if by its benefits there is created and imposed the slightest obligation for payment or remuneration. Grace is unrecompensed favor. Its riches must be bestowed and received only on the ground that it is an uncomplicated *gift*. "I give unto them eternal life," and "The gift of God is eternal life through Jesus Christ our Lord" (John 10:28; Rom. 6:23).

In order that the field might be absolutely clear for the manifestation of uncomplicated divine grace, God has perfectly eliminated every work of man— past, present, and future—from the terms of salvation by grace: "not of works, lest any man should boast"; and, "if by grace, it is no more works"; "Now to him that worketh is the reward not reckoned of grace, but of debt. But to him that worketh not, but believeth on him that justifieth the ungodly, his faith is counted [reckoned] for righteousness"; "Not by works of righteousness which we have done, but according to his mercy he saved us." Man must take salvation as a *gift*. He need only *believe* in order to be saved. The complete setting aside of human obligation as payment for divine blessings is the only ground upon which God can be free to act in unlimited divine grace toward sinners; but every human work and obligation is now set aside, and pure grace is offered to all men in the Gospel of the grace of God.

Third. *Any Recognition of Human Merit.*

This third opposing principle to divine grace has been disannulled by the fact that humanity is now stripped of every conceivable merit before God. As has been stated, revelation concerning the present relation of fallen man to God goes far beyond a disclosure of the fact that man is a sinner both by nature and by practice. This of itself would be a sufficient cause for condemnation; but, beyond all this, God has now pronounced an all-inclusive, judicial, condemning sentence on the whole race, both Jew and Gentile. By this universal sentence every individual has been reduced to the lowest level, so far as human merit before God is concerned. In the affairs of men, there is a legitimate field in which they may compare themselves one with another as to relative moral character and action; but such comparison is now completely eliminated from all *divine* estimations of unregenerate men. This important fact is one of the characterizing features of this age and forms an essential factor in the present supreme purpose of God in which He purposes to manifest His grace. Apart from this judicial sentence against all men, the grace of God could never be manifested. The following Scriptures disclose this present universal decree of divine judgment against all men, and in considering them it is important to note that this universal judgment is not a mere estimation of the various degrees of human guilt; it is an arbitrary leveling of *every* human being to a basis which is *absolutely* without merit or standing before God.

"For we have before proved both Jews and Gentiles, that they are all under sin" (Rom. 3:9); "But the scripture hath concluded all under sin, that the promise by faith of Jesus Christ might be given to them that believe" (Gal. 3:22); "For God hath concluded them all [Jew and Gentile] in unbelief [disobedience,] that he might have mercy upon all" (Rom. 11:32); "That every mouth may be stopped,

and all the world may become guilty before God"
(Rom. 3:19). It is true that "all have sinned, and
come short of the glory of God," which indicates
that man is a sinner by practice; but it is a far
deeper revelation that *all,* by judicial sentence, are
under *"sin"* and *"unbelief"* and are *all* now equally
"guilty" before God.

In exact agreement with the present universal
leveling of all humanity to the place of supreme
and unconditioned condemnation is the equally important revelation that, through the substitutionary
death of Christ for *all* men as Sin-Bearer (John 1:29;
2 Cor. 5:14, 19), the ground of universal divine
condemnation is no longer the sins which men have
committed and which Christ has borne; but rather
the condemnation is now because of the personal
rejection of the Saviour who bore the sin.[1] This is
set forth in His Word: "He that believeth on him is
not condemned: but he that believeth not is condemned already, because he hath not believed in the
name of the only begotten Son of God" (John 3:18);

[1]Should question be raised at this point as to the fact
that a vast portion of humanity have not actually rejected
a Saviour since they have had no knowledge of the Gospel,
it should be borne in mind that two divine provisions have
been determined for this age, and they are interdependent:
(1) God has commissioned that the Gospel of His grace shall
be preached to *every* creature, and, (2) *every* creature will
stand or fall, according to his personal attitude toward this
Gospel of saving grace. The fact that the messengers have
failed to bear the message to every creature has created
a situation in the world about which the divine provisions
are not revealed; nor could they be revealed reasonably.
The essential age-characterizing fact must stand,—God holds
men as condemned, or not condemned, on the sole basis of a
personal rejection, or acceptance, of all that is revealed in
the Gospel of His grace.

"But he that believeth not shall be damned" (Mark 16:16). In confirmation of the fact that men are now condemned because of unbelief, it should be noted that when the Spirit of God approaches the unsaved to convince them of sin, He does not shame them, or blame them, concerning the sins they have committed; He rather convicts them of *one* sin only: "Of sin, because they believe not on me" (John 16:9). So, also, Christians are said to be free from all condemnation on the sole ground that they have *believed* on the Saviour: "He that believeth on him is not condemned" (John 3:18. Cf 5:24; Rom. 8:1; 1 Cor. 11:32; 2 Cor. 5:19).

The conclusion to be derived from this investigation into the present standing of man before God is that he is universally *"condemned," "under sin,"* and reckoned to be in *"unbelief."* This divine decree permits of no variations or gradations. It represents the very lowest level of standing before God to which it is possible for any human being to descend, and *all* unregenerate men are now placed on that level.

At this point God offers but one remedy. That remedy is GRACE. By the complete removal of all consideration of human merit, God is now unconditionally free to act in grace in behalf of man. On no other ground could grace be exercised. Hence all preaching of law-observance, or moral reform, to unregenerate men is unwarranted, misleading, and is contrary to the essential fact of divine grace; for no moral appeal, or appeal to human works, can be made apart from the assumption that, should unregenerate people comply with such appeals, they would not be discredited to the same extent before God as they would otherwise be.[1]

In this dispensation there is no middle ground for half-good people. Men are either *utterly* condemned under the universal decree of the Judge of all the earth, or they are *perfectly* saved and safe in the grace of God as it is in Jesus Christ.

It is either Christ or Hell.

The divine objective in reducing humanity to the lowest level of all conceivable grades of human standing before God is not merely to give adequate expression to His hatred of evil: it is the expression of His infinite goodness and love; for only thus could the riches of His grace be extended to them. He has reckoned them to be in unbelief "that he might have mercy [grace] upon all"; and "The scripture hath concluded all under sin, that the promise by faith of Jesus Christ might be given to them that believe." Only when human merit has thus been removed forever, can divine grace undertake its saving work.

The grace of God which is offered so freely to the sinner is not a variable quantity which might be adapted to the different degrees of human sinfulness; it is an unchangeable whole. It is standardized and cannot be increased or diminished. It is *all* that God can ever do for the sinner in time or eternity. It is as infinite as He is infinite. Such measureless grace is now freely offered to the sinner. He has but to receive Christ in whom all

1 Let it be restated that there is, in the field of human government and social order, a legitimate recognition of varying degrees of moral fitness; but these find no place as a basis of divine grace, or as the ground of salvation.

fulness dwells. Men are either "under sin," or "under grace." They are, in the most unequivocal sense, either *lost* or *saved*.

In order that grace might be measured in all its limitless riches and glory, the objects of that grace are lifted from the lowest level of human standing before God to the highest pinnacle of heavenly glory. Everything has been divinely arranged so that this transition may be a measurement of divine grace. To this end the widest extremes that are possible for God to decree in human positions have been determined. Such is the present low estate of the lost under the universal divine decree, and such will be the exalted estate of the saved in the highest glory when grace shall have completed its work. Of no archangel has the Lord prayed as He has prayed for the objects of His grace: "Father, I will that they also, whom thou hast given me, be with me where I am; that they may behold my glory, which thou hast given me" (John 17:24). These two extremes, represented by the present estate of the lost, on the one hand, and the coming heavenly glory of the saved when finally transformed into the very image of Christ, on the other hand, are the boundaries which measure the infinite grace of God. The positional transference of man from the lowest level that divine judgment can decree to the highest altitude of heaven, the change from a death-doomed, hell-deserving sinner to a son of God and a partaker of the eternal glory, are demonstrations of the measurement of His own grace which God has decreed and with which He is to be forever satisfied.

Since God's grace is to be manifested in glory, it is required that every aspect of the saving transformation shall be wrought in grace alone. All human merit is of necessity excluded. So, also, since the ultimate estate of the saved in glory is to be such that they will then be "like Christ" and "conformed to the image" of God's Son, and "faultless before the presence of his glory," it is equally demanded that this divine transformation shall be free from every human touch. Such measureless results can be secured and guaranteed only as the work of God is uncombined with any human work. The best human work could but mar and spoil the divine ideal. Therefore it is by grace that ye are saved through faith; and that not of yourselves: it is the gift of God: not of works, lest any man should boast (Eph. 2: 8, 9).

Having in the most absolute sense disposed of the three grace-opposing principles—human sin, human obligation, and human merit,—God, in the same absolute sense, is now free to lavish His undiminished grace upon whomsoever He will. He purposes thus to manifest His grace: not merely as a selfish gratification of display on His part; but rather as a satisfaction of His love which knows no bounds.

Only as grace is seen to be the realization of the supreme purpose of God, can the expressions used in the Scriptures concerning the outflow of that grace be understood. The resources of language have been exhausted in the attempt to indicate the infinite grace of God in terms of human speech. Probably these resources of language have been more exhausted at this point than concerning any other theme of the Word of God. How could it be otherwise? God through grace purposes the realization of the greatest undertaking and accomplishment in all the universe. The following Scriptures unfold the limitless character of His grace:

"And of his fulness have all we received, and grace for [added to, or heaped upon] grace" (John 1:16); "Abundance [superabundance] of grace" (Rom. 5:17); "But where sin abounded, grace did much more abound" (superabound. Rom. 5:20); "What shall we say then? Shall we continue in sin, that grace may abound?" (superabound. Rom. 6:1); "And by their prayer for you, which long after you for the exceeding [above measure] grace of God in you" (2 Cor. 9:14); "The abundant [more than enough] grace" (2 Cor. 4:15).

Grace heaped upon grace, superabounding, and without measure, is the description given of the limitless outflow of divine favor. The grace of God belongs to the realm of the infinite. His measureless love and goodness are released from every restraint. They are unshackled and free. The supreme divine objective is then, that infinite love may manifest itself in superabounding grace. His love is knowledge-surpassing, infinite, and eternal. So, also, is His grace.

III. THE GRACIOUS WORK OF GOD FOR MAN.

The uncomplicated work of God for man, which is to measure His grace, is presented in the Word of God in seven major aspects:

First. *The Finished Work of Christ.*

This is no less than the combined values of His redemption, reconciliation, and propitiation, as these aspects of His cross are related to the whole world lost in sin (1 Tim. 2:6; 2 Cor. 5:19, 20; 1 John 2:1, 2). This aspect of the divine work is forever *"finished"* for every soul, and its glorious achievement is the good news of the Gospel of saving grace.

Second. *The Convicting Work of the Spirit.*

By this work of God the Gospel of His saving grace is revealed to the mind and heart of the unsaved by the Spirit of God. He convinces of sin, of righteousness, and of judgment (John 16:7-11). Only by this illuminating work of the Spirit can the Satan-blinded mind of the unsaved (2 Cor. 4:3, 4) understand the way of life in Christ Jesus.

Third. *The Saving Work of God.*

This divine undertaking includes every aspect of the work of God that is accomplished at the instant when the sinner believes on Christ. It is no less than many transforming miracles which are wrought instantaneously and simultaneously in the saving power of God.

Fourth. *The Keeping Work of God.*

The clear Biblical testimony is to the effect that the believer is kept always and only through the grace and power of God. Because of the work of Christ on the cross, God is presented as not only being free to *save* meritless sinners; but He is presented as being free to *keep* those whom He has saved. Under legal relationships men endured in order that they might be saved (Mt. 24:13). Under grace relationships men endure because they are saved (John 10:28). God alone is "able" to keep.

Fifth. *The Delivering Work of God.*

The Christian who is perfectly saved from the guilt and penalty of sin needs also to be saved from the reigning power of sin. God alone can save in any case, and therefore deliverance from sin, weakness and failure is provided, not by human effort, but by the power of the indwelling Spirit; and is secured, not on the principle of works, but on the principle of faith. "Walk in the Spirit, and ye shall not fulfil the lust of the flesh" (Gal. 5:16). Deliverance, too, is always and only a work of God.

Sixth. *The Work of God in Christian Growth.*

Too often Christian growth is confused with spirituality, or deliverance from the power of sin. A very immature believer, as to growth, may be delivered and be in the full blessing of the Spirit. He has yet much to learn from experience and from the Word of God; but this need not limit his immediate blessing of heart and life. In fact only spiritual Christians grow. Carnality in life means perpetual babyhood in spirituality. "But grow in grace, and in the knowledge of our Lord and Saviour Jesus Christ" (2 Pet. 3:18); "But we all, with open face beholding as in a glass the glory of the Lord, are changed into the same image from glory to glory, even as by the Spirit of the Lord" (2 Cor. 3:18).

Seventh. *The Final Presenting Work of God.*

It is the final and consummating work of God to present the believer faultless before the presence of His glory to His own exceeding joy. It is promised that when we see Him we shall be "like him." We shall then be conformed to the image of the Son of God.

No one will persuade himself that he will assist in this final transformation and translation. No more can any believer assist in any of these aspects of the work of God. Salvation is the work of God alone. It is *from* Him, *by* Him, and *unto* Him. In every stage of the development it is the work of God alone which can avail, and that work is now provided and offered in marvelous grace. Particular emphasis is needed at this point. Salvation is of God; and man's responsibility is only that of being a recipient of it. Man is called upon to make only such personal adjustment to God as will place him in the normal position to receive the divine blessing. The undertaking is of such a character that man can contribute in no wise to its accomplishment. It aims to reproduce the very perfection of Christ Himself, which perfection would be ruined could man touch it. And it is all to the demonstration of the grace of God in the ages to come and hence, as certainly, precludes the thought of any complication with human merit, else the greatest motive of God which has been working from before the foundation of the world would be defeated,—a contingency impossible in the light of revelation.

According to the Scriptures, the human element

is never included beyond the essential adjustment of man to the work of God. This human responsibility is always expressed in terms which suggest that man is the recipient of the benefits of the work of God. Some of these Bible terms are: "Believe," "Receive," "Faith," "By me if any man enter in," "Come unto me," "Whosoever will may come," "Whosoever calleth," "Turned to God," being "Reconciled to God." Thus it is seen that man is saved from the guilt and penalty of sin, not by expiating his own sins, but by *believing* in the One who has suffered in his stead. After he is thus saved, he is delivered from the power of sin in his daily life, not by anxious striving, but by yielding and by relying on the all-sufficient, indwelling Spirit. He will be saved from the presence of sin into the coming glory and likeness of Christ, not by any effort or human device, but by the power which wrought in Christ to raise Him from the dead, and by which he will be translated instantly from the earth to heaven. In every instance the divine responsibility is seen to be within the sphere of the actual accomplishment of the mighty undertaking; but man's responsibility is in the sphere of the reception of that work. The whole transaction is free from every consideration of remuneration, barter, or trade. It is the love of God expressing itself in His gracious work for those who, within themselves, will ever be hopelessly undeserving and therefore eternally debtors to infinite grace.

Salvation is the work of God for man; it is not the work of man for God.

Salvation is the bestowal and actual impartation of

eternal life; it is not the beauties and artifical imitations of ethical living.

Salvation is the imputed righteousness of God; it is not the imperfect righteousness of man.

Salvation is according to the faithful calling of God; it is not according to the fitful carefulness of man.

Salvation is a divine reconciliation; it is not a human regulation.

Salvation is the canceling of *all* sin; it is not the cessation from *some* sin.

Salvation is being delivered from, and dead to, the law; it is not delighting in, or doing, the law.

Salvation is divine regeneration; it is not human reformation.

Salvation is being acceptable to God; it is not becoming exceptionally good.

Salvation is completeness in Christ; it is not competency in character.

Salvation is possessing every spiritual blessing; it is not professing any special betterment.

Salvation is always and only of God. It is never of man. It is the unsearchable riches of Christ. It is *unto* good works which God hath before ordained that we should walk in them.

IV.   THE GRACE OF GOD IS SOVEREIGN.

Not every member of the human family will be included in the glorious, grace-revealing company of the redeemed in heaven. Nothing is more clearly taught in the Scriptures than this; but the salvation of those who are being gathered into that company, it is revealed, will be according to the sovereign purpose of God, and not according to any merit in the individual. There are two fields of divine undertaking wherein the work of God stands alone: (1) The creation of the universe and (2) the redemption of sinners. Certain aspects of work, however, are entrusted to men. They are appointed to preach the Gospel to the lost, to edify the saints by teaching, and to co-operate in the gathering and care of the assemblies of believers. Yet even this human service is impotent apart from the enabling power of the Spirit of God.

So, also, while God is sovereign in the salvation of men, He has allowed sufficient latitude within the larger circles of His unalterable purpose for the exercise of the human will. "Whosoever will may come." This is the invitation to the unsaved. Likewise He addresses the believer concerning the possible blessings of a Spirit-filled life by such words of human responsibility as "yield," "reckon," and "confess." It is equally revealed in the Scriptures that such action of the human will is never apart from the divine enablement. God must move the heart of the unsaved: "No man can come to me, except the Father which hath sent me draw him" (John 6:44). He must move the heart of the saved as well: "For it is God which worketh in you both to will and to do of his good pleasure" (Phil. 2:13).

There is no Biblical ground for the theory that even the minutest detail of the eternal purpose of God will ever be uncertain because of a supposed unanticipated action of the human will. God cannot be disappointed, defeated, or surprised. The glorious company of the redeemed will, therefore, be gathered according to an "election of grace."

Two out-standing facts are disclosed in the Scriptures in regard to the attitude of God toward this world: (1) Back of the secondary question of the human choice for which man is held responsible, is the more important fact that God has permitted men to be born and live who He as certainly knows will reject His grace with all the woe that their choice entails. Thus there is no escape from the fundamental fact of the sovereignty of God by emphasizing the superficial issues of a human choice. And (2) God is under the compelling force of His own boundless love to be the Saviour of all men. He so loved the *world* that He gave His only begotten Son that whosoever believeth on Him should not perish, but have everlasting life. Thus, if divine love for a lost world can form any incentive in the heart of God, according to the Scriptures, there is formed an equal incentive toward *all*. These statements are seemingly contradictory one to the other, and the solution of the problem they present is never found in seeking to minimize the one in the hope of preserving the other. Theological systems have been developed, made their appeal, and failed at this very point. The solution of the problem is never found in the range of human reason; it is perfectly solved in the range of divine righteousness. Being unable to penetrate the infinite issues involved, man may rest on the absolute righteousness of God. The glorified saint, looking back over the steps of the divine accomplishment, will then see that all God did was *right*. Here faith alone can minister rest to the soul. The consummation of the age will be seen to be according to infinite wisdom, love, and power. It will be to the eternal satisfaction of God whose tender heartedness is boundless and whose justice can never be diminished. It will be all-satisfying to His saints; for it is declared that they will be "satisfied" when they awake in His likeness. The Gospel of the grace of God is to be preached to all men with an appeal to their will. The result will be a selection and election according to sovereign grace. It will be in absolute accord with infinite goodness, and the result will be to His own exceeding joy.

Every form of evangelism which tends to force the decision of the will beyond the sovereign movements of the Spirit on the hearts of men is fraught with infinite perils.

No emphasis on the importance of preaching the Gospel of grace in its purity can be too strong. Biblical preaching must present saving grace with no admixtures of limitations because of human sin, human obligation, or human merit. Only thus can there be the fullest co-operation of the Spirit of God, and only thus can the messenger be saved from the unrevoked anathema which is pronounced (Gal. 1:8, 9) on all those who pervert the Gospel of the grace of God.

CHAPTER III

SAFE-KEEPING IN GRACE

NOT only is the believer said to be saved by grace, but he is said to *"stand"* in grace. The word *stand*, as used in the New Testament, gives expression to the thought of continuing and enduring, and to "stand" in grace is to abide unchanged, to endure, and to continue in grace. We read: "We have access by faith into this grace wherein we stand" (Rom. 5:2), and, "This is the true grace of God wherein ye stand" (1 Pet. 5:12).

The continued exercise of divine grace toward the Christian is the one and only basis upon which he may hope to endure; for, as certainly as grace is the one and only basis upon which God can save a meritless sinner, so certainly grace alone is the basis upon which God can righteously keep him saved. Having begun in the Spirit, or wholly in the power and grace of God, there is no hope for continuance to be found in the flesh, or the resources of human strength. Human ability can no more *maintain* a right standing before God than it can *attain* such a standing.

Since the application of divine grace for the salvation of the sinner precedes, in point of time, the application of that grace for the keeping of the one who is saved, it is perhaps permissible to contemplate the operation of divine grace in a two-fold classification—the grace which saves, and the grace which keeps. But, on the other hand, an over-emphasis of this two-fold classification is misleading in the extreme; for in no sense are there two efforts, or operations, of divine grace. The keeping ministry of God in grace is but the realization of that which is purposed, programmed, and wholly provided for in His saving ministry in grace. In reality, God offers no saving ministry of grace which does not include and guarantee His keeping ministry of grace. The varied operations of divine grace in behalf of the sinner which contemplate his every need to the end of eternity are one indivisible purpose of God.

The wholly artificial, two-fold classification of the ministries of grace into that which saves, and that which keeps, has been emphasized by certain theological systems. These systems, while professing to believe in the doctrine of salvation by grace, ignore or repudiate at the same time, the doctrine of the keeping power of God through grace. The promoters of these systems have contended that God in grace might save a sinner for the moment; but the *endurance* in that salvation would, of necessity, be conditioned on human merit and works. In other words, the saved one would remain saved only as long as he remained good. Such a conception of saving grace is so far removed from the fundamental ground upon which all grace must be based, that it must be concluded that the framers and supporters of these doctrines have in no sense discovered the true character of saving grace and are, therefore, unable to advance on the true lines of revelation which lead to the perfectly secured consummation of all saving grace. This consummation is no less than the keeping of the saved one throughout all time and eternity. Multitudes who have been trained in these false doctrines are saved, but they are saved in *spite* of their doctrines, and those who are saved have in every case been kept from the moment they were saved; not because they remained good, but because of the fact that unmerited favor is provided for every one who is saved by grace.

Since there is a difference as to time of application of the indivisible operations of divine grace and since certain theological systems have forced this division to the point of an avowed belief and confidence toward the grace which saves, and to the point of avowed disbelief and discredit toward the grace which keeps, grace will be treated throughout this and remaining chapters as though it were subject to this two-fold classification.

The fact that God keeps the saved one on a grace principle alone has been anticipated already in the preceding chapters; but turning to a more specific consideration of the fact and force of divine grace as related to the keeping power of God, the subject may be given a three-fold classification: (1) The keeping power of God through grace is included in every consideration of the principles of grace. (2) The keeping power of God through grace is implied in every revelation wherein is presented the truth that grace reaches into the coming ages for its consummation. (3) The keeping power of God through grace is seen in the manifold provisions and safeguards which He has made to that end. These three viewpoints of the keeping power of divine grace are essential.

I. THE KEEPING POWER OF GOD THROUGH GRACE IS INCLUDED IN EVERY CONSIDERATION OF THE PRINCIPLES OF GRACE.

If God has found a way whereby He can righteously save hell-deserving, meritless sinners, apart from all complications with human resources or limitations, He has, by the *continued* application of those principles, found a way whereby, without reference to merit or demerit, the saved one can be kept saved to the ages of the ages. This, though most reasonable, is purely a question of divine revelation, and, therefore its consideration should not be influenced by rationalistic systems of thought. From observation of the natural workings of the human mind, it may be concluded that it is a greater test of faith for the individual to repose on the *keeping* power of God through grace, than it is to repose on the *saving* power of God through grace; yet, as has been stated, to have accepted the true grace principles in salvation is to be committed to those selfsame principles which, in turn, form the very basis of the keeping power of God through grace. To restate,—The basis upon which God can exercise grace in the salvation of the sinner is three-fold: (1) There must be the disposal of every condemnation which divine righteousness could impose because of sin. This has been perfectly accomplished in the cross of Christ. (2) There must be a disposal of every human obligation. This has been provided in the offer of salvation to man as a gift from God. And, (3) there must be a disposal of all human merit. This has been supplied by the divine decree which places the whole world "under sin" before God. If these great principles of grace, which belong to salvation, 'shall be applied and continued to the believer after he is saved, there is formed thereby, the same righteous freedom for the infinite love of God to be exercised to its own satisfaction in the eternal keeping of the one who has been saved. With more specific reference to these three principles in grace, it may be observed:

First, *There must be the Disposal of Every Condemnation which Divine Righteousness could Impose Because of Sin.*

Since the problem of the keeping power of God is related only to the believer, the crucial question which is confronted at this point may be stated thus: Are the sins which Christians commit *after* they are saved divinely judged and disposed of in the cross equally with the sins of the unsaved? The Scripture is clear on this point: "And he is the propitiation for our [Christians] sins: and not for ours only, but also for the sins of the whole world"; "The blood of Jesus Christ his Son cleanseth us [Christians] from all sin" (1 John 1:7; 2:2). To these passages may be added all the Scripture which contemplates the universality of the efficacious death of Christ for sin; for sin is *sin* in any and every case, whether it be committed by the saved or the unsaved, and it can be cured only by the precious blood of the Son of God. All sin taken together formed the unmeasurable burden which was laid on Him. The supposition that the sins of Christians were *excluded* from the redeeming work of Christ, can be entertained only without serious thought. Equally erroneous is the supposition that God does not deal judicially with the Christian's sins until they are committed. Every sin that humanity—saved or unsaved —had committed, or ever would commit, was dealt with in perfect divine judgment by Christ at the cross. He was God's Lamb that "taketh away the sin of the world." Being universal, this divine judgment contemplated the sin of the saved as much as the sin of the unsaved.

As certainly, then, as grace may be extended to the unsaved on the basis of the fact that Christ has *already* borne the condemnation of his sin, so certainly grace may be extended and continued to the saved on the basis of the fact that Christ has *already* borne the condemnation of the Christian's sin. In this dispensation, the unsaved are not said to be condemned primarily because of their sins which Christ has borne; they are condemned because they do not *believe* on Christ who bore their sins. "He that believeth not is condemned already, because he hath not believed in the name of the only begotten Son of God" (John 3:18). In like manner, the Christian will never be condemned because of the sin which Christ has borne. So, also, the Christian, having accepted Christ, can never be condemned for lack of saving faith. It is therefore said: "Verily, verily, I say unto you, He that heareth my word, and believeth on him that hath sent me, hath everlasting life, and shall not come into condemnation; but is passed from death unto life" (John 5:24). "There is therefore now no condemnation to them that are in Christ Jesus" (Rom. 8:1, R. V.). "He that believeth on him is not condemned" (John 3:18).

By this Scripture it is seen that the cross of Christ is the foundation of the Christian's eternal security and standing in grace; but it should never be disassociated from the supplementary, though wholly unrelated, truth that God, while never condemning either the saint or the sinner because of sin, since Christ has died, does undertake, upon an entirely different basis, to safeguard the Christian from every practice of sin, and He chastens, where there is need, as only a righteous Father can do.

Does sin unsave the Christian? This is a fair question, and if it be answered in the affirmative, there are but two possible positions in which the Christian might stand: he must, at a given time, be either sinlessly perfect, or a lost soul. There could be no intermediate ground. The true reply to this important question will be found (1) in the Scriptures and (2) in human experience.

1. *Revelation* not only infers, but directly states that Christians sin. It also presents the cure for such sin, which, it may be added, is wholly different from that which is provided for the cure of the sins of the unsaved. This body of truth, both directly and indirectly, constitutes a very large proportion of the Epistles of the New Testament; for the Epistles are written to believers only, and disclose both the believer's eternal standing and his present state before God. This message, while plainly declaring that Christians do sin, as plainly declares that Christians are not condemned. This seeming moral inconsis-

tency is not adjusted by blindly supposing the Christian to be lost because of his sin; it is adjusted by that higher morality made possible through the death of Christ, which, alas, too few have comprehended or acknowledged, either for their salvation or keeping.

2. *Human experience* also testifies to the indisputable fact that Christians *do* remain saved in spite of their evident imperfections and sin. This fact must not be slighted. Christians *are* now standing, and the continuance of any Christian as such for an hour, or a moment, is a final proof that there is some divine provision for their keeping; for in no sense could it reasonably be supposed that they are standing in any goodness or perfection of their own. The fact that they *are* now standing, is final proof, also, that they are neither lost when they sin, nor sinless when they remain saved. They are, rather, "kept through the power of God," and that power is not only directly exercised in their behalf; but it has been made righteously *free* to act through the shed blood of the Lamb of God. Sin does not overcome the blood; it is blood that overcomes sin.

Thus grace is extended toward the believer for time and eternity, not on the ground of impossible perfection, nor by slighting the fact of sin; it is extended to him because it is the Father's good pleasure to keep His child, and the Father is unconditionally free to do this through the blood that has been shed.

Second, *There Must be a Disposal of Every Human Obligation.*

It is most evident from the Scriptures that every human work has been set aside and salvation is now

offered to men, only as the *gift* of God. There are
no payments to be made, past, present, or future;
else grace is no longer grace. This fact is the second
foundation principle of grace as grace is exercised
toward the sinner. This aspect of divine favor is
equally effective when grace is exercised toward the
Christian. Do Christians pay their way, or do they,
by their good lives and service, make it imperative
for God to keep them saved? The answer is evident.
There could be no peace of heart under such relations to God. Who could ever assure himself that
he had accomplished *all* his Christian duty, or complied with *all* the demands found in the holy ideals
of God? Who can repay God for the riches of His
grace? To attempt to do so, is to place a sordid
value on the priceless treasures of heaven's glory.
God proposes to keep every believing soul, for He
has said, "I will in no wise cast out." But His keeping will not be on a basis of exchange wherein Christian faithfulness, as important as it is, will be made
the purchasing medium of the measureless goodness
and blessing of God. He will keep by *grace* alone.

Third, *There Must be a Disposal of Every Human
Merit.*

Through the divine decree, as has been seen, every
human merit has been set aside in order that pure
grace might reign unchallenged and uncomplicated.
That salvation might be by grace alone, God has removed every possible conflicting issue which might
arise because of human merit. The whole human
family is now "under sin"; for only thus are they
objects of pure grace. Such grace can be exercised

only toward the meritless. Salvation is based on the
loving goodness of God and never on the supposed
worthiness of the sinner. In like manner, God is now
equally free to continue the exercise of His boundless
grace toward the Christian without reference to the
Christian's merit. All that the love of God may
prompt Him to do in grace, He is free to do. His
unconditional covenant of eternal blessings is the
guaranty of His abiding purpose. This leads to the
consideration of the second classification:

II.   THE KEEPING POWER OF GOD THROUGH GRACE
IS IMPLIED IN EVERY REVELATION WHEREIN IS PRE-
SENTED THE TRUTH THAT GRACE REACHES UNTO THE
COMING AGES FOR ITS CONSUMMATION.

Through the cross of Christ, which has dealt with
sin, and through His decree against all human obligation and merit as related to salvation, God is righteously free to preserve His child forever. And since
His supreme purpose in all the ages will not be realized until the sinner is saved, transformed into the
image of Christ, and lifted up to the highest glory,
He will continue the exercise of His grace toward
every believer until the divine objective is consummated. How perfectly He has delivered Himself from
every limitation! How absolutely gracious are all His
ways with those whom He saves! And how irresist-
ible in His purpose and power!

The great covenant promises of salvation are not
limited to the moment when the sinner accepts the

saving grace that is in Christ Jesus; they all reach on and guarantee every step of the way from the first moment of faith to the last moment of fruition. Even the word *salvation,* in its largest Biblical meaning, covers all that is past, all that is present, and all that is future, in the out-working of the grace of God for the one who believes. "He which hath begun a good work in you will perform it until the day of Jesus Christ" (Phil. 1:6). "For God so loved the world, that he gave his only begotten Son, that whosoever believeth in him should not perish, but have everlasting life" (John 3:16). In the great promises of grace there is no measurement as to time, nor any human condition imposed other than believing. "But as many as received him, to them gave he power [right] to become the sons of God, even to them that believe on his name" (John 1:12). "He that believeth on the Son hath everlasting life" (John 3:36). "Verily, verily, I say unto you, He that heareth my word, and believeth on him that sent me, hath everlasting life, and shall not come into condemnation; but is passed from death unto life" (John 5:24). "And him that cometh to me I will in no wise cast out" (John 6:37). "For I am not ashamed of the gospel of Christ: for it is the power of God unto salvation to every one that believeth" (Rom, 1:16). "That he might be just, and the justifier of him which believeth in Jesus" (Rom. 3:26). "For Christ is the end of the law for righteousness to every one that believeth" (Rom. 10:4). Such is the unalterable and unconditional covenant of God in grace.

III. THE KEEPING POWER OF GOD THROUGH GRACE
IS INDICATED BY THE MANIFOLD PROVISIONS AND SAFE-
GUARDS WHICH HE HAS MADE TO THAT END.

The eternal purposes of God in grace can never
fail since He has anticipated and provided for every
emergency that could arise. Some of these provisions
are:

First. *The Power of God.*

His power, which is supreme, is ceaselessly engaged in the keeping of His own unto the realization
of His eternal purpose. *Able* is the great New Testament word that is used to indicate the omnipotent
power of God. By use of this word, God is said to
be of sufficient power to do whatever is predicated
of Him. "My Father, which gave them me, is greater
than all; and no man [nothing] is able to pluck them
out of my Father's hand" (John 10:29). "For I
am persuaded, that neither death, nor life, nor angels, nor principalities, nor powers, nor things present, nor things to come, nor height, nor depth, nor
any other creature [created being], shall be able to
separate us from the love of God, which is in Christ
Jesus our Lord" (Rom. 8:38, 39).[1] "Who art thou
that thou judgest another man's servant? to his own
master he standeth or falleth. Yea, he shall be holden
up: for God is able to make him stand" (Rom. 14:4).
And God "is able to do exceeding abundantly

[1] It should be observed that there is no reference in this
list either to things past, or to sin, as having possible power
to separate the believer from God. The past and all sin is
under the blood and, therefore, not even to be considered.

above all that we ask or think" (Eph. 3:20). "According to the working whereby he is able even to subdue all things unto himself" (Phil. 3:21). "For I know whom I have believed, and am persuaded that he is able to keep that which I have committed unto him against that day" (2 Tim. 1:12). "For in that he himself hath suffered being tempted, he is able to succor them that are tempted" (Heb. 2:18). "Wherefore he is able also to save them to the uttermost [without end] that come unto God by him" (Heb. 7:25). "Now unto him that is able to keep you from falling, and to present you faultless before the presence of his glory with exceeding joy" (Jude 24). "And being fully persuaded that, what he has promised, he was able to perform" (Rom. 4:21). "What shall we then say to these things? If God be for us, who can be against us?" (Rom. 8:31).

Second. *The Love of God.*

Not only is God *able* to do according to His eternal purpose, but His love as a supreme motive will never fail. "Having loved his own which were in the world, he loved them unto the end" (without end, John 13:1). "But God commendeth his love toward us, in that, while we were yet sinners, Christ died for us. Much more then, being now justified by his blood, we shall be saved from wrath through Him. For if, when we were enemies, we were reconciled to God by the death of his Son, much more, being reconciled, we shall be saved by his life" (Rom. 5:8-11). As he loved the unsaved enough to give His Son to die for them, even when they were "yet without strength" and "enemies"; "Much more then, being now justified by his blood" and "reconciled," they shall be "saved from wrath through him," and "saved by his life." Such is the unchangeable love of God. "Much more" than His love for the "enemies," which drew out the unspeakable gift of His Son, is His love for His own who are now "justified" and "reconciled." So, also, there is a boundless assurance as to the future: "saved from wrath through him," which points to the unchangeable position of the believer "in Christ," and "saved by his life" which points to the living presence and ministry of Christ in glory. With such provisions, God's love can know no disappointment concerning those whom He has saved in grace.

Third. *The Prayer of the Son of God.*

Christ prayed while here on earth: "I pray for them: I pray not for the world, but for them which thou hast given me; for they are thine. And all mine are thine, and thine are mine; and I am glorified in them. And now I am no more in the world, but these are in the world, and I come to thee. Holy Father, keep through thine own name those whom thou hast given me, that they be one, as we are. While I was with them in the world, I kept them in thy name: those that thou gavest me I have kept, and none of them is lost, but the son of perdition." "I pray not that thou shouldest take them out of the world, but that thou shouldest keep them from the evil." "Neither pray I for these alone, but for them also which shall believe on me through their word" (John 17: 9-12, 15, 20). It is wholly impossible that any prayer of the Son of God should be unanswered. Too much emphasis cannot be placed on this assuring fact. While the "son of perdition," who was never saved, was lost that, in his case, "the Scripture might be fulfilled," the Son of God could say of the saved ones: "And none of them is lost." Thus, since He has prayed, as well, for "them also which shall believe on me through their word," He will yet say, of *all* believers: "And none of them is lost," and in the same manner will the Scriptures be fulfilled in the presentation of every saved one in glory.

As Christ began to pray for his own while He was yet here in the world, so He has continued to pray for them, and will continue to pray for them, in heaven: "Seeing he ever liveth to make intercession for them" (Heb. 7:25). Who can measure the security of the children of God when they are the objects of the ceaseless intercession of the Son of God, whose prayer can never be denied?

Fourth. *The Substitutionary Death of the Son of God.*

The death of the Son of God is the sufficient answer to the condemning power of sin; even as sin appears before the righteous throne of God. Not even the unsaved are now condemned because of sin which Christ has borne; how much more are the saved free from condemnation through the death of Christ! Thus the Holy Spirit boldly inquires: "Who is he that condemneth?" The answer He also gives: "It is Christ that died"; "There is therefore now no condemnation to them which are in Christ Jesus";

"When I see the blood, I will pass over you." The eternal purpose of God in grace is assured through the death of the Son of God.

Fifth. *The Resurrection of the Son of God.*

When he is saved, every believer partakes of the resurrection life of the Son of God. He receives a new life from God. It is the gift of God which is eternal life, and it is "Christ in you, the hope of glory." Speaking of this imparted life, Christ said: "I am come that they might have life," and, "He that believeth on the Son hath everlasting life." So, again, "I give unto them eternal life; and they shall never perish" (John 3:36; 10:10, 28). It is the imperishable life of the eternal Son of God which is imparted to every believer. God never gave this gift in blindness, not knowing what might be the future character of the one He thus saved. He knew the end from the beginning. He anticipated every failure and sin; yet, through Christ, He can assure us that, having received the gift of eternal life, we shall *never* perish. According to the unalterable gift of eternal life, made possible through the death and resurrection of the Son of God, the purposes of God in grace are secured.

Sixth. *The Present Advocacy of the Son of God.*

The Lord Jesus Christ is now "appearing" in the presence of the Father as Advocate for every one who is saved by grace. As Advocate, He is concerned with the actual sins of the Christian. He is not there before the Father making excuses for their sins, nor is He imploring the Father to be merciful; He is rather presenting His own blood before that throne as the answer to the condemnation of every sin. "If any man sin, we [Christians] have an advocate with the Father, Jesus Christ the righteous" (1 John 2: 1). In Rom. 8: 34, assurance is given by four great facts that the child of God will never be condemned. One of these is that Christ "is even at the right hand of God." To the same purpose it is declared in Heb. 9: 24, that "Christ is not entered into the holy places made with hands, which are the figures of the true; but into heaven itself, now to appear in the presence of God for us." In view of the presence of the Advocate before the Father's throne, meeting the force of every sin, even meeting the challenge of Satan who is there to accuse the brethren night and day before God (Rev. 12: 10), there can be no doubt remaining as to the realization of the eternal purposes of God in grace.

Seventh. *The Intercession, or Shepherdhood, of the Son of God.*

The intercession of Christ extends beyond His present ministry of prayer for the saved, which has just been considered, and includes, as well, His shepherd-care over them. As Shepherd, He is guarding their path against the snares of the evil one, and guiding their feet in the ways of His blessing and peace. Peter knew nothing of the fact that Satan had designs against him, or that Christ had anticipated those designs and had prayed for him. All this was revealed to him when Christ said: "Simon, Simon, behold, Satan hath desired to have you [obtained thee by asking], that he may sift you as wheat: but

I have prayed for thee, that thy faith fail not" (Lk. 22: 31, 32). Peter's ignorance of that which had transpired in heaven concerning him did not change the fact that he was, nevertheless, under the shepherd-care of Christ the Lord. So it is at every moment concerning the child of God.

As Shepherd and Intercessor, Christ is now the High Priest in heaven for His own. The priesthood ministry of the old dispensation was continually interrupted by the dying of the priests; but this Priest —Christ—hath an "unchangeable priesthood," and that is assured because "he continueth ever"—Christ will never die again. His priesthood will never cease. Because of this it is also said: "Wherefore he is able also to save them to the uttermost [without end] that come unto God by him, seeing he ever liveth to make intercession for them" (Heb. 7: 23-25). He will save them as long as He lives, which is *forever*.

David, too, had learned of the shepherd-care of his Lord: for he said, "The Lord is my shepherd; I shall not want." His confidence concerning the future which is expressed by the words, "I shall not want," is that which is even more to be expected in the believer of this dispensation, who has all the added revelation regarding the present ministry of Christ in heaven. The instructed believer is thus made certain that the eternal purposes of God in grace will never fail.

Eighth. *The Regenerating Work of the Spirit.*

By the regenerating work of the Spirit the believer

is made a legitimate child of God. God being actually his Father, he is impelled by the Spirit to say, "Abba, Father." Being born of God, he has partaken of the "divine nature," and, on the ground of that birth, he is an heir of God, and a joint-heir with Christ (John 1:13; 3:3-6; Tit. 3:4-6; 1 Pet. 1:23; 2 Pet. 1:4; 1 John 3:9).

The impartation of a nature is an operation so deep that the nature thus imparted is never said to to be removed for any cause whatsoever. This statement may be verified from the Scriptures. The vital fact of relationship through birth is never said to be disannulled. Thus, again, the fulfillment of the eternal purpose of God in grace is to be anticipated with unwavering confidence.

Ninth. *The Spirit's Indwelling.*

The fact that the Spirit of God now indwells every believer may also be verified from the Word of God (John 7:37-39; Rom. 5:5; 8:9; I Cor. 2:12; 6:19; 1 John 3:24). It is also clearly revealed that the Spirit has come to "abide" in the heart He has once entered. This abiding presence of the Spirit is in answer to the prayer of the Son of God, which prayer cannot be unanswered. "And I will pray the Father, and he shall give you another Comforter, that he may abide with you for ever" (John 14:16). The Christian may "grieve," and "quench" (resist) the Spirit; but there is no Scripture which teaches that the Spirit will be grieved *away,* or quenched *away.* So long as the Spirit indwells, the eternal purposes of God in grace are sure, and He *must* abide forever.

Tenth. *The Baptism with the Spirit.*

The Christian has been so vitally united to Christ by the baptism with the Spirit that he is said to be "in Christ," and Christ is said to be "in" the believer. According to the Scriptures, there is no other meaning to the baptism with the Spirit than this (1 Cor. 12 : 13). Thus, being placed by the Spirit in organic union with Christ, the believer is related to Christ as the branch is to the vine, or as a member of the human body is to its living head. Because of this most vital union to Christ through the baptism with the Spirit, the believer is said to be a partaker in all that Christ is, all that Christ has done, and all that Christ will ever do. This is a limitless theme since it opens before one the eternal realities of an unchangeable identification with Christ. One of these eternal realities is " the imputed righteousness of God." This garment in which every believer is now clothed. and because of which he is now, and will be forever, accepted before God, is reckoned unto him because he is "in Christ": "That we might be made the righteousness of God in him" (2 Cor. 5 : 21); "But of him are ye in Christ Jesus, who of God is made unto us . . . righteousness" (1 Cor. 1 : 30); "That I may win Christ, and be found in him, not having mine own righteousness, . . . but that which is through the faith of Christ, the righteousness which is of God by faith" (Phil. 3 : 8, 9). "In him" we are made nigh through the blood of Christ, and we are "made accepted in the beloved." There is a righteousness from God which is *unto* all and *upon* all who believe (Rom. 3 : 22).

This is the imputed righteousness of God. It covers the Christian, because he is "in Christ," and God sees him only as Christ is seen. Being "in Christ" he is in God's sight what Christ is. This position is that of being accepted as a living member in the body, of which Christ is the living Head. God sees the member only in the body of His Son. As long, then, as Christ abides and is Himself what He is—the very righteousness of God—, so long the member of His body will abide under the imputed righteousness of God. Thus the eternal purposes of God in grace are certain through the baptism with the Spirit.

Eleventh. *The Sealing with the Spirit.*

Likewise, every believer is now sealed with the Spirit. The immediate value of this accomplishment seems to be more for the sake of God, than for the sake of the believer. This particular ministry is mentioned only three times in the New Testament; but it is of vital import: "Who hath also sealed us, and given the earnest of the Spirit in our hearts" (2 Cor. 1:22); "Having also believed, ye were sealed with the Holy Spirit of promise" (Eph. 1:13, R. V.); "And grieve not the Holy Spirit of God, whereby ye are sealed unto the day of redemption" (Eph. 4:30). It is also said of Christ that He was sealed of the Father (John 6:27. Cf Isa. 42:1). The sealing of the believer with the Spirit is "unto the day of redemption." It is the very presence of the Spirit in the heart. He is the Seal. The thing accomplished by His sealing is so vital and enduring that it precludes the possibility of interruption or deflection. Thus, as for reasons given above, the eternal purposes of God in grace are to be received without distrust, because of the sealing with the Spirit.

Twelfth. *The New Covenant made in His Blood.*

The several great covenants into which God has been pleased to enter with men are either conditional covenants, or unconditional covenants. A covenant is conditional whenever it is made to depend at any point on the faithfulness of man. The law as given by Moses was a conditional covenant. Its terms might be stated in the words, "If ye will do good, I will bless you." On the other hand, a covenant is unconditional when it stands as a simple declaration from God as to what He purposes to do, and without relation to the faithfulness, or unfaithfulness, of man. The Abrahamic Covenant (Gen. 12:1-4; 13:14-17; 15:1-7; 17:1-8) is an unconditional covenant. It will be seen that God relied at no point on the character or conduct of Abraham. He simply declared to Abraham what He purposed to do. This was based on Abraham's faith; but not on Abraham's faithfulness. The covenant was, and is, assured through the faithfulness of God alone. In like manner, the New Covenant made in His blood, by which every Christian is now related to God, is an *unconditional* covenant. It is God's declaration of what He proposes to do for the one who places his faith in Christ. Belief in Christ, it should be noted, is not a condition within the covenant; it is the one condition of entrance into the covenant. Turning to the great promises of the keeping of God through grace, it will be discovered that they are always *unconditional*. These promises are made to depend only on the goodness and faithfulness of God. As a fruitage of the saved life, good works are closely related to the Christian's life under God, and are the ground of all future rewards; but human works, as important as they are, do not enter as a *condition* into either the divine plan of salvation by grace, or of divine keeping through grace. This, too, may be verified from the Word of God. Three very brief and unconditional promises of eternal security are here given: "I will in no wise cast out" (John 6:37); "They shall never perish" (John 10:28); and, "shall not come into condemnation" (John 5:24). Under such unconditional promises the eternal purposes of God in grace may be received with unwavering confidence.

Certain passages, it should be noted, have been interpreted by some writers to teach that, in spite of this overwhelming body of revelation concerning the purpose and power of God in grace, the Christian who is truly saved might be lost again. The passages are worthy of careful consideration but such consideration cannot be entered into here.[1] Scripture does not present a contradiction, and, as must be concluded from what has gone before, it will be found upon careful examination of these Scriptures, considering their context and dispensational character, that there is no Scripture which lessens the force, or discredits the revelation, concerning the eternal purposes of God in grace.

Salvation by grace is, then, the indivisible whole of God's redeeming purpose in Christ and that which

---

[1] See author's book *Salvation* for extended analysis of these passages.

rescues a sinner from the lowest depths of human standing, and transforms, preserves, and presents that sinner in the highest eternal glory. At infinite cost, God has made Himself free to do *all* of this. His unmeasured love will suffer Him to do no less in behalf of every one who comes to Him through His Son. Divine grace is God's *all*. It is the expression of the last degree of His love. In no sense could He exercise a part of His grace. It must be all or none. He must save perfectly for all time and eternity, or not at all. There is no other salvation offered in the Word of God.

Failure to trust in Christ alone is disclosed when salvation is supposed to depend on anything other than *believing* in Christ, and when security is made to depend at any point whatsoever on human faithfulness. Men are saved and kept in sovereign grace through simple faith in Christ alone. This is the heart of the Gospel of divine grace. If any other Gospel than his be preached, it must fall under the unrevoked anathema of God (Gal. 1:8, 9).

The zeal engendered by modern religious movements which are even accompanied with signs and wonders is no guaranty of sound doctrine. The enthusiasts responsible for these movements almost universally deny that salvation is by simple faith in Christ, and that the grace of God will keep those who are saved as His own forever. Those who discredit the absolute reign of grace in the salvation and keeping of a soul, should ponder well the fact that there is no other way of salvation.

We have thus complete evidence that the eternal purposes of God in grace are unalterable, since His keeping power through grace is *included* in every consideration of the principles of grace, His keeping power is *implied* in every revelation in which is presented the truth that grace reaches into the coming ages for its consummation, and His keeping power is *indicated* by the manifold provisions and safeguards which He has made to that end. Should His eternal purpose fail by the slightest degree, the object of salvation, the object of the death and resurrection of Christ, and the object of creation itself, will have failed. It shall not fail; for the mouth of the Lord has spoken it.

CHAPTER IV

Introductive.

The salvation in grace which God accomplishes for those who believe includes, among other things, the placing of the saved one in position as a son of God, a citizen of heaven, and a member of the family and household of God; and, since every position demands a corresponding manner of life, it is to be expected that a rule of conduct as exalted as heaven itself will be committed to the believer. This is precisely what we find; for grace not only provides a perfect salvation and eternal keeping for the one who believes on Christ; but grace provides, as well, the instruction for the daily life of the one who is saved, while he is being kept through the power of God. This instruction for the daily life, it will be found, is a particular revelation from God to Christians only. As it is wholly gracious in character, it is entirely separate from, and independent of, any other rule of life which is found in the Word of God. The Bible, being the one Book from God for all people of all the ages, contains the detailed expression of the will of God concerning the manner of life of various dispensational classes of people as they are related to God in different periods of time, and under the several corresponding covenants. Among these revelations, is the rule of conduct regarding the daily life of those who are saved by grace in this dispensation which occupies the time between the cross and the second coming of Christ. This gracious rule of life is complete in itself and stands alone in the Scriptures, disassociated from any other and uncomplicated. It is the teachings of grace.

The remainder of this discussion will be occupied, in the main, with the identification and application of the extended body of Scripture relative to the teachings of grace. The value of knowing this revelation cannot be estimated, (1) because no Christian may hope to live well-pleasing to God who does not know the facts of the revealed will of God for his daily life, and (2) because appalling ignorance exists on every hand concerning these vital truths and distinctions of the Word of God.

No careful reader of the New Testament can fail to observe the fact that doctrinal strife obtained at the very opening of the Christian dispensation. This controversy was concerned mainly with the question of whether law or grace furnishes the governing principle for Christian conduct. Although the New Testament contains specific and lengthy warnings against both the legalizers and their teachings, and their systems are therein proven to be opposed to the doctrines of pure grace, their successors from generation to generation to the present time have ever sought to discredit the grace of God. Their messages, though steeped in error, have often exhibited great zeal and sincerity; but zeal and sincerity, greatly to be desired when well directed, fail utterly in God's sight as substitutes for a consistent presentation of the truth. The only hope of deliverance from the false doctrines of legalizing teachers is through unprejudiced consideration of the exact revelations of Scripture. This examination of the Scriptures should be free from a blind following of the teachings of men, and should be made with a heart willing to receive "reproof" and "correction" from the Word of God as well as "instruction in righteousness" (2 Tim. 3 : 16). Only the one to whom these teachings are crystal clear can appreciate the transcendent value of understanding the teachings of grace.

In presenting this introductory consideration of the extensive theme of the teachings of grace, it is necessary in some instances to assume conclusions the fuller proof of which are taken up in subsequent treatments of the discussion. Likewise, in completing the various lines of argument, repetition at certain points is unavoidable.

SECTION ONE

GRACE PROVIDES A PARTICULAR RULE OF LIFE

In chapter 2 of the Epistle by Paul to Titus, beginning at verse 11, we read: "For the grace of God that bringeth salvation hath appeared to all men, teaching us that, denying ungodliness and worldy lusts, we should live soberly, righteously, and godly, in this present world [age]; looking for that blessed hope, and the glorious appearing of the great God and our Saviour Jesus Christ; who gave himself for us, that he might redeem us from all iniquity, and purify unto himself a peculiar people, zealous of good works."

Two widely different ministries of grace are set forth in this passage:

First, the grace of God which bringeth salvation hath appeared unto *all* men. This, it is clear, refers to the saving grace of God which has come into the world by Christ Jesus, and is now to be proclaimed to *all* men. It is a message for *all* men, since its provisions are universal and its invitation is to "whosoever will." Grace upon grace is bestowed both now and unto the consummation of the ages upon those who believe.

Second, the passage reveals, as well, that it is the

same grace which has brought salvation to *all* men, that teaches *"us."* The word *us*, it should be observed, does not refer to the wider class of *all* men mentioned before; but it refers only to the company of those who are saved. The importance of this distinction is evident; for whatever grace proposes to teach, its teachings are addressed only to those who are saved by grace. This qualifying aspect of the teachings of grace is not limited to this one passage, though that would suffice; it is an out-standing characteristic of the whole body of grace teachings as they appear throughout the New Testament. These teachings, being addressed to Christians only, are never intended to be imposed on the Christ-rejecting individual, or the Christ-rejecting world. This fact cannot be emphasized too forcibly. The word of God makes no appeal to the unsaved for a betterment of life. There is but one issue in this dispensation between God and the unregenerate man, and that is neither character nor conduct; it is the personal appeal of the Gospel of the grace of God. Until the unsaved receive Christ, who is God's gift in grace, no other issue can be raised. Men may moralize among themselves, and establish their self-governments on principles of right conduct; but God is never presented in the unfoldings of grace as seeking to *reform* sinners. Every word regarding the quality of life is reserved for those who are already rightly related to Him on the greater issues of salvation.

Could it be demonstrated that God has made the slightest moral appeal to the unregenerate other than that which is implied in the Gospel invitation, then it must be admitted that, should that moral appeal be complied with by any individual, that individual would have moved nearer to God. The works of man would become meritorious, and thereby a third classification of humanity would be created, standing somewhere between those who are "under sin" and those who are "in Christ," or "under grace." In this age, no such intermediate group of people is possible. If such a class existed, they could not be saved; for they would no longer be fit objects of grace. Men are either lost and condemned "under sin," or wholly and eternally saved by grace in Christ Jesus. The common practice of presenting the great standards of Christian living indiscriminately to mixed congregations by preaching, and to people in general through public print, is a tragedy of infinite proportions. If the unsaved are present when the teachings of grace are discussed, there should be a Gospel appeal made by which the unsaved are classified and excluded from any share in those teachings. Apart from this appeal, it is impossible to save the unregenerate from receiving the impression that God is now seeking their reformation before He seeks their regeneration. Nothing is more wholesome for the unsaved than lovingly to be reminded that they, according to the Word of God, have no part in the Christian life, and that they are shut up to the acceptance of Christ. Saving results are sure to follow the continued, clean-cut, discriminating preaching of the Word in its right application to both the saved and the unsaved. It is alarming to the unsaved to be warned that they are lost until they receive Christ, and such faithful preaching, being the Truth of God, is owned and used of the Spirit of God.

Nothing need be said here of the crime against high heaven which is committed by men who are *purposely* urging moral betterment on the unsaved in lieu of the Gospel of grace. The unrevoked anathema of God rests upon them; "But though we, or an angel from heaven, preach any other gospel unto you than that which we have preached unto you, let him be accursed. As we said before, so say I now again, If any man preach any other gospel unto you than that ye have received, let him be accursed" (Gal. 1: 8, 9). There is a possibility, however, that, through carelessness or ignorance, some, whose intentions are good, may make the same fatal error in presenting God's Truth. As certainly as the exercise of pure grace is the supreme divine purpose unto the eternal glory, so certainly to hinder an understanding of that grace, or to mislead one soul by a misstatement, is the supreme blunder. How momentous is the practice of preaching and of personal work, both for those who hear and for those who speak! Well might the high crime of dealing damnation to the souls of men in the name of Christian preaching be treated, from a mere humanitarian viewpoint, with a thousand-fold greater penalty than the crime of dealing deadly poison to the bodies of men. Sinners are to be saved by grace. It is Satan's device to complicate this simple fact with the lesser issues of Christian living.

The teachings of grace, it will be found, comprise all of the teachings of the Epistles, the Acts, and also certain portions of the Gospels apart from their mere historical features. Returning to the passage already quoted from Titus, we discover that only a portion of the whole appeal of the teachings of grace are mentioned in this Scripture; but here the believer is taught that he is to deny ungodliness and worldly lusts, and to live soberly, righteously, godly, and looking for the personal return of his Lord from heaven. This describes a life of peculiar devotion and sweetness. Thus would God "purify unto himself a peculiar people, zealous of good works."

According to the Scriptures, Christians are confronted with a two-fold danger: On the one hand, they may go in the way of the irresponsible, careless sin of the Gentiles, or, on the other hand, they may go into the legality of the Jews. They may "walk as do the Gentiles," or they may "fall from grace." They are warned as much against the one mistake as against the other. The doctrines of grace may be so perverted that, while there is a holy horror of slipping into careless sin, it is deemed most pious to assume the cursing burden of law. The teachings of grace give equal warning against the sin of turning either in the way of Gentiles or in the way of the Jews.

In discovering the fact and scope of the teachings of grace, it will be noted that, (1) The Christian's daily life is to be directed only by the teachings of grace, (2) The law is excluded from the grace teachings of Christ, (3) The law is excluded from the teachings of the Apostles, and (4) The life and service of the Apostle Paul is an illustration of a life which is lived under grace.

I. THE CHRISTIAN'S DAILY LIFE IS TO BE DIRECTED ONLY BY THE TEACHINGS OF GRACE.

In exact accord with the fact that Christians are to be governed only by the teachings of grace, the Biblical appeal in grace never contemplates an observance of the law. Through the death of Christ, the law is not only disannulled; but, as a rule of life, it is never mentioned, or included in the teachings of grace. It is rather excluded. The believer is to walk by a "rule," but that rule, it will be seen, is never an adaptation of the law (Cf Gal. 6:16; Phil. 3:16). This important fact should be carefully verified by the reading of all the Epistles. It is impossible to refer here to this extensive body of Scripture beyond a very few illustrative passages. In the following Scriptures, as in all grace teachings, the law, it will be found, is not once applied to believers:

"For we are his workmanship, created in Christ Jesus unto good works, which God hath before ordained that we should walk in them" (Eph. 2:10).

"For the kingdom of God is not meat and drink; but righteousness, and peace, and joy in the Holy Ghost. For he that in these things serveth Christ is acceptable to God, and approved of men. Let us therefore follow after the things which make for peace, and things wherewith one may edify another" (Rom. 14:17-19).

"And this I pray, that your love may abound yet

more and more in knowledge and in all judgment; that ye may approve things that are excellent; that ye may be sincere and without offence till the day of Christ; being filled with the fruits of righteousness, which are by Jesus Christ, unto the glory and praise of God" (Phil. 1:9-11).

"Finally, brethren, whatsoever things are true, whatsoever things are honest, whatsoever things are just, whatsoever things are pure, whatsoever things are lovely, whatsoever things are of good report; if there be any virtue, and if there be any praise, think on these things. Those things, which ye have both learned, and received, and heard, and seen in me, do: and the God of peace shall be with you" (Phil. 4:8, 9).

"But God forbid that I should glory, save in the cross of our Lord Jesus Christ, by whom the world is crucified unto me, and I unto the world. For in Christ Jesus neither circumcision availeth anything, nor uncircumcision, but a new creature [creation]. And as many as walk according to this rule, peace be on them, and mercy, and upon the Israel of God" (Gal. 6:14-16).

"For we through the Spirit wait for the hope of righteousness by faith. For in Christ Jesus neither circumcision availeth anything, nor uncircumcision; but faith which worketh by love" (Gal. 5:5, 6.)

"But now the righteousness of God without the law is manifested, being witnnessed by the law and the prophets" (Rom. 3:21).

"For Christ is the end of the law for righteousness to every one that believeth" (Rom. 10:4).

"But put ye on the Lord Jesus Christ, and make no provision for the flesh, to fulfil the lusts thereof" (Rom. 13:14).

"False brethren. . . .who came in privily to spy out our liberty which we have in Christ Jesus, that they might bring us into bondage: to whom we gave place by subjection, no, not for an hour; that the truth of the gospel might continue with you" (Gal. 2:4, 5.)

"For it seemed good to the Holy Ghost, and to us, to lay upon you no greater burden than these necessary things; that ye abstain from meats offered to idols, and from blood, and from things strangled, and from fornication: from which if ye keep yourselves, ye shall do well" (Acts. 15:28, 29).

"As touching the Gentiles which believe, we have written and concluded that they observe no such things" (issues of the law. Acts 21:25).

"Stand fast therefore in the liberty wherewith Christ hath made us free, and be not entangled again with the yoke of bondage" (Gal. 5:1).

By these passages, selected from the whole body of New Testament teaching concerning the believer's walk in grace, it is seen that the teachings of grace do not *include* the precepts of the law as such; but that they *exclude* those precepts. However, no vital principle contained in the law is abandoned. It will be observed that these principles of the law are carried forward and are restated in the teachings of grace; not as law, but as principles which are revised, adapted, and newly incorporated in the issues of pure grace.

II. THE LAW IS EXCLUDED FROM THE GRACE TEACH-
INGS OF CHRIST.

Concerning the admixture of the principles of law
and grace, it will be seen that these principles are
wholly separated in the teachings of Christ. Are
Christians to keep the law as the rule of their conduct either because of a command from Christ, or
because of the example of Christ? No light will be
gained on these questions until the two-fold aspect
of the ministry of Christ is distinguished. According to Rom. 15: 8, 9, Christ was, first, "a minister
of the circumcision for the truth of God, to confirm
the promises made unto the fathers"; and, second,
"that the Gentiles might glorify God for his mercy."
This two-fold distinction obtains at every point in
the Gospels and Epistles. So, also, it obtains in the
Old Testament types and prophecies relating to
Christ. Christ sustained a particular and unique
relation to the nation Israel as the One who fulfilled
the great Messianic covenants given to that people.
At the opening of His ministry He said, "I am not
sent but unto the lost sheep of the house of Israel"
(Mt. 15: 24); and when, at the same time, sending
His disciples out with the Jewish message of "the
kingdom of heaven," He instructed them, saying,
"Go not into the way of the Gentiles, and into any
city of the Samaritans enter ye not: but go rather to
the lost sheep of the house of Israel. And as ye go,
preach, saying, The kingdom of heaven is at hand"
(Mt. 10: 5-7). As a Jew, and as the Consolation
and Hope of Israel, He personally acknowledged,

kept, taught, and enforced the law. As the Saviour
and Hope of the world, He established the new manner of life and relationship which belongs to the believer under grace. Speaking to the Jewish ruler,
Christ said: "If thou wilt enter into life, keep the
commandments" (Mt. 19:17).[1] True to the Jewish
dispensation, He said with reference to the law of
Moses: "This do and thou shalt live"; but when
contemplating the cross and Himself as the bread
come down from heaven to give His life for the
world, He said: "This is the work of God, that ye
believe on him whom he [God] hath sent" (John
6:29). These opposing principles are not to be
reconciled. They indicate that fundamental distinction which must exist between those principles that
obtain in an age of law, on the one hand, and an age
of grace, on the other hand.

What interpretation should be given, then, to the
word *commandments* as used by Christ or as related
to Christ, according to the following passages: "If
ye love me, keep my commandments"; "He that
hath my commandments, and keepeth them, he it is
that loveth me"; "If ye keep my commandments,
ye shall abide in my love"; "And hereby we do

[1] In the Synoptic Gospels, *life*, it should be noted, is sometimes that aspect of divine blessing which is provided for
those who enter the kingdom of heaven (Note Mt. 18: 1-10;
25: 31-46), and being somewhat different, should not be confused with the present gift of God, which is eternal life
through Jesus Christ our Lord. One was offered, and is
yet to be granted, on the basis of faithful, law-keeping
works: the other is gained only through the grace which is
by Jesus Christ our Lord. One is provided for the age to
come (Lk. 18: 30). The other is a present possession; for He
has said: "He that believeth on the Son hath everlasting
life" (John 3: 36).

know that we know him, if we keep his commandments''; ''And whatsoever we ask, we receive of
him, because we keep his commandments, and do
those things that are pleasing in his sight'';
''He that keepeth his commandments dwelleth in
him, and he in him''; ''By this we know that we
love the children of God, when we love God, and
keep his commandments''; ''Teaching them to observe all things whatsoever I have commanded you'';
and, ''Blessed are they that do his commandments''
(John 14:15, 21; 15:10; 1 John 2:3; 3:22, 24;
5:2; Mt. 28:20; Rev. 22:14)? Is Christ here requiring the commandments as given by Moses?

In considering this crucial question, it should be
noted that, when dealing with Jews as such, He gave
no ''commandments'' of His own relative to the
rule of their lives. He recognized only the law of
Moses and the law of the kingdom. In matters of
life-relationship to God He said, ''What readest
thou in the law?''; but when He began to instruct
those who were saved by grace through His cross,
He began to announce what He was pleased to term
''my commandments.'' This term is not found in
all the Gospels until the record is given of His farewell words in the upper room on the night before
His death (John, chapters 13-17).[1] This is most
significant; for it is evident that the upper-room
discourse was addressed, not to Israelites, but to
those who were ''clean'' through the word He had
spoken to them. In this portion of the Scriptures,
the cross is treated as an accomplished fact (John

---

[1] Mt. 28:20 not only follows the cross, in point of time; but
also follows the forty-days post-resurrection teaching concerning the kingdom of God as recorded in Acts 1:3.

16:11. Cf 12:31); the whole body of teaching is dated by Christ beyond the cross by the words, "And now I have told you before it come to pass, that, when it is come to pass, ye might believe" (14:29); and, finally, the only reference to the law in this great message of the upper room is so stated as to place those Jews to whom He was speaking *outside* its authority: "But this cometh to pass, that the word might be fulfilled that is written in their [not your] law" (John 15:25).

The upper-room discourse is the genesis of the Epistles of the New Testament; for in it, in germ form, the great doctrines of grace are announced. The phrase *my commandments* is reserved until this grace-revelation, because this term refers to the teachings of grace, rather than to the law.

Added proof that the term, *my commandments,* refers to the teachings of grace may be seen when the passages which indicate the character of His commandments are considered. Some of these are: "A new commandment I give unto you, That ye love one another; as I have loved you"; "This is my commandment, That ye love one another, as I have loved you"; "And this is his commandment, That we should believe on the name of his Son Jesus Christ, and love one another, as he gave commandments"; "And this commandment have we from him, That he who loveth God love his brother also"; "For this is the love of God, that we keep his commandments: and his commandments are not grievous";[1] "I rejoice greatly that I found of thy

1 This could not be said of the law of Moses; for of that law it is written: "Now therefore why tempt ye God, to put a

children walking in truth, as we have received a commandment from the Father. And now I beseech thee, lady, not as though I wrote a new commandment unto thee, but that which we had from the beginning, that we love one another." To this the Apostle Paul has added a testimony concerning the commandments of the Lord. By the testimony of Paul, the whole teaching of grace, as set forth by himself, is related to the commandments of the Lord: "If any man think himself to be a prophet, or spiritual, let him acknowledge that the things that I write unto you are the commandments of the Lord"; "For ye know what commandments we gave you by the Lord Jesus"; "Bear ye one another's burdens, and so fulfil the law of Christ" (John 13: 34, 15: 12; 1 John 3: 23; 4: 21; 5: 3; 2 John 4: 5; 1 Cor. 14: 37; 1 Thes. 4: 2; Gal. 6: 2).

The "commandments" of Christ are not, therefore, the law, or any aspect of the law; they rather constitute "the law of love," and "the perfect law of liberty." They enter into the teachings of grace as those teachings are set forth by Christ, and by those to whom He gave authority and commandment (Mt. 28: 18; Acts 1: 3; Lk. 24: 46-48; Heb. 2: 3, 4).

yoke upon the neck of the disciples, which neither our fathers nor we were able to bear?" (Acts 15: 10). Reference is here made to the law of Moses, and to place it on the children of grace is to "tempt God." It is an unbearable "yoke"; but Christ said, when anticipating the relationships of grace, "My yoke is easy, and my burden is light" (Mt. 11: 30). Christians are not to be "entangled" with the "yoke of bondage" (Gal. 5: 1). So, also, the "old commandment" of 1 John 2: 7, is, in 3: 11, seen to be the same message of grace.

III.   THE LAW IS EXCLUDED FROM THE TEACHINGS OF THE APOSTLES.

From the teaching of the Apostles it will be seen that the principles of law and grace are not to be mixed. There can be no question but that their teachings are exactly according to Christ's message concerning grace. As an example, and in harmony with the teaching of all the Apostles, it may be observed that the Apostle Paul spoke by the authority of Christ (1 Tim. 1:1; Tit. 1:3; 1 Thes. 4:15; 1 Cor. 15:3; Gal. 1:11, 12; Eph. 3:1-11). It is equally evident that he contended only for the blessings of pure grace. At no point would he suffer the principle of law to intrude. The Jewish element in the early church was slow to abandon the law, and there is evidence that, by the provisions of men, a double standard was suffered to exist for a time—one, a legality for the Jews, and the other, pure grace for the Gentiles. This fact of a double standard is revealed in connection with the first council of the church in Jerusalem (Acts 15:19-21. Cf 21:18-26); but the Apostle Paul never countenanced this double standard (Rom. 1:16, 17). The change from law to grace was revolutionary, and the age-long covenant of works did not readily yield to the new teachings of grace, nor has it wholly yielded to this day. There are some who, ignorant of the dispensational divisions of God's Word, and seeking to qualify the clear grace teachings of the Apostle Paul, are encouraging themselves in legalism on the strength of the fact that Christ kept and vindicated the law in the days of His particular ministry to Israel. The teaching of these legalists is a circumvention of the whole revelation of divine grace.

IV. THE PERSONAL EXPERIENCE OF THE APOSTLE PAUL IS AN ILLUSTRATION OF THE TEACHINGS OF GRACE.

The personal position and practice of the Apostle Paul is evidence that the principles of law and grace should not be mixed. The Spirit has prompted the Apostle to make a six-fold exhortation to believers to be followers of himself (1 Cor. 4:6; 11:1; Phil. 3:17; 1 Thes. 1:6; 2 Thes. 3:7, 9). This appeal was warranted because his doctrine was revealed to him from Christ (Gal. 1:11, 12; Eph. 3:1-10), and was in fact, therefore, the very teachings of Christ; because he was an Apostle; and because his own attitude toward Judaism and his own experience was a living illustration of the power of a life in grace.

The Epistles of Paul are an uncompromising protest against the intrusion of law, or any phase of law, into the reign of grace. Among very many Scriptures, there is one passage in particular which reveals the Apostle's own position. Speaking of his hope of a reward because of faithful service, he proceeds to describe the details of that service. In this connection he is incidentally led to disclose his own position at that time, as compared to other possible positions before God. We read: "For though I be free from all men, yet have I made myself servant unto all, that I might gain the more. And unto the Jews I became as a Jew, that I might gain the Jews; to them that are under the law, as under the

law, that I might gain them that are under the law;
to them that are without law, as without law, (being
not without law to God, but under the law to Christ),
that I might gain them that are without law'' (1 Cor.
9:19-21). These various relationships should be
considered:

First. *"And unto the Jews I became as a Jew,
that I might gain the Jews."*

Was not the Apostle a Jew? Did he not make
that his boast (Phil. 3:4, 5)? He was a Jew by
origin, birth, and training; but when he became
saved by grace he passed over onto new ground where
there "is neither Greek nor Jew, circumcision nor
uncircumcision, Barbarian, Scythian, bond nor free:
but Christ is all, and in all" (Col. 3:11). In like
manner, Gentiles when saved, are no longer Gentiles
in the flesh: "Wherefore remember, that ye being
in times past Gentiles in the flesh, ...now in
Christ Jesus ye who sometimes were far off are made
nigh by the blood of Christ" (Eph. 2:11-13). The
new creation in Christ is in view here. Through
the new birth by the Spirit, a new humanity is being
formed, and, though drawn from both Jews and Gentiles, it is neither Jew nor Gentile; it is the Church
of God—the redeemed of all generations from Pentecost until the Lord returns for His own. According to the Scriptures, humanity is now classified
under three major divisions: "Give none offence,
neither to the Jews, nor to the Gentiles, nor to the
church of God" (1 Cor. 10:32). The Apostle made
an effort to become "as a Jew, that he might gain
the Jews." Thus he left his own position, as it

were, to adapt himself to the position of the Jew. To what length he went, it is not revealed. As regarding himself, it is clear, however, that he everywhere disclaimed every Jewish relation to God. There are very many questions which might be discussed between a Jew and a Christian; but the Apostle passed these by that he might get to the heart of the Jew with the one issue of the Gospel of the grace of God.

Second. *"To them that are under the law, as under the law, that I might gain them that are under the law."*

While it is evident that the law was never addressed to any outside the one nation Israel, and also that, since the death of Christ, no Jew, Gentile, or Christian is now under the law either for justification, or as a rule of life (which statement will receive fuller proof at another place), there was a multitude of people in Paul's day, both Jews and Christians, as there are to-day, who have placed themselves under the law. This does not suggest that God has placed them there, or that He recognizes them as standing in their self-imposed position. However, having assumed a position under law they are morally obligated to "do the whole law" in the interests of consistency. It is not a mere repetition, then, when the Apostle makes reference first to the Jews and then to those that are under the law. The important point to be observed here is that the Apostle did not consider *himself* to be under the law; for he represents himself as leaving his own position that he might approach the man who is under the law. What endless discussions might he have waged with the one who was under the law! He set all these questions aside that he might rather present the more vitally important blessings of grace. The supreme issue was not, and is not, one of correcting the outward life by the application of one rule or another: it was, and is, one of believing on Christ unto salvation by grace. When that is accomplished, and because of the very character of salvation, the saved one, of necessity, is subject only to the governing principles of grace.

Third. *"To them that are without law, as without law, . . . that I might gain them that are without law."*

Thus the Apostle implies that, as to the rule of his life, he is not "without law." The class referred to as being "without law" is not the heathen to whom no missionary has ever gone; it refers, rather, to the great Gentile world to whom the law was never addressed. To these the Apostle went, acknowledging as he went, that he, as a Christian, had no part with the lawless and ungoverned.

Fourth. *"Not being without law to God, but under the law* [literally, inlawed] *to Christ."*

Here the Apostle reveals the exact truth as to his own relation to God as a Christian. It is unfortunate that the theological discussion which has proceeded on the supposition that a Christian must either be under the law of Moses, or else be absolutely lawless and ungoverned, could not have made place for the fact that there is a third ground of relationship to God which is neither the law of Moses, nor the ungoverned lawlessness of the world. To be "inlawed to Christ" is to be under the teachings of grace as a rule of life. These teachings include the "commandments" of Christ which are addressed to Christians as such in the upper room, and these "commandments" of Christ have been taken up, enlarged, and advanced, under the guidance of the Spirit in the book of the Acts and the Epistles of the New Testament. They constitute a separate and sufficient rule of life for the believer which is divinely adapted to his position in grace, and these great governing principles of grace are addressed to the believer alone, and not to the Christ-rejecting world. The message of God to the unsaved world is that they believe on the Saviour who is offered to them in limitless grace. The message to the saved is that they "walk worthy" of the calling wherewith they are called.

SECTION TWO

THE TEACHINGS OF THE LAW

In seeking an understanding of the teachings of grace, it is necessary to give due consideration to the teachings of the law; for, according to the Scriptures, the latter, with its covenant of works, is the one principle which is opposed to the teachings of grace. The law may be considered in a three-fold way: (1) As to the meaning of the word *law* as used in the Bible; (2) As to the relation the law sustains to the time of its reign; and, (3) As to the application of the law.

I. AS TO THE MEANING OF THE WORD *LAW* AS USED IN THE SCRIPTURES.

The foundation of all divine law is the Person of God. What He requires is only the expression of what He is. Since He is holy, just and good, His ideals, standards and requirements must be holy, just and good. The ideals and ways of fallen men are, of necessity, far removed from these divine standards which reflect the character of God. Comparison of these two standards has ever demonstrated the measure of human failure. Throughout the history of God's dealings with the world this comparison has brought into bold relief the unmeasured gulf which exists between God and man, between holiness and sin, and the complementary revelation of the divine compassion which led God to bridge that gulf.

The word *law*, as commonly used, means a rule which regulates conduct. It naturally implies the adequate authority and power on the part of the law-giver for its enforcement, and the proper penalty to be inflicted in case of its violation. The use of the word in the Bible is, however, much wider than its common usage. At least a seven-fold use of the word *law* is found in the Word of God.

First, *The Ten Commandments*.

The Ten Commandments have the peculiar distinction of having been written by the finger of God on tables of stone. They are therefore the direct writings of God. They are themselves a crystallization of the entire law given to Moses. They are summarized by Christ when He said to the Jewish lawyer: "Thou shalt love the Lord thy God with all thy heart, and with all thy soul, and with all thy mind. This is the first and great commandment. And the second is like unto it, Thou shalt love thy neighbor as thyself. On these two commandments hang all the law and the prophets" (Mt. 22: 36-40). The Apostle Paul summarized the law in two great statements: "Love is the fulfilling of the law"; and, "For all the law is fulfilled in one word, even in this; Thou shalt love thy neighbor as thyself" (Rom. 13: 10; Gal. 5: 14). So, also, James has written: "If ye fulfil the royal law according to the scripture, Thou shalt love thy neighbor as thyself, ye do well'' (Jas. 2:8). In no sense is the law applied to the believer by these Scriptures; they merely imply that the law is fulfilled by the exercise of that love which is most vitally the duty of every child of God.

That this limited declaration of commandments from God is termed *"the law,"* is proven beyond question in Rom. 7:7-14. In this passage the Apostle records: "I had not known lust, except the law had said, Thou shalt not covet." The same precept is also called a *commandment;* for he goes on to say: "But sin, taking occasion by the commandment, wrought in me all manner of concupiscence." Further, it is evident that the Decalogue is the heart of the law as the law is stated in the Old Testament. Particular emphasis is given to the fact that the Commandments are a part of the law, because there are those who teach that the whole law might be set aside without affecting the Ten Commandments. They claim that these commandments were never any part of the law, and, though the reign of the law ceased with the death of Christ, the binding authority of the Ten Commandments did not cease. The Bible teaches that the Commandments are a part of the law, and though their principles are restated under grace, the Commandments ceased to be the *rule* of conduct when Christ fulfilled the law, and it came to its end in Him.

Second. *The Whole System of Government for Israel in the Land.*

The law in this larger aspect was divided into three major parts:

1. The Commandments, which were the revealed law of God relative to His righteous will. Of this revelation, the Decalogue was the center (Ex. 20: 1-17).

2. The Judgments, which were the revealed law of God relative to the social life of Israel (Ex. 21:1 to 24:11).

3. The Ordinances, which were the revealed will of God relative to the religious life of Israel (Ex. 24:12 to 31:18).

This three-fold governing system of law covered *all* divine requirements which were imposed on an Israelite in the land. The three divisions of the system were both interrelated and interdependent. This three-fold system provided its own instruction as to what was good, and its own prohibitions against that which was evil. In the prescribed sacrifices its own divine remedy was provided for the wrong committed. No other provision for a broken law has ever been disclosed to man than that of the animal sacrifices, and the final, and fulfilling sacrifice of the cross where every demand of the law was met forever. The projection of the Commandments into this dispensation disassociated from the ritual and sacrifices to which they are interrelated, is done with seeming plausibility only at the expense of one of the most vital dispensational distinctions in the Word of God.

Third. *The Kingdom Rule of Messiah.*

The still future dispensation of the reign of Messiah, which will be the fulfillment of all God's covenants with Israel, is to be a reign of pure law.

This, it will be seen at a later point of the discussion, is proven both by the precise statements of Scripture, and by a careful study of the character of those injunctions which constitute the laws of the kingdom, and which find their application in the yet future dispensation of the kingdom.

Fourth, *The Whole Revealed Will of God for any Individual, or Nation, when Contemplated as a Covenant of Works which is to be Wrought in the Energy of the Flesh.*

The essential principle of the law was embodied in the covenant of works. The divine blessing was conditioned on the performance of the entire law of God. Under the new covenant of grace, the undivided, undiminished, divine blessing is first bestowed by God's favor, and by this bestowal, an obligation is created for a life corresponding to the divine blessing. When any work is undertaken for God by which it is hoped thereby to gain divine favor, that work is wrought of necessity on the basis of pure law. On the other hand, when any work is undertaken for God because it is recognized that divine favor and blessing already have been received, it is wrought in harmony with pure grace. Thus the highest ideal of grace if prostituted by the motive of securing divine favor, takes on the character of law.

Moreover, the will of God for the daily life of the one who is perfectly saved in grace has been clearly revealed by extended and explicit injunctions, or beseechings. These injunctions and beseechings, being gracious and heavenly in character, anticipate the imparted and inwrought enabling power of the indwelling Spirit for their fulfillment. The covenant of grace is a covenant of faith. Thus when the injunctions or teachings of grace are attempted in the strength of the flesh, the very teachings of grace thereby become, in principle, a covenant of works. Therefore any revelation of the righteous will of God for any individual or company of 'individuals is, apart from the one exception of a personal reliance of faith on the power of the Spirit, a covenant of works, or a law of God. One illustration may suffice:

In Romans 8:4 the statement is made that the "righteousness of the law" is to be fulfilled *in* us, rather than *by* us. To this end Christ has died, and to this end the energizing Spirit has been sent into the world (8:2, 3). The phrase, "the righteousness of the law," which is here said to be fulfilled *in* us, proposes more than a fulfillment of the limited demands found in the Mosaic system; it proposes nothing less than the divine energy of the Spirit realizing continuously every aspect of the revealed and unrevealed will of God *in* the believer. It is conditioned on one thing only: "Who walk not after the flesh, but after the Spirit."

No better example of a man-made, self-imposed law can be found than the experiences of every unsaved person who is trying, even in the slightest degree, to live the Christian life. He is doing what he does with a view to being accepted of God, not because he is accepted; and he is doing what he does in the energy of the flesh, not in the power of the Spirit. To such an one, the Christian's manner of life in grace is only a yoke of bondage.

Likewise, there is reference to the whole will of God in the following Scriptures wherein that revelation is termed the *law*: "For I delight in the law of God after the inward man" (Rom. 7:22). There is the possibility of a wide difference between what is indicated by the two terms, "The law of Moses," and "The law of God." The law of Moses is the law of God, but the law of God may be much more than the law of Moses. "Whosoever committeth sin transgresseth also the law: for sin is the transgression of the law" (1 John 3:4). Since the Decalogue contained no reference to the great issues of Christian service and prayer, or the details of the character of the believer's walk in the world, no one, upon serious thought, will be willing to limit this great definition of sin as merely the transgression of the law of Moses. "The sting of death is sin; and the strength of sin is the law" (1 Cor. 15:56). Sin, again, is nothing less than failure in any aspect of the will of God. When this fuller requirement of the will of God is considered in its present application under grace, it is termed "the perfect law of liberty" (Jas. 1:25. Cf Rom. 8:21; 1 Cor. 8:9; 10:29; 2 Cor. 3:17; Gal. 2:4; 5:1-13; Jas. 2:12).

Fifth. *Any Rule of Conduct Prescribed by Men.*

Here the use of the word *law* is extended to the regulations men may make among themselves. We read: "But we know that the law is good, if a man use it lawfully; knowing this, that the law is not made for a righteous man, but for the lawless and disobedient, for the ungodly and for sinners" (1 Tim. 1:8, 9). "And if a man also strive for masteries, yet is he not crowned, except he strive lawfully'' (2 Tim. 2:5. Cf Mt. 20:15; Lk. 20:22).

Again, to this classification of law as being man-made, may be added any self-imposed law. Thus the law of Moses or the law of the kingdom when assumed as a rule of life by Jews, Gentiles, or Christians, becomes a man-made and self-imposed law. It is written: "For when the Gentiles [the same is equally true now of Jews or Christians], which have not the law, do by nature [usage] the things contained in the law, these, having not the law, are a law unto themselves" (Rom. 2:14). The law, though not addressed to them is self-imposed and becomes to that extent a mere man-made obligation.

Sixth. *Any Recognized Principle in Operation.*

In this aspect of the meaning of the word *law* it is seen to be used as the equivalent of *power*. In common usage, reference is made to the *law* of gravitation. Which is likewise the *power* of gravitation. Thus it is used in the Word of God: "For the law [power] of the Spirit of life in Christ Jesus hath made me free from the law [power] of sin and death" (Rom. 8:2).

Seventh. *The Necessary Sequence Between a Cause and its Effect.*

This particular aspect of the use of the word *law* is seen in Rom. 7:21: "I find then a law, that, when I would do good, evil is present with me."

Discrimination of these widely different meanings of the word *law* is imperative for a right understanding of this great theme in the Scriptures.

II. AS TO THE RELATION THE LAW SUSTAINS TO THE
TIME OF ITS REIGN.

The Scriptures teach that the law given by Moses,
which was a covenant of works, was given from God
to man at a particular time. The human family had
walked before God upon the earth for upwards of
2500 years prior to the imposition of the law. Thus
it had been demonstrated that God is able to deal
with men in the earth without reference to the law
of Moses.

In the Word of God the period between Adam and
Moses is particularly contrasted with the dispensation
of the law. The revelation is final: "Wherefore, as
by one man sin entered into the world, and death by
sin; and so death passed upon all men, for that all
have sinned: (For until the law sin was in the
world: but sin is not imputed where there is no law.
Nevertheless death reigned from Adam to Moses, even
over them that had not sinned after the similitude
of Adam's transgression)" (Rom. 5:12-14).

Physical death, the unavoidable penalty for sin,
antedates the giving of the law, and death reigned
from Adam to Moses; but sin was not *"imputed"*
where there was no law. As it does now, death
reigned over sinless infants, good people, and bad
people alike. Sin, in this connection, is evidently
the inbred fallen-nature which all have received from
Adam; and not the transgressions personally committed. Thus the penalty—death—is due to the
fallen-nature which all have received and is not due
to individual transgressions. Since the sin-nature

from Adam is universal, its penalty is universal. Should one member of the human family be delivered from the possession of the sin-nature, the fact would be proven by a like deliverance from its penalty—death. None are delivered from physical death so long as Christ tarries. It is "by the offence of one" that "judgment came upon all men to condemnation" (Rom. 5:18).

The all important distinction between the sin-nature of man, which is the universal possession, and the personal wrongdoing of the individual, is maintained throughout the Scriptures, including the revelation of the cross. There are two aspects of the death of Christ as that death is related to sin: He died "for our sins," which fact is the basis of the divine cure for personal sin by justification (Rom. 3:21 to 5:11); and He died "unto sin," which fact is the basis of the divine cure for the reigning power of the sin-nature (Rom. 6:1 to 8:4).

Sin and death reigned from Adam to Moses because sin, in its essence, is the fallen-nature itself, and death is its penalty; but sin, which is the personal wrongdoing of the individual, "is not imputed where there is no law." Thus is the relation of man and God described covering the great period between Adam and Moses.

The pertinent question—"Wherefore then serveth the law?"—is both propounded and answered in the Scriptures (Gal. 3:19). Continuing we read, the law "was added because of transgressions." That is, it was "added" to give to sin the augmented character of transgression. Sin had always been evil in itself and in the sight of God; but it became *disobedience* after that the holy commandments were disclosed. The fact of the sin-nature is not changed by the introduction of the law; it was the character of personal wrongdoing which was changed. It was changed from sin, which is not imputed where there is no law, to sin which is the rebellion against the command of God, and which must reap all the punishment attendant upon broken law. Israel, to whom the commandments were given, being a chosen, exalted people, were, by the imposition of the law, constituted a more responsible people before God; but they were wholly unable to keep the law. The giving of the law to Israel did not result in an obedient people; it rather proved their utter sinfulness and helplessness. The law became a ministry of condemnation to every one who failed to keep it. Nor did the giving of the law really tend to their betterment at heart, or retard the power of sin; it provoked them to sin. As the Apostle says: "But sin, taking occasion by the commandment, wrought in me all manner of concupiscence" (Rom. 7. 8).

There can be no question as to the righteous character of the law; for it is written: "Wherefore the law is holy, and the commandment holy, and just, and good. Was then that which is good made death unto me? God forbid. But sin, that it might appear sin, working death in me by that which is good; that sin by the commandment might become exceeding sinful" (Rom. 7: 12-13). Thus the purpose of the giving of the law is stated: "That sin by the commandment might become exceeding sinful."

Apart from the Man Christ Jesus, there was universal failure in the keeping of the law. This is not to say that the law was imperfect in itself. The universal failure in keeping the law is the revelation of the helplessness of man under the power of "sin in the flesh." Two passages give evidence as to the failure of the law through the weakness of the flesh to which it made its appeal: "For what the law could not do, in that it was weak through the flesh" (Rom. 8:3); and, "But now, after that ye have known God, or rather are known of God, how turn ye again to the weak and beggarly [poverty-stricken] elements, whereunto ye desire again to be in bondage?" (Gal. 4:9). The appeal is strong: Why, after having come to know the power of God through the Spirit, do ye turn to a relationship to God which as a means of victory and blessing has always been, and must always be, "weak" and "poverty-stricken"?

The law was never given as a means of salvation or justification: "Therefore by the deeds of the law there shall no flesh be justified in his sight: for by the law is the knowledge of sin" (Rom. 3:20. Cf Gal. 3:11, 24). Though given as a rule of conduct for Israel in the land, it, because of the universal failure in its observance, became a curse (Gal. 3:10), condemnation (2 Cor. 3:9), and death (Rom. 7:10-11). The law was effective only as it drove the transgressor to Christ. It became a means of turning the people to God for His mercy as that mercy is provided in Christ. The law was a "schoolmaster," or child trainer, to bring the offender to Christ. This was immediately accomplished in his turning to the sin-offerings which were provided, and which were the type of Christ in His death; but more fully, was this accomplished when the dispensation itself came to its end in the death of Christ. "The law made nothing perfect, . . . but the bringing in of a better hope," and the law was a "shadow of good things to come" (Heb. 7:19; 10:1).

The reign of the law is limited to a period of about 1500 years, or from Sinai to Calvary—from Moses to Christ. These boundaries are fixed beyond question in the Word of God.

First. *The Law Began its Reign at Mount Sinai.*

The law was never imposed upon any people or generation before it was given to Israel at the hand of Moses. "And Moses called all Israel, and said unto them, Hear, O Israel, the statutes and judgments which I speak in your ears this day, that ye may learn them, and keep, and do them. The LORD our God made a covenant with us in Horeb. The LORD made not this covenant with our fathers, but with us, even us, who are all of us here alive this day" (Deut. 5:1-3). When the law was proposed, the children of Israel deliberately forsook their position under the grace of God which had been their relationship to God until that day, and placed themselves under the law. The record is given thus: "And Moses went up unto God, and the LORD called unto him out of the mountain, saying, Thus shalt thou say to the house of Jacob, and tell the children of Israel; Ye have seen what I did unto the Egyptians, and how I bare you on eagles' wings, and brought you unto myself. Now therefore, if ye will obey my voice indeed, and keep my covenant, then ye shall be a peculiar treasure unto me above all people: for all the earth is mine: and ye shall be unto me a kingdom of priests, and an holy nation. These are the words which thou shalt speak unto the children of Israel. And Moses came and called for the elders of the people, and laid before their faces all these words which the LORD commanded him. And all the people answered together, and said, All that the LORD hath spoken we will do. And Moses returned the words of the people unto the LORD" (Ex. 19: 3-8).

While it is certain that Jehovah knew the choice the people would make, it is equally certain that their choice was in no way *required* by Him. His description of the relation they had sustained to Him until that moment is most tender and pleading: "Ye have seen what I did unto the Egyptians, and how I bare you on eagles' wings, and brought you unto myself." Such is the character of pure grace. By it the sinner is carried on eagles' wings and brought to God. It is all of God. Until that hour they had been sustained in the faithfulness of Jehovah and without the slightest reference to their wickedness; but His plan and purpose for them had remained unchanged. He had dealt with them according to the unconditional covenant of grace made with Abraham. The marvelous blessedness of that grace-relationship should have appealed to them as the priceless riches of the unfailing mercy of God, which it was. The surrender of the blessings of grace should have been allowed by these people on no condition whatever. Had they said at the hearing of the impossible law, "None of these things can we do. We crave only to remain in that boundless mercy of God, who has loved us, and sought us, and saved us from all our enemies, and who will bring us to Himself," it is evident that such an appeal would have reached the very heart of God. And the surpassing glory of His grace would have been extended to them without bounds; for grace above all else is the delight of the heart of God. In place of the eagles' wings by which they were carried unto God, they confidently chose a covenant of works when they said: "All that the LORD hath spoken we will do." They were called upon to face a concrete choice between the mercy of God which had followed them, and a new and hopeless covenant of works. They fell from grace. The experience of the nation is true of every individual who falls from grace at the present time. Every blessing from God that has ever been experienced came only from the loving mercy of God; yet with that same blasting self-trust, people are now turning to a dependence upon their works. It is far more reasonable and honoring to God to fall helpless into His everlasting arms, and to acknowledge that we rely on His grace alone.

Upon the determined choice of the law, the mountain where God was revealed became a terrible spectacle of the unapproachable, holy character of God. "And mount Sinai was altogether on a smoke, because the LORD descended upon it in fire: and the smoke thereof ascended as the smoke of a furnace, and the whole mount quaked greatly. . . . And the Lord said unto Moses, Go down, charge the people, lest they break through unto the LORD to gaze, and many of them perish" (Ex. 19:18-21). He who had brought them to Himself under the unconditional blessings of His grace, must now warn them lest they break through unto the LORD and perish. That the burning mountain was a sign of the unapproachableness of God under the new covenant of works, is again declared in Heb. 12:18-21. Speaking there of the glory and liberty of grace, it is said: "For ye are not come unto the mount that might be touched, and that burnt with fire, nor unto blackness, and darkness, and tempest, and the sound of a trumpet, and the voice of words; which voice they that heard intreated that the word should not be spoken to them any more: (For they could not endure that which was commanded, And if so much as a beast touch the mountain, it shall be stoned, or thrust through with a dart: and so terrible was the sight, that Moses said, I exceedingly fear and quake:). But ye are come unto mount Sion, and unto the city of the living God, the heavenly Jerusalem, and to an innumerable company of angels, to the general assembly and church of the firstborn, which are written in heaven, and to God the Judge of all, and to the spirits of just men made perfect, and to Jesus the mediator of the new covenant, and to the blood of sprinkling, that speaketh better things than that of Abel." By this passage, the great contrast between the relationship to God under the law covenant of works, and the relationship to God under grace, is set forth clearly. Under their works, Israel could not come unto God lest they die; but under grace they were carried on eagles' wings unto God, and so, under grace, all come unto God, and to Jesus, and to the blessed association and glory of heaven itself.

The children of Israel definitely chose the covenant of works, which is law, as their relationship to God.

In like manner, every individual who is now under
the law, is self-placed, and that law under which he
stands is self-imposed. In every case such relationship is clung to in *spite* of the appeal of pure grace.
Had the legalists minds to understand and hearts to
feel, they would realize that there is no access to God
by a covenant of works and merit. To such as seek
to come to Him by the law, God is as unapproachable
as flaming Sinai.

Second. *The Reign of Law was Terminated with
the Death of Christ.*

The truthfulness of the statement that the reign of
the law was terminated with the death of Christ is
to be determined by the Word of God, rather than
by the traditions and suppositions of men. The law,
when given, was only a temporary, or *ad interim*,
dealing "until the seed should come" (Gal. 3:19),
and the "seed" is Christ (3:16). This conclusive
passage (vs. 22-25) continues: "But the Scripture
hath concluded all under sin, that the promise by
faith of Jesus Christ might be given to them that
believe." The distinction between Jew and Gentile
is broken down and *all* are "under sin." There is
provided and offered in Christ a new access and
relationship to God. It is "through Christ" and "in
Christ." It is gained upon a principle of faith alone.
Christ is the object of faith. It is nothing less than
the "promise by faith of Jesus Christ," and it is
given to them who *"believe."* Thus the new covenant of grace through faith in Christ is placed in
contrast to the old covenant of works. The passage
goes on to state: "But before faith [the new prin-

ciple in grace] came, we [Paul is here speaking as a Jew of his own time] were kept under the law, shut up unto the faith which should afterwards be revealed. Wherefore the law was our schoolmaster [child leader] to bring us unto Christ, that we might be justified by faith [the new principle in grace]. But after that faith [the new principle in grace] is come, we are no longer under a schoolmaster" (the law).

As a standard of holy living, the law presented the precise quality of life which was becoming a people who were chosen of God and redeemed out of the bondage of Egypt. At the cross, a new and perfect redemption from sin was accomplished for Jew and Gentile alike. The redemption from Egypt was a type of the redemption from sin. As the redemption from Egypt created a demand for a corresponding holy life, so the redemption from sin creates a demand for a corresponding heavenly walk with God. One is adapted to the limitations of the natural man; the other is adapted to the infinite resources of the spiritual man. One is the teaching of the law; the other is the teaching of grace.

III. AS TO THE APPLICATION OF THE LAW.

The law was given only to the children of Israel. This statement admits of no discussion when the Scriptures are considered. A very few passages from the many are here given: "And Jesus answered him, The first of all the commandments is, Hear, O Israel; The Lord our God is one Lord: and thou shalt love the Lord thy God with all thy heart"

(Mk. 12:29-30); "And what nation is there so great, that hath statutes and judgments so righteous as all this law, which I have set before you this day?" (Deut. 4:8); "And Moses called all Israel, and said unto them, Hear, O Israel, the statutes and judgments which I speak in your ears this day, that ye may learn them, and keep, and do them. The LORD our God made a covenant with us in Horeb. The LORD made not this covenant with our fathers, but with us, even us, who are all of us here alive this day" (Deut. 5:1-3). The message given from the mount was that great covenant of works of the law contained in the Ten Commandments, which is here included in the "statutes and judgments." This covenant was never made with any other nation or people; for God made no covenants with people other than Israel. "The LORD gave me the two tables of stone, even the tables of the covenant" (Deut. 9:11). Speaking of the covenants in relation to Israel, it is said: "Who are Israelites; to whom pertaineth the adoption, and the glory, and the covenants, and the giving of the law, and the service of God, and the promises; whose are the fathers, and of whom as concerning the flesh Christ came, who is over all, God blessed forever" (Rom. 9:4, 5). Speaking of the Gentiles it is said: "Wherefore remember, that ye being in times past Gentiles in the flesh, . . . that at that time ye were without Christ, being aliens from the commonwealth of Israel, and strangers from the covenants of promise, having no hope, and without God in the world" (Eph. 2:11, 12).

It is expressly declared that the Gentiles have not the law: "For when the Gentiles, which have not the law, do by nature [usage] the things contained in the law, these, having not the law, are a law unto themselves'' (Rom. 2:14). In harmony with this, Pontius Pilate, a Gentile ruler, denied any responsibility to Israel's law: ''Then said Pilate unto them, Take ye him, and judge him according to your law'' (John 18:31).

We conclude, therefore, that the law which was given by Moses was a covenant of works, that it was ''added'' after centuries of human history, that its reign was terminated by the death of Christ, that it was given to Israel only, and that, since it was never given to Gentiles, the only relation that Gentiles can sustain to it is, without any divine authority, to impose it upon themselves. Additional proof of these facts concerning the law are yet to be presented.

According to the Scriptures, all time is divided into seven periods, or dispensations. The Bible is occupied, in the main, with the last three of these periods. All that lies between Exodus, chapter 19, and Revelation, chapter 20, is the unfolding of the exact scope and character of these three ages. These ages are: The age of the law of Moses, which is measured by the duration of the reign of that law, or from Sinai to Calvary; The age of the kingdom, which is measured by the earth-reign of the King, or from the second coming of Christ when He comes to occupy His throne (Mt. 25:31), to the bringing in of the eternal state in the new heavens and new earth (Rev. 21:1; 1 Cor. 15:24-28); And lying between the age of the law of Moses, which is wholly past, and the age of the kingdom, which is wholly future, there is the present age of grace, bounded by the death of Christ, on the one hand, and by His second advent, on the other. The revelation concerning the out-standing ordinance for this age also marks the limit of duration of the age itself with a future event—dateless, but never-the-less sure: "For as often as ye eat this bread, and drink this cup, ye do shew the Lord's death till he come."

Due recognition of the essential character of each of these ages is the key to the understanding of the exact manner of the divine rule in each age. The rule of God in each case is adapted to the conditions which obtain. Since the respective characteristics of the ages are widely different, the manner of the divine rule is correspondingly different. The practice of confusing these three ages in respect to their characteristics and the manner of the divine rule in each is common, and is, doubtless, the greatest error into which many devout Bible interpreters fall. It is perhaps easier to confuse the present age with that which immediately precedes it, or with that which immediately follows it, than to confuse it with conditions which are more remote; although there need be no confusion of these immediately suceeding but sharply separated periods of time, for they are divided by age-transforming events. The age of the law of Moses is separated from the present age of grace by the death of Christ, when He bore the curse of the law and finished the work by which man may stand justified before God forever, and justified as he could not have been justified by the law of Moses. The age of grace is separated from the age of the kingdom by the second coming of Christ to the earth—the time when He comes to reign, to bind Satan, to terminate human governments, and to cause righteousness and peace to cover the earth as the waters cover the face of the deep.

The divine government could not remain the same in the earth after the world-transforming, spiritual victories of the cross, as it had been under the law of Moses. So, likewise, the divine government cannot remain the same in the earth after the world-transforming temporal victories of the second coming, as it has been under the reign of grace. All this is reasonable; but, what is far more impelling and compelling, this is what is precisely revealed by God in His Word.

There are, then, three separate and distinct systems of divine government disclosed in the Scriptures, corresponding to three separate and distinct ages to be governed.

In respect to the character of divine government, both the age before the cross and the age following the return of Christ represent the exercise of pure law; while the period between these two ages represents the exercise of pure grace. It is imperative, therefore, that there shall be no careless co-mingling of these great age-characterizing elements, else the preservation of the most important distinctions in the various relationships between God and man are lost, and the recognition of the true force of the death of Christ and His coming again is obscured.

Kingdom teachings will be found in those Psalms and prophecies of the Old Testament which anticipate the reign of Messiah in the earth, and in the kingdom portions of the Gospels. These teachings as found in the Old Testament and the New are purely legal in essence; both by their inherent character, and by the explicit declaration of the Word of God. The legal requirements of the kingdom teachings are greatly advanced, both in severity and detail, beyond the requirements of the law of Moses. This intensification of legal requirements, as it appears in the kingdom teachings, should not be looked upon as a mere continuation of the law of Moses. The kingdom teaching is a system complete and perfect in itself. Moreover, this intensification of legal requirements in kingdom revelations does not move the teachings of the Mosaic law nearer the heart of the teachings of grace. On the contrary, it removes them still farther in the opposite direction, inasmuch as the teachings of the kingdom increase the burden of meritorious workers over that which was required by the law of Moses. In the kingdom law, anger is condemned in the same connection where only murder had been prohibited in the law of Moses, and the glance of the eye is condemned where only adultery had previously been forbidden.

The kingdom Scriptures of the Old Testament are occupied largely with the character and glory of Messiah's reign, the promises to Israel of restoration and earthly glory, the universal blessings to Gentiles, and the deliverance of creation itself. There is little revealed in the Old Testament Scriptures concerning the responsibility of the individual in the kingdom; it is rather a message to the nation as a whole. Evidently the details concerning individual responsibility, were, in the mind of the Spirit, reserved for the personal teaching of the King, at the time when the kingdom would be "at hand." As to the reign of the King, two important disclosures are made in the kingdom portions of the Old Testament: (1) His will be a rigid reign of righteousness that shall go forth from Jerusalem with swift judgment upon the sinner (Isa. 2:1-4; 11:1-5); and (2), according to the new covenant which He will have made with his people, He will have put His laws into their minds, and will have written them on their hearts (Jer. 31:31-40; Heb. 8:7-12). The writing of the law upon the heart is a divine assistance toward the keeping of the kingdom law which was in no wise provided under the reign of the law of Moses. However, the written law on the heart, as it will be in the kingdom, is not to be compared with the power of the indwelling Spirit which is the present divine enablement provided for the believer under grace.

Under the new covenant, God will have put away the former sin of the nation forever. This, it is revealed, He is free to do through the blood of His Son who, as God's Lamb, took away the sin of the world (Mt. 13:44; Rom. 11:26, 27).

The great key words under the Mosaic system were "law" and "obedience"; the great key words in the present age are "believe" and "grace"; while the great key words in the kingdom are "righteousness" and "peace." The following are brief excerpts from the Old Testament Scriptures bearing on the kingdom:

"The word that Isaiah the son of Amoz saw concerning Judah and Jerusalem. And it shall come to pass in the last days, that the mountain of the LORD's house shall be established in the top of the mountains, and shall be exalted above the hills; and all nations shall flow unto it. And many people shall go and say, Come ye, and let us go up to the mountain of the LORD, to the house of the God of Jacob; and he will teach us of his ways, and we will walk in his paths: for out of Zion shall go forth the law, and the word of the LORD from Jerusalem. And he shall judge among the nations, and shall rebuke many people: and they shall beat their swords into plowshares, and their spears into pruninghooks: nation shall not lift up sword against nation, neither shall they learn war any more'' (Isa. 2:1-4).

"And there shall come forth a rod out of the stem of Jesse, and a Branch shall grow out of his roots: and the Spirit of the LORD shall rest upon him, the spirit of wisdom and understanding, the spirit of counsel and might, the spirit of knowledge and of the fear of the LORD; and shall make him of quick understanding in the fear of the LORD: and he shall not judge after the sight of his eyes, neither reprove after the hearing of his ears: but with righteousness shall he judge the poor, and reprove with equity for the meek of the earth: and he shall smite the earth with the rod of his mouth, and with the breath of his lips shall he slay the wicked. And righteousness shall be the girdle of his loins, and faithfulness the girdle of his reins'' (Isa. 11:1-5).

"And I will gather the remnant of my flock out of all countries whither I have driven them, and will bring them again to their folds; and they shall be fruitful and increase. And I will set up shepherds over them which shall feed them: and they shall fear no more, nor be dismayed, neither shall they be lacking, saith the LORD. Behold, the days come, saith the LORD, that I will raise unto David a righteous Branch, and a King shall reign and prosper, and shall execute judgment and justice in the earth. In his days Judah shall be saved, and Israel shall dwell safely: and this is his name whereby he shall be called, THE LORD OUR RIGHTEOUSNESS. . . . And they shall dwell in their own land'' (Jer. 23:3-8).

"For the children of Israel shall abide many days without a king, and without a prince, and without a sacrifice, and without an image, and without an ephod, and without teraphim: afterward shall the children of Israel return, and seek the LORD their God, and David their King; and shall fear the LORD and his goodness in the latter days" (Hosea 3:4,5).[1]

Turning to the New Testament Scriptures bearing on the kingdom, it is important first to consider again the two-fold character of the work and teachings of Christ. He was both a minister to Israel to confirm the promises made unto the fathers, and a minister to the Gentiles that they might glorify God for His mercy (Rom. 15:8, 9). These two widely different revelations are not separated in the Scriptures by a well-defined boundary of chapter and verse; they are intermingled in the text and are to be identified wherever found by the character of the message and the circumstances under which it is given. This, it should be remembered, is the usual divine method of presenting truth. To illustrate: there is no chapter and verse boundary in the prophetic books of the Old Testament between that portion of the Scriptures which presented the *immediate* duty of Israel, and that portion of the Scriptures which presented their *future* obligation in Messiah's kingdom. The prophets, while unfolding both of these widely differing obligations, co-mingle these messages in the text and the different messages are discerned only through an observance of the character

[1] Note additional passages: Ps. 72: 1-20; Isa. 4: 2-5; 9: 6, 7; 14: 1-8; 35: 1-10; 52: 1-15; 59: 20 to 60: 22; 62: 1-12; 66: 1-24; Jer. 31: 36, 37; 33: 1-26; Joel 3: 17-21; Amos 9: 11-15; Zeph. 3: 14-20; Zech. 14: 16-21.

of the truth revealed. Likewise, there is, to some
extent, a co-mingling in the Gospels of the message of
the kingdom and the teachings of grace. Moreover,
these teachings were given while the law of Moses
was in full authority. In harmony with the demands
of that dispensation, many recognitions of the Mosaic
system are embedded in the teachings of Christ.
The Gospels are complex almost beyond any other
portion of Scripture, since they are a composite of
the teachings of Moses, of grace, and of the kingdom. In attempting to discover and to identify the
kingdom teachings of Christ as they are co-mingled
with the teachings of grace, and of the law, it is of
value to note the peculiar feature of each Gospel:

The Gospel by Matthew is a message to Israel of
her King and His kingdom. In that Gospel He is
introducd first as the ''Son of David'' (1:1), which
title immediately relates Him to the Davidic covenant, and that covenant eternally secures for Israel
a throne, a King, and a kingdom. Christ, being the
Son of David, is the Messiah-King—the Hope and
Consolation of Israel. While this Gospel is primarily
of the King and His kingdom, the closing portion is
of Christ as the Son of Abraham.

The Gospel by Mark presents Christ as the Servant
of Jehovah. It records more concerning His service
than of His teaching, and, like Matthew's Gospel, it
is almost wholly addressed to Israel.

The Gospel by Luke presents Christ in His humanity, and, while written to Jews, the avowed purpose
of the writer is to ''set in order'' and establish the
''certainty of those things which are most surely believed among us.'' This certainty of testimony is

thus sealed: "Having had perfect understanding of all things from the very first" ("from above." Cf John 3:31; 19:11; Jas. 1:17; 3:15, 17).

The Gospel by John was also written for a particular purpose: "But these are written, that ye might believe that Jesus is the Christ, the Son of God; and that believing ye might have life through his name" (20:31). Thus the saving grace of God in Christ is declared to be the theme of this Gospel. While the ministry of Christ to Israel is acknowledged by the words, "He came to his own, and his own received him not" (1:11), the Gospel by John is primarily of the grace of God in salvation through Christ. The Gospel by John divides the teachings of Christ into two parts: chapters 1 to 12, the grace of God that saves; and chapters 13 to 16, and 19 to 21, the grace of God that teaches.

From this brief consideration of the four Gospels it may be concluded that those teachings of Christ which confirm the covenants made unto the fathers, or Israel, will be found primarily in the Synoptic Gospels, and that these kingdom teachings are crystallized in the first portion of the first Gospel. The position of this kingdom portion in the context of the Scriptures is also significant—following immediately, as it does, on the Old Testament. The Old Testament closed with its great hopes unrealized and its great prophecies unfulfilled. These hopes were based on covenants from Jehovah, to which He had sworn with an oath. These covenants guarantee to the nation an earthly kingdom in their own land, under the abiding reign of Messiah, sitting on the throne of His father David. No such promise was fulfilled in the Old Testament period. The kingdom as provided for in the faithfulness of Jehovah was revealed in the Old Testament only in predictive prophecy. No such kingdom situation existed when Christ was born. It is expressly declared that Israel's great hope and consolation was yet in expectation when Christ came (Lk. 1:31-33; 2:25). The children of Israel were then largely scattered among the nations and their land was under the authority of Rome.

At this point and under these circumstances, a new message went forth: "The kingdom of heaven is at hand." It was proclaimed by the forerunner—John the Baptist (Mt. 3:1-2), by Christ (Mt. 4:17), and by His disciples (Mt. 10:5-7). The strongest prohibition was imposed against the giving of this message to any Gentile, or even to a Samaritan (Mt. 10:5, 6. Cf 15:24). The message, though brief, was calculated to arouse all the national longings of the people to whom it was spoken. The messengers needed no analytical training to sense the exact meaning of their theme. As instructed Israelites, the kingdom hope had been their expectation and meditation from birth. Later on, and in contrast to this, their utter slowness of heart to understand the new facts and teachings of grace is most obvious. Even when, after His resurrection, Christ had given forty days of instruction in things pertaining to the kingdom of God, they said: "Lord, wilt thou at this time restore again the kingdom to Israel?" (Acts 1:6), so little had they grasped the meaning of His death and the immediate purpose of grace. On the other hand, there is no record that the messengers needed or received one moment of exposition as to the meaning of the message relative to the Gospel of the kingdom before they were sent forth to deliver it. It was evidently Israel's hope.

The phrase, *the kingdom of heaven,* is peculiar to the Gospel by Matthew, and refers to the rule of God in the earth. In that particular, it is to be distinguished from the kingdom of God, which is the rule of God throughout the bounds of the universe. One, in certain aspects, is included in the other, and there is, therefore, much that is common to both. The Messianic rule of God in the earth was the theme of the prophets; for the prophets only enlarged on the covenants which guaranteed a throne, a King, and a kingdom, over regathered Israel, in that land which was sworn to Abraham. The term, *the kingdom of heaven,* was used by Christ to announce the fact that the covenanted kingdom blessings were "at hand." This good news to that nation was the "gospel of the kingdom," and should in no wise be confused with the Gospel of saving grace.

The national hope was centered in the genuineness of the claims of both the King and His forerunner. The evidence was carefully weighed, it may be believed, and it was found unimpeachable; but the wickedness of heart prevailed. They imprisoned the forerunner, who was later beheaded by Herod, and they crucified the King. Both the forerunner and the King fulfilled prophecy in respect to the office of each in every detail. The forerunner was the voice of one crying in the wilderness. The King was of the seed of Abraham, of the tribe of Judah, a son of David born of a virgin, in Bethlehem of Judæa, He came out of Egypt, and was called a Nazarene. At

His birth He was proclaimed, "King of the Jews." In His public ministry He took up the message of a King. At His entrance into Jerusalem He was hailed as Israel's King. At His trial before Pilate, He claimed to be a King. And He died under the accusation, "This is Jesus, the King of the Jews." The crown of thorns had no significance in relation to His sacrificial death for sin: it was the emblem of the nation's derision for His kingship claim. They thus fulfilled by act the very prophecy the King had made: "We will not have this man to rule over us." There should be no confusion at this point. The rulers of the nation who demanded His death were not personally rejecting a Saviour, as sinners are rejecting Him now; they were rejecting their King. They did not say, "We will not believe on the Saviour to the salvation of our souls"; they said, "We have no king but Cæsar."

The rejection of the King was according to "the determinate counsel and foreknowledge of God" (Acts 2:23); for His rejection and humiliation were foreshadowed in the types, and foreseen in the prophecies of the Old Testament; He was the "Lamb slain from the foundation of the world." At every step in the record His rejection and death are said to be the fulfilling of the Scriptures. It is recorded of Him in sixteen passages that He, by His rejection and death, fulfilled the Old Testament Scriptures. It is also recorded of Him in nine passages that He was the fulfillment of Old Testament prophecies concerning the King.

The first ministry of Christ was, then, to Israel as her King. In this He appeared; not as a personal

Saviour, but as her long expected Messiah; not as a Lamb, but as a Lion; not as a sacrifice by which a Church—the spotless Bride—might be purchased to Himself from among all nations, but as the Son of David, with every right to David's throne, over Israel, at Jerusalem, in the land of promise. In the Synoptic Gospels, there is, therefore, no record of any step toward the formation of the Church, or any reference to that great purpose, until, from His own nation, His rejection as King is evident. According to the Synoptic Gospels, the early teachings of the King were of that nation, and were in no wise related to the great results which would afterwards be accomplished through His death and resurrection in the calling out of His Church from all the nations of the earth. Upon His rejection, He began to speak, in anticipation of His death, of the formation of His Church, and of His coming back again to the earth. He likewise related the sure fulfillment of every covenant with Israel to the time of His return.

Was, then, the Gospel of the kingdom, as announced by John, by Christ, and by His disciples, a *bonafide* message? Did it really mean what it announced? Was Israel's long predicted kingdom at hand? If so, and had they received their King, what would have become of the divine purposes of redemption as they were to be accomplished through His death? These questions are insistently asked to-day; but the answers are not difficult.

The Gospel of the kingdom was a *bonafide* message to Israel. To treat it otherwise, is to accuse God of trickery and deception. It is likewise a serious misrepresentation of all the related Scriptures to apply the message and teaching of the King to the present purposes of God in this age of grace. All confusion which arises concerning the kingdom message in its relation to the cross arises from the failure to recognize the important distinction between the divine viewpoint and the human viewpoint. It is only another application of the rationalistic trick of playing the free will of man against the sovereignty of God. On the human side, there was a clear-cut issue with unrestrained power to choose, or reject, the King. On the divine side, there was a genuine offer of the kingdom in the Person, presence and ministry of the King; but back of this was the foreknowledge of God which was absolute as to the choice they would make. Their choice would be but the outworking of the eternal purpose of God in Christ, and for that choice they would be held guilty. On the divine side, it is said: "Therefore they could not believe" (John 12:39), and on the human side, it is said: "They hated me without a cause" (John 15:25). Is this the only example of such a problem in the Scriptures? By no means.

Every dispensation represents a new divine purpose in the testing of man. In every case man is seen to fail, and to be guilty before God; yet we behold God patiently and faithfully bringing man face to face with the issues involved. After a brief experience in the wilderness, He took Israel to Kadesh Barnea where He provided and offered an immediate entrance into their own land. The choice was theirs; they refused to enter. They were guilty. God knew they would refuse to enter the land; yet His offer was genuine, and His purposes were realized. In chastisement, God sent them back into the wilderness for forty years of added discomfort. In His own time, and by His own power, they finally entered the land. This portion of Israel's history may be taken to be typical. When Christ came, the nation had then experienced over five hundred years of trial in dispossession of their land and the vacancy of David's throne. When their Messiah came, they refused the divine provisions centered in the King, and, as typified at Kadesh, they returned to what has now proven to be two thousand years of added affliction. The day is coming, however, when, according to the faithfulness of God, they will receive their King and abide under His undimmed glory.

Turning to the Old Testament, the student is confronted with the problem of the right adjustment as to the time of fulfillment of two great lines of prophecy concerning Christ. On the one hand, He was prophesied to come as a Monarch whose reign and kingdom would be everlasting (Cf 2 Sam. 7:16; Ps. 72:1-20; 89:35-37; Isa. 9:6, 7). The thought of His death is foreign to this body of prophecy. It is no function of a king to die,—"Long live the king!" But, on the other hand, there is prophecy equally as explicit regarding the sacrificial, substitutionary death of Christ (Ps. 22:1-21; Isa. 53:1-12). Manifestly, these two lines of undertaking could not be accomplished simultaneously. Christ could not be the resistless, undying King, and be an unresisting sacrifice, at one and the same time. It was this very time-element in the problem which Peter declared was not disclosed to the prophets. He writes: "Of which salvation the prophets have inquired and searched diligently, who prophesied of the grace that should come unto you: searching what, or what manner of time the Spirit of Christ which was in them did signify, when it testified beforehand the sufferings of Christ, and the glory that should follow'' (1 Pet. 1:10, 11). Since the present age of grace and its purpose was not revealed to the writers of the Old Testament, the time-element relating these two lines of prophecy could not be disclosed. When the fullness of time came, it pleased God to present His King in fulfillment of prophecy and according to all His covenants to Israel. Both by the "determinate counsel and foreknowledge of God" and by the free choice of the nation, the King was rejected and crucified. It is evident, therefore, that the prophecies concerning the King and His earthly kingdom remain unfulfilled to this hour. They are not forgotten or abandoned. Neither are they receiving a *spiritual* fulfillment. They are yet to be fulfilled when the King returns to the earth.

In like manner, the same clear light as to the divine purpose is revealed through Daniel when he predicts the order of events to be fulfilled in the period between his own time and that of the reign of Messiah. In this prophecy the "cutting off of Messiah" precedes the reign of the King. Thus did God anticipate what would take place; but this in no wise lessens the exercise of free choice on the part of the nation Israel in rejecting the King.

It is puerile to assert that the cross of Christ was held in jeopardy until Israel's choice concerning the King had been consummated. Let those who traffic in such tricks of argument be consistent to the point of applying their rationalism to all the great issues wherein the sovereignty of God and the free will of man are found to meet. The ministry of Christ was genuine. He was a minister to the circumcision to confirm the promises made unto the fathers. He was likewise the open door into the grace of God that Gentiles might glorify God for His mercy. Though real, His rejection as King was the necessary step in all redemption, and God in faithfulness will yet fulfill every covenant related to the throne, the King, the nation, and the land. This He will do when the King comes back to the earth again.

It has been necessary to outline the relation of the covenanted, earthly kingdom to the first advent of Christ, in order that the kingdom teachings of Christ may be seen in their true setting.

Referring to the first section of the Gospel by Matthew (chapters 1 to 12), wherein the Gospel of the kingdom is preached to Israel, it will be found that this precise message of the kingdom Gospel was first announced by John the Baptist, of whom it is said: "For this is he that was spoken of by the prophet Esaias, saying, The voice of one crying in the wilderness, Prepare ye the way of the Lord, make his paths straight" (Mt. 3:1-3); it was announced by the King Himself (Mt. 4:17); and by the disciples (Mt. 10:5-7). Embedded in this context wherein only the Gospel of the kingdom is in view, and completely bounded by the records of these proclamations, is the "Sermon on the Mount," which is evidently, the Manifesto of the King (Mt. 5:1 to 7:29). In this Manifesto the King declares the essential character of the kingdom, the conduct which will be required in the kingdom, and the conditions of entrance into the kingdom. This kingdom rule of life is purely legal, both in its inherent qualities and by its own claim (Mt. 7:12). It is, however, very different from the law as given by Moses. In the kingdom teachings, as has been stated, the commands of Moses are advanced into requirements vastly more impossible as to detail, and this does not relieve, but rather intensifies, its character as strictly legal. Christ does not disown the principles of the law in the unfoldings of kingdom requirements any more than He does in all His dealings with Israel before His death. He is rather presenting a new degree and standard of law which is adapted to the conditions which shall obtain in the kingdom, and which He *contrasts* with the law of Moses. The great kingdom words— *righteousness* and *peace*—are dominant, and there is never a reference either to salvation, or grace. Nor is there the slightest reference to those great realities of relationship which belong to the new creation wrought by Christ through His death and resurrection. Such a complete omission of any reference to any feature of the present age of grace, is a fact which should be carefully weighed.

The minute accuracy of the Scripture is seen in Christ's use of the phrase *my commandments*. During the days of His ministry to the nation Israel, He enforced the commandments of Moses, and spoke of the new principles which were to be applied in the kingdom as "these sayings of mine," and "I say unto you"; but at no time did He use the term *my commandments* until He used it with His disciples in the upper room, and at the time when He was unfolding the new principles which were to condition the daily living of those who should stand on resurrection ground, in the new creation, and under grace. It is also significant that the *first* use of the term *commandment* in this grace message is when He said, "A new commandment I give unto you" (John 13:34). There is, therefore, a possible limitation to be placed on the extent of the responsibility imposed by Christ in His great commission wherein He said: "teaching them to observe all things whatsoever I have commanded you" (Mt. 28:20). It is hardly probable that He intends all the Mosaic law, the governing principles of the kingdom, and the teachings of grace, to be combined and applied to those who receive the message of the great commission.

In the teachings of the kingdom, the characterizing phrase is, "hear and do" (Mt. 7:24), while the characterizing phrase under grace is "hear and believe" (John 5:24). The essential character of the teachings of the kingdom as they are contrasted with the teachings of Moses, and as they are contrasted with the teachings of grace, will, at another point of the discussion, be considered at length.

There is a sense in which the kingdom of God, as the rule of God in the hearts of individuals, is present in the world to-day. This should not be confused with the Messianic kingdom which is to be set up over a nation, and extended through them to all nations, with the King ruling, not in the individual heart, but on the throne of David, in the city of Jerusalem. As the King came nearer to His death, and the rejection became more evident, He made mention of that aspect of the rule of God in the individual heart which was to characterize the hitherto unannounced age of grace. The following passage (like Mt. 13:1-52), taken from the later teachings of Christ as recorded by Luke, is an example: "And when he was demanded of the Pharisees, when the kingdom of God should come, he answered them and said, The kingdom of God cometh not with observation [outward show] : neither shall they say, Lo here! or, lo there! for, behold, the kingdom of God is within you" (in your midst. Lk. 17:20, 21).

In no sense could it be truthfully said that the kingdom of God was *in* the hearts of those Christ-rejecting Pharisees. There was, however, a real sense in which the kingdom of God was to be, as it is now, in the hearts of individual believers; but the direct statement of Christ is to the effect that the kingdom was then, in the Person of the King, in their midst. So, also, the phrase, *the kingdom of God cometh not with outward show,* anticipates the present aspect of the rule of God in the individual heart; but after this, and according to all prophecy, the kingdom of heaven will come with outward show. There is much promise of a transformed earth, which condition will be ushered in, not by unseen forces and processes; but through the resistless power and presence of the returning King.

So, also, He could say to Israel: "The kingdom of God is come nigh unto you" (Lk. 10:9). As certainly as the King was before the nation, so certainly their kingdom was before them, and this was the appeal of the Gospel of the kingdom which was given to "the children of the kingdom" only. When the King was rejected, His kingdom was rejected. When

His kingdom was rejected and its realization delayed until the return of the King, the application of all Scripture which conditions life in the kingdom was delayed, as well, and will be delayed as long as the King tarries. This necessary delay is easily accepted with reference to the earthly, national glory, which is the theme of the kingdom teachings of the Old Testament; but it is equally true that there is a necessary delay in application of the last detail of human obligation related to the earthly kingdom as set forth in the New Testament.

The kingdom teachings are a sufficient and complete statement of all that it will be necessary for one to know concerning the terms of entrance into, and conduct in the Messianic kingdom on the earth. Much in these kingdom teachings is similar to that which is found in the teachings of Moses. Much is similar, also, to the teachings of grace; but these facts do not constitute these teachings an indivisible whole, nor do they justify a careless co-mingling of these great systems of rule in the earth. The characterizing elements in each will be found to be those principles which are peculiarly applicable to the dispensation to which they belong, rather than in the principles wherein they are similar.

THE LIFE UNDER GRACE
(continued)

CONTRASTS BETWEEN LAW AND GRACE TEACHINGS

Having considered the fact that God provides different rules of life, as recorded in the Scriptures, to fit His succeeding dispensational dealings with man, it is important to consider the wide difference which exists between the principle of law, and the principle of grace, as applied to the divine government of man.

While the purpose of this section is to emphasize the fact that the three systems of divine government are essentially separate, each one from the others, and each one, being wholly complete and sufficient in itself, is in no wise exchangeable for either of the others, and cannot be co-mingled; it should be observed that there are important fields of Bible interpretation and instruction besides the limited aspect of truth which is suggested by the various rules of conduct. The Scriptures unfold many highways of truth with unbroken development from "the blade, then the ear, after that the full corn in the ear." The important features of this unity in the Scriptures are:

1. *The revelation concerning God.* He is first revealed in the Old Testament by His names and

works, and to this the New Testament adds the fuller emphasis upon the Trinity, the relation of the Persons of the Godhead to mankind, and the various aspects of saving grace. The continuity of the Old Testament testimony concerning Christ was proven by Himself on the Emmaus road, as it is recorded: "Beginning at Moses and all the prophets, he expounded unto them in all the scriptures the things concerning himself" (Lk. 24:27).

2. *Prophecy and its fulfillment.* Every recorded instance of the fulfillment of prophecy shows that every detail of the prediction was fulfilled to the letter.

3. *The union between type and antitype.* Almost every important truth of the New Testament was typified and foreshadowed in the Old Testament. This fact proves the symmetry of all Scripture (See 1 Cor. 10:1-11).

4. *The revelation concerning Satan and evil.* In this body of revelation, likewise, the Bible story is uninterrupted, save for the new material added in the development of the divine message.

5. *The doctrine of man and his sin.* The exact manner of the application of the divine remedy for sin varies from dispensation to dispensation; but there is no variation in all the record concerning the essential facts of human failure, and the gracious, divine remedy through blood alone.

6. *The requirement of holiness in the conduct of saints.* While there is wide difference between the rules of conduct which are imposed in the various ages, there is unity in the revelation that a holy manner of life is the divine requirement in every age.

7. *The continuity of purpose in the program of the ages.* In this aspect of the truth it should be observed that, while each age possesses a character exclusively its own, the divine purpose throughout all the ages is one, ending in the ultimate consummation which God has decreed. This fact is stated in Heb. 1:2. Speaking of God as revealed in, and related to, the Son, it is written: "By whom he programmed the ages" (literal).

Such is the wonderful unity of the Scriptures throughout; but in no sense are the various systems regulating human conduct the same, and the exact application of these systems must be guarded at every point. If truth for the children of God under grace is to be drawn from the teachings of the law of Moses, or the kingdom, it should be acknowledged that it is taken from a system foreign to grace, and that it is applicable only by way of illustration.

These governing principles differ in three particulars: (1) They present independent, sufficient, and complete systems of divine rule in the earth. (2) In these systems the order varies as to the sequence of the divine blessing and the human obligation. (3) These systems differ according to the degree in which the divine enablement has been provided.

I. THEY PRESENT INDEPENDENT, SUFFICIENT, AND COMPLETE SYSTEMS OF DIVINE RULE IN THE EARTH.

As has been stated, there are three of these systems of divine government. (1) The teachings of the law of Moses; (2) The teachings of grace;

and (3) The teachings of the kingdom. Naturally there is field here for wide expansion, since these three systems of authority occupy the major portion of the Bible. A brief review only of the essential character of these systems is here given:

(1) *The Teachings of the Law of Moses.*

This rule of life was revealed from God and accepted by Israel at Sinai, and was at no time addressed to the nations of the world. It was a peculiar form of government for a peculiar people, and accomplished a peculiar purpose in condemning the failure of man and in leading him to Christ. Its full detail is revealed in the writings of Moses; but the history of Israel under the law occupies the rest of the Old Testament, and the major part of the Gospels up to the record of the death of Christ. In the doctrinal teachings of the New Testament, very much additional light is given to the character and purpose of the law of Moses. There the law is held in contrast with the teachings of grace. There, also, as will be seen more fully in the later discussion, the law is represented as having passed out of force through the death of Christ; and, it may be observed, that, after the death of Christ, the law is in no instance treated as being directly in force.

The law of Moses was complete within itself. It was sufficient to regulate the conduct of an Israelite under every circumstance that might arise. No other rule of life had been revealed during the days in which the law of Moses was in effect, hence there was no temptation for Israel to complicate her governing principle with any other. In her relation to God, that nation remained for fifteen hundred years under pure law. "The law was given by Moses, but grace and truth came by Jesus Christ."

(2) *The Teachings of Grace.*

Like the teachings of the law of Moses, the teachings of grace have not applied to men in all ages. These teachings were revealed from God through Christ and His apostles. Moreover, they are never addressed to the world as applicable to it in the present age; but are addressed to a peculiar people who are in the world, but are not of the world. These teachings constitute the divine instruction to the heavenly citizen and unfold the exact manner of life that such a citizen is expected to manifest even here in the earth. The full detail of this rule of life is found in portions of the Gospels, portions of the Book of Acts, and the Epistles of the New Testament. As light is given in these particular Scriptures of the New Testament by way of contrast, concerning the character and purpose of the law of Moses, so, in like manner, the very foundations of grace and its relationships are laid in the types and prophecies of the Old Testament. It is revealed that God dealt graciously with the human family from Adam to Moses; but it is also revealed that the precise form of divine government which is the present teaching of grace was not then disclosed, nor was it applied to men until the reign of the law had been terminated in the death of Christ. It is likewise revealed that the death of Christ was the necessary foundation for the present, full manifestation of super-abounding grace. It is equally as certain from revelation that the teachings of grace will apply to the children of God under grace as long as they are in the world, and these principles will cease to rule, of necessity, when the people to whom they alone apply are gathered out and taken from the earth at the coming of Christ. This period between the death of Christ and His coming again is not characterized in the Scriptures as a time when the supreme purpose of God is the governing of the nations of the earth; this age is rather spoken of as "the times of the Gentiles" in all matters of human government in the earth. Nor is this age the period in which God is realizing the fulfillment of His unchanging covenants with the nation Israel; that nation is now said to be scattered, peeled, blinded, broken off, and hated of all nations, and they are to remain so to the end of the age. This age is not the time of the salvation of society; that great undertaking is clearly in the purpose of God, but it is reserved for the age which is yet to come. The present age is characterized by a unique emphasis on the individual. The death of Christ contemplated above all else the need of the *individual* sinner. The Gospel of grace, which the death of Christ made possible, is an appeal to the *individual* alone, and the very faith by which it is received is exercised only by the *individual*. The message of grace is of a personal faith, a personal salvation, a personal enduement of the Spirit, a personal gift for service, and a personal transformation into the image of Christ. The company of individuals thus redeemed and transformed, are to be in the ages to come the supreme manifestation of the riches of God's grace. Unto this eternal purpose the whole universe was created and all ages have been programmed by God. The glory of this dispensation is lost to a large extent when the reign of the law is intruded into this age which followed the death of Christ, or when the social order of the kingdom, promised for a future age, is expected before the return of the King. The Bible affords no basis for the supposition that the Lord will come to a perfected social order. At His coming He will gather the saved to Himself, but the wicked He will judge in righteousness. The transcendent glory of this age is that grace which will have been either accepted or rejected by the *individual*.

The teachings of grace are perfect and sufficient in themselves. They provide for the instruction of the child of God in every situation which may arise. There is no need that they be supplemented, or augmented, by the addition of precepts from either the law of Moses, or the teachings of the kingdom.

(3) *The Teachings of the Kingdom.*

The teachings of the kingdom have not been applied to men in all the ages; nay, more, they have not yet been applied to any man. Since they anticipate the binding of Satan, a purified earth, and the personal reign of the King, they cannot be applied until God's appointed time when these accompanying conditions on the earth have been brought to pass. The kingdom laws will be addressed to Israel and beyond them to all the nations who will enter the kingdom. It will be the first and only universal reign of righteousness and peace in the history of the world. One *nation* was in view when the law of Moses was in force in the earth; the *individual* is in view during this age of grace; and the whole *social order* of mankind will be in view when the kingdom is set up in the earth.

The reign of the King is never said to be ushered in by a gradual process of world improvement; it is introduced suddenly and with great violence. The return of the King to rule is like a smiting stone, and will demolish the structure of world empires, will grind them to powder, and will scatter them as the wind scatters the chaff of the summer threshing floor (Dan. 2: 31-45). Satan and the satanic deception will have been removed from the earth, Israel will have realized the glory of her covenants, and the long predicted blessing will have come upon all the Gentiles, and upon creation itself. The church is not once mentioned in relation to the teachings of the kingdom, nor are those teachings applied to her; for her part in the kingdom is not to be reigned over, but to reign with Christ—her Head. She, being the Bride of the King, is His consort. She will still be under the heavenly teachings of grace, and her home will be in the bosom of the Bridegroom in the ivory palace of the King. The King will reign with a rod of iron. Sin and iniquity will be rebuked instantly and judged in perfect righteousness. Clear conception of the glory of the kingdom is lost if it is confused with the age of grace which precedes it, or with the sinless new heavens and new earth of the eternal state which follows it. The kingdom closes with a demonstration of the failure of man and thus it adds the last message of the converging testimony to the wickedness of the fallen heart, and to the fact that in the exceeding grace of God alone is their salvation.

The teachings of the kingdom are found in portions of the Psalms, the kingdom prophecies of the Old Testament, and the kingdom teachings in the Synoptic Gospels. These teachings are complete and sufficient to direct the life of the children of the kingdom in every condition that may arise under the rule of the King. There is no need that these teachings be supplemented or augmented by additions from either of the other governing systems.

Under God's classification, there are only three major divisions of the human family—"The Jew, the Gentile and the church of God." Wherever they are mentioned in any portion of the Bible they are recognized as distinctly separate peoples, and it is important to follow the divine record concerning each from its beginning to its end.

The Jew, or Israel, began with Abraham, was favored in relationship to God above all the nations of the earth for fifteen hundred years in the promised land, is the object of all of Jehovah's purposes and covenants in the earth, is now as free from the law, and is as effectually shut up to the Gospel of the grace of God as are the Gentiles, and will yet inherit the limitless blessings of all the kingdom covenants in the earth.

The Gentile began with Adam, received no direct instruction or covenant from Jehovah in all the ages past, is now the object of appeal, with the Jew, in the Gospel of grace, and will share in the glory of the kingdom to come, when the divine blessing will be poured out on all the Gentiles (Acts. 15:17).

The Church began with the death of Christ and the descent of the Spirit, is the divine objective in this age, is a heavenly people taken from both Jews and Gentiles, and will reign with the King as His Bride, in the ages to come.

Since there is so wide a difference in the character of these ages—of law, of grace, and of the kingdom —and in the peoples of the earth—the Jew, the Gentile, and the Church—as they stand related to God throughout the ages, it is to be expected that there will be a variation in the divine government according to the essential character of the several ages. This is not only reasonable; it is the precise teaching of the Bible. Since these great governing systems are wholly separate and sufficient in themselves, and since there is much which is held in common in them all, a brief comparison of the systems is here undertaken:

First. *The Similarity and Dissimilarity Between the Teachings of the Law of Moses and the Teachings of Grace.*

In this discussion, the law of Moses will be limited to the Decalogue; for no legalist proposes to carry forward into grace the judgments which governed the social life of Israel, or the ordinances which governed their religious ritual in the land. However, the moral commandments of the Decalogue are almost universally imposed upon the church by these legalists. In justification of this imposition, the plea is usually made that apart from the direct application of the Decalogue there could be no divine authority or government in the earth.

In no sense does this question involve the issues of world government; for God has never addressed either the teachings of the law, or the teachings of grace to the whole world. The world has borrowed certain moral precepts from the Bible for its self-government; but it does not follow that God has accepted the world on the basis of the teachings of the law, or the teachings of grace. In reality, the world is shut up to the one appeal of the Gospel of grace. Until this appeal is heeded, the individual is neither under law, nor grace, as a rule of life; but is "under sin."

The issue is, therefore, between law and grace as governing principles in the life of the Christian. Must Christians turn to the Decalogue for a basis of divine government in their daily lives? Scripture answers this question with a positive assertion: "Ye are not under the law, but under grace." If this be true, are the great moral values of the Decalogue discarded? By no means; for it will be seen that every moral precept of the Decalogue, but one, has been restated with increased emphasis in the teachings of grace. These precepts do not reappear under grace in the character and coloring of the law, but, rather, in the character and coloring of pure grace. The following brief comparison will demonstrate the fact that the moral values of the law are reincorporated in the teachings of grace.

1. "Thou shalt have no other gods before me."

1. "We . . . preach unto you that ye should turn from these vanities unto the living God" (Acts 14: 15).

2. "Thou shalt not make unto thee any graven image; . . . thou shalt not bow down to them nor serve them."

2. "Little children, keep yourselves from idols" (1 John 5: 21).

3. "Thou shalt not take the name of the LORD thy God in vain."

3. "But above all things brethren, swear not, neither by heaven, neither by the earth, neither by any other oath" (Jas. 5:12).

4. "Remember the sabbath day to keep it holy."

4. No such command is found in the teachings of grace.

5. "Honour thy father and thy mother."

5. "Children obey your parents in the Lord: for this is right" (Eph. 6: 1).

6. "Thou shalt not kill."

6. "Whosoever hateth his brother is a murderer: and ye know that no murderer hath eternal life abiding in him" (1 John 3: 15).

7. "Thou shalt not commit adultery."

7. "Neither fornicators, nor idolaters, nor adulterers . . . shall inherit the kingdom of God" (1 Cor. 6: 9, 10).

8. "Thou shalt not steal."

8. "Steal no more" (Eph. 4: 28).

9. "Thou shalt not bear false witness."

9. "Lie not" (Col. 3: 9).

10. "Thou shalt not covet."

10. "Covetousness, let it not be named among you" (Eph. 5: 3).

While some principles of the Mosaic law are restated under grace, those aspects of the law which are foreign to grace are omitted. The command to keep the seventh day is omitted wholly. This fact and the reason thereof will be considered more at length later in the discussion. So, also, the one promise of the Decalogue is omitted. This promise occurs in connection with the precept concerning the obedience of children. It reads: "Honour thy father and thy mother; that thy days may be long upon the land which the LORD thy God giveth thee." The fact that the law presented a promise to obedient children is pointed out in the New Testament (Eph. 6: 1), with no inference that the promise is in effect now; but as a reminder of that which obtained under the law. It would be difficult for any individual, or child, in the Church to establish a claim to a God-given land, or to demonstrate that any law now obtains by which long life is guaranteed to those who are now obedient to parents. Again, concerning Israel and her relation to the land it is written: "Trust in the LORD, and do good; so shalt thou dwell in the land, and verily thou shalt be fed"; "The righteous shall inherit the land, and dwell therein for ever"; "For the upright shall dwell in the land" (Ps. 37: 3, 29; Prov. 2: 21). No land has been given to the Christian. He is a "stranger and pilgrim" here, an "ambassador," a citizen of heaven. If he is taught in the Scriptures, he is not looking for a long life here; but he is looking for the coming of his Lord. He is not clinging to this life; for "to depart, and to be with Christ, . . . is far better." The serious manner in which people apply an

Old Testament promise, impossible under grace, to themselves is a revelation of the measure of inattention with which the Scriptures are too often read and quoted. Since every adaptable precept of the law is restated in grace, it is not necessary to violate the Scriptures by forcing the law into the sphere of grace.

The Decalogue, in its moral principles, is not only restated in grace, but its principles are greatly amplified. This is illustrated, again, by the same precept concerning the obedience of children. In the teachings of grace, the whole issue of obedience is taken up at length, and to this is added the instructions to parents as well. Under the teachings of grace, the appeal of the first commandment is repeated no less than fifty times, the second twelve times, the third four times, the fourth (about the sabbath day) not at all, the fifth six times, the sixth six times, the seventh twelve times, the eighth six times, the ninth four times, and the tenth nine times.

Yet further, that which is even more vital should be noted: The teachings of grace are not only gracious in character and of the very nature of heaven itself, but they are extended to cover the entire range of the new issues of the life and service of the Christian. The Ten Commandments require no life of prayer, no Christian service, no evangelism, no missionary effort, no gospel preaching, no life and walk in the Spirit, no Fatherhood of God, no union with Christ, no fellowship of saints, no hope of salvation, and no hope of heaven. If it is asserted that we have all these because we have both the law and grace, it is replied that the law adds nothing to grace but confusion and contradiction, and that there is the most faithful warning in the Scriptures against this admixture.

A few times the teachings of the law are referred to by the writers of the Epistles by way of illustration. Having stated the obligation under grace, they cite the fact that this same principle obtained under the law. There is, however, no basis here for a co-mingling of these two governing systems.

The law of Moses presents a covenant of works to be wrought in the energy of the flesh; the teachings of grace present a covenant of faith to be wrought in the energy of the Spirit.

Second. *The Similarity and Dissimilarity Between the Teachings of the Law of Moses and the Teachings of the Kingdom.*

As will be seen more fully further on, these two systems of divine government are both legal in character and order. If this is true, it is to be expected that there is much in common between them. (1) They are similar because they are both based on a covenant of works. (2) They are similar because of elements which are common to both. (3) They are dissimilar because of certain points in which they differ.

1. *They are similar because they are based on a covenant of works.*

The nature of a covenant which is based on human works is obvious. Whatever God promises under such a covenant, is conditioned on the faithfulness of man. Every blessing under the law of Moses was so conditioned, and every blessing in the kingdom relationship will be found to be so ordered. Turning to the kingdom teachings of Christ wherein the issues of personal conduct and obligation in the kingdom are taken up, it will be seen that all the kingdom promises to the individual are based on human merit. The kingdom blessings are reserved for the poor in spirit, the meek, the merciful, the pure in heart, and the peace maker. It is a covenant of works only and the emphatic word is *"do."* "This do and thou shalt live," is the highest promise of the law. As men judge, so shall they be judged. A tree is approved, or rejected, by its fruits. And not every one that saith Lord, Lord, shall enter into the kingdom of heaven; but he that *doeth* the will of "my Father" which is in heaven. As the individual forgives, so will he be forgiven. And except personal righteousness shall exceed the righteousness of the scribes and Pharisees, there shall be no entrance into the kingdom of heaven. To interpret this righteousness which is required to be the imputed righteousness of God, is to disregard the teaching of the context, and to introduce an element which is not once found in this whole system of divine government. The kingdom teachings of the "Sermon on the Mount" are concluded with the parable of the house built on the rock. The key to this message is given in the words, "Whosoever heareth these sayings of mine, and doeth them."

Turning to the law of Moses, we discover that it presents no other relation to God for the individual than this same covenant of works: "And it shall come to pass, that if thou shalt hearken diligently unto the voice of the L ORD thy God, to observe and to do all his commandments which I command thee this day [including the Decalogue], that the L ORD thy God will set thee on high above all nations of the earth: and all these blessings shall come on thee, and overtake thee . . . Blessed shalt thou be . . . " (Deut. 28:1-14). "But it shall come to pass, if thou wilt not hearken unto the voice of the L ORD thy God, to observe and to do all his commandments and his statutes which I command thee this day; that all these curses shall come upon thee, and overtake thee . . . Cursed shalt thou be . . . " (Deut. 28:15-68). "Honour thy father and thy mother: that thy days may be long upon the land which the L ORD thy God giveth thee" (Ex. 20:12). "All that the L ORD hath spoken we will do" (Ex. 19:8). "Master, what shall I do to inherit eternal life? He said unto him, What is written in the law? how readest thou? And he answering said, Thou shalt love the Lord thy God . . . And he said unto him, Thou hast answered right: this do, and thou shalt live" (Lk. 10:25-28).

By these references to the law of Moses and the law of the kingdom, it may be seen that both of these systems are based wholly on a covenant of works.

2. *They are similar because of elements which are common to both.*

In the law of the kingdom, the Mosaic law is carried forward and intensified. "Think not that I am come to destroy the law, or the prophets: I am not come to destroy but to fulfil. For verily I say unto you, Till heaven and earth pass, one jot or one tittle shall in no wise pass from the law, till all be fulfilled. Whosoever therefore shall break one of these least commandments, and shall teach men so, he shall be called the least in the kingdom of heaven. . . . Ye have heard that it was said by them of old time, Thou shalt not kill . . . But I say unto you, That whosoever is angry with his brother without a cause shall be in danger of the judgment. . . . Ye have heard that it was said by them of old time, Thou shalt not commit adultery; but I say unto you, That ⁎whosoever looketh on a woman to lust after her hath committed adultery with her already in his heart'' (Mt. 5:17-28. Cf 31-48; 6:1-18, 25-34). ''Therefore all things whatsoever ye would that men should do to you, do ye even so to them; for this is the law and the prophets'' (Mt. 7:12).

By these illustrative passages it is clear that the law of Moses and the law of the kingdom are similar in that they contain elements which are common to both.

3. *They are dissimilar because of certain points in which they differ.*

In the law of the kingdom, certain features are added which are not found in the law of Moses. These new features can be mentioned here only in part.

It has been revealed in the Scriptures above quoted that the law is intensified in the kingdom teachings. From these no element of the law of Moses has been subtracted. Rather, to the Mosaic revelation are added the kingdom teachings of Christ concerning marriage and divorce, the taking of an oath, and the personal obligation to others. The law demanding ''an eye for an eye, and a tooth for a tooth'' is replaced

by required submission. The other cheek is to be
turned, the second mile is to be traveled, and to him
that asketh, there is to be no refusal. Even the
enemies are to be loved. These things are to be done
"that ye may be the children of your Father which is
in heaven," and are only further evidences that in
fact and force they issue from the covenant of works.
There is a new appeal for sincerity in alms-giving,
in prayer, and in fasting. There is a new revelation
concerning prayer; but it is prayer for the kingdom
and according to conditions in the kingdom alone.
Special instruction is given concerning the use of
riches in the kingdom and also concerning anxiety
and care.

Third. *The Similarity and Dissimilarity Between
the Teachings of Grace and the Laws of the Kingdom.*

The importance of an unprejudiced consideration
of these Scriptures which disclose the whole field
of comparison between the teachings of grace and the
laws of the kingdom cannot be too strongly emphasized. The theme is extensive, but an outline-treat-
ment only can be given here. While this study of
contrasts should be extended into all the kingdom
teachings of the Gospels, the plan will be to follow
a brief analysis of the Manifesto of the King as recorded in Matthew, chapters 5 to 7, and to compare
the various precepts there revealed with the precepts
given to the believer under grace. It will be necessary, also, to compare these precepts with the kingdom teachings of the Old Testament; for it will be
found that the teachings of the kingdom presented
in Matthew, chapters 5 to 7, are in exact accord

with the Old Testament predictions regarding the kingdom, and are almost wholly in disagreement with the teachings of grace.

In Luke 16:16 it is written: "The law and the prophets were until John: since that time the kingdom of God is preached, and every man presseth into it." The message of John the Baptist was something new. It was in no sense the preaching of the "law and the prophets" as a direct application of the Mosaic system. Nevertheless, his preaching was purely legal in character. An important exception to this is found in the Gospel by John. In that Gospel, the characterizing words, selected from all the sayings of John the Baptist are, "Behold the Lamb of God, which taketh away the sin of the world" (1:29). The Gospel by John is distinctly of salvation and grace through believing, and the selection of this one message from John the Baptist beautifully illustrates the mind and purpose of the Spirit in the selection of material for the construction of that Gospel of divine grace. This exceptional word from John the Baptist, fitted to the message of grace in the Gospel by John, should not be confused with his legalistic preaching as recorded in the Synoptic Gospels, where his real ministry as the forerunner is set forth. What he preached, is clearly stated in Luke 3:7-14: "Bring forth therefore fruits worthy of repentance . . . And the people asked him, saying, What shall we do then? He answered and saith unto them, He that hath two coats, let him impart to him that hath none; and he that hath meat, let him do likewise. Then came also publicans to be baptized, and said unto him, Master, what shall we do? And he said unto them, Exact no more than that which is appointed you. And the soldiers likewise demanded of him, saying, And what shall we do? And he said unto them, Do violence to no man, neither accuse any falsely; and be content with your wages.''

The intense emphasis on the covenant of meritorious works is obvious in this message; but John did not preach Moses and the prophets. The law and the prophets were *until* John. It is to be concluded that the preaching of John the Baptist was wholly new, and was according to his mission as herald of the King; but that message is legalistic, and not gracious. It is a covenant of works, and not a covenant of faith.

Added light is also given in Luke 16:16 as to the kingdom character of John's preaching. The divine rule in the earth which Matthew terms "the kingdom of heaven" is by Luke termed "the kingdom of God." This is justified since the kingdom of God includes the kingdom of heaven, or the earth-rule of the King. Since Matthew and Luke are so evidently referring to the same divine rule in the earth, and often reporting the same message when employing these two phrases, it is conclusive that Luke's use of the term, "the kingdom of God," here, and elsewhere, is with reference to the limited divine rule in the earth. Into that kingdom, men who enter are said to be "pressing in." "To crowd oneself in," is the literal meaning, and the word suggests intense human effort, and implies the need of merit, which is required for entrance into the kingdom.

There are at least three major distinctions which

will appear when the teachings of grace are contrasted with the teachings of the kingdom.

(1) In the kingdom message, hope is, in the main, centered in the kingdom of heaven, and, in Mark and Luke, in that aspect of the kingdom of God which corresponds with the kingdom of heaven. This, it should be remembered, is not heaven: in this connection, it is the rule of the Messiah-King in the earth. However, the larger rule of the kingdom of God is mentioned once (Mt. 6:33), and at a point when all the divine interests are in view, and three times the kingdom message holds the anticipation of heaven itself before its children (Mt. 5:12; 6:20; 7:23). In the teachings of grace it is heaven itself which is in view, with never a reference to the kingdom of heaven, other than that the saints shall reign with the King. Christians, on the other hand, are often related to the larger sphere of the kingdom of God (See John 3:3).

(2) These two lines of teaching may be identified, also, by the use of the great words they employ. According to both the Old Testament and the New, *righteousness* and *peace* are the great words of the kingdom. The "Sermon on the Mount" is the expansion of the full meaning of the personal righteousness which is required in the kingdom. The great words in this age are *believe* and *grace*. Not once do these words appear in connection with the kingdom teachings of Matthew, chapters 5 to 7. Mercy is unfolded in grace, rather than in righteousness.

(3) The kingdom teachings, like the law of Moses, are based on a covenant of works. The teachings of grace, on the other hand, are based on a covenant of

faith. In the one case, righteousness is demanded; in the other it is provided, both imputed and imparted, or inwrought. One is of a blessing to be bestowed because of a perfect life, the other is of a life to be lived because of a perfect blessing already received.

Too often it has been supposed that the kingdom reign of Messiah will be a period of sinlessness on the earth, corresponding to the new heavens and new earth which will follow. Every Scripture bearing on the kingdom emphasizes the moral conditions which will obtain in the kingdom. Because of the binding of Satan, and the immediate judgment for sin, the high moral requirements in the kingdom will be possible; but there will be evil to judge, the enemy will persecute, and many who have professed will fail because they have not actually *done* the will of the King. So great will be the moral advance in world conditions in the kingdom over the present age, that righteousness will then "reign"; while at the present time, righteousness "suffers" (2 Tim. 3:12).

The various topics presented in the "Sermon on the Mount," are here considered in order:

1. *The Beatitudes* (Mt. 5:1-12).

This kingdom message opens with the record of the nine-fold blessing which is promised and provided for the faithful child of the kingdom. These blessings are won through merit. This is in sharp contrast to the blessings in the exalted position of the Christian to which he instantly attains through Christ at the moment he believes.

a. "Blessed are the poor in spirit [humble]: for

theirs is the kingdom of heaven." As the little child, "of such is the kingdom of heaven." In the Old Testament vision of the coming manifestation of the King, it is said: "I dwell in the high and holy place, with him also that is of a contrite and humble spirit, to revive the spirit of the humble, and to revive the heart of the contrite ones" (Isa. 57:15). To the Christian it is said: "Put on therefore, as the elect of God, holy and beloved, bowels of mercies, kindness, humbleness of mind" (Col. 3:12). These virtues are not put on by the Christian to gain heaven; much less the kingdom of heaven. They are put on because these elements of character belong to the one who is already "elect of God, holy and beloved." Christ is the pattern (Phil. 2:8), and God resists aught but humbleness of mind (Jas. 4:6). In the teachings of grace, "put on" does not mean to pretend, or assume; it is the manifestation of the life through the power of the Spirit (See Eph. 4:24; 6:11; Col. 3:12).

b. "Blessed are they that mourn: for they shall be comforted." Mourning does not belong to the Bride of Christ. To her a different message has been given: "Rejoice, and again I say, Rejoice." Mourning is the portion of Israel until her King comes, and when He comes, it will be "to proclaim the acceptable year of the LORD, and the day of vengeance of our God; to comfort all that mourn; to appoint unto them that mourn in Zion, to give unto them beauty for ashes, and the oil of joy for mourning, and the garment of praise for the spirit of heaviness" (Isa. 61:2, 3. Cf Isa. 51:3; 66:13; 35:10; 51:11; Zech. 1:17).

c. "Blessed are the meek: for they shall inherit the earth." Under grace, meekness is wrought in the believer by the Spirit, and is *never* rewarded; but the judgments of the King will be to "reprove with equity for the meek of the earth" (Isa. 11:4. Cf Isa. 29:19; Zeph. 2:3; Ps. 45:4; 76:9). The earth is to be inherited in the kingdom reign. The glory of the King will be in the earth. It could hardly be supposed that the meek are inheriting the earth now, or that this is any promise to the Church, to whom no earthly promise is made. Those who are kept by the power of God through faith unto salvation ready to be revealed in the last time, have an inheritance incorruptible, and undefiled, and that fadeth not away, reserved in heaven.

d. "Blessed are they which do hunger and thirst after righteousness: for they shall be filled." The Christian may crave a closer walk with God; but he is already "made the righteousness of God in him." In distinction to this, righteousness is that quality which must be *attained* in the kingdom (Mt. 5:20). "For Zion's sake will I not hold my peace, and for Jerusalem's sake will I not rest, until the righteousness thereof go forth as brightness, and the salvation thereof as a lamp that burneth. And the Gentiles shall see thy righteousness, and all kings thy glory" (Isa. 62:1, 2. Cf Ps. 72:1-4; 85:10, 11, 13; Isa. 11:4, 5).

e. "Blessed are the merciful: for they shall obtain mercy." The exact condition revealed in this promise should be carefully considered; for in this passage, mercy from God is made to depend wholly on the exercise of mercy toward others. This is pure law. Under grace the Christian is besought to be merciful, as one who has already obtained mercy (Eph. 2:4, 5;

Tit. 3:5). The mercy of God will go forth in grace to the nation Israel when He gathers them into their own land (Ezk. 39:25); but He will, at the same time, deal with them as individuals by law: "But the mercy of the Lord is from everlasting to everlasting upon them that fear him, and his righteousness unto children's children; to such as keep his covenant, and to those that remember his commandments to do them" (Ps. 103:17, 18). "Therefore hath the Lord recompensed me according to my righteousness, according to the cleanness of my hands in his eyesight. With the merciful thou wilt shew thyself merciful; and with the upright man thou wilt shew thyself upright; with the pure thou wilt shew thyself pure; and with the froward thou wilt shew thyself froward" (Ps. 18:24-26). Under grace, He is rich in mercy, even when we were "dead in sins."

f. "Blessed are the pure in heart; for they shall see God." Opposed to this, and under grace it is written: "But we see Jesus," and "God, who commanded the light to shine out of darkness, hath shined in our hearts, to give the light of the knowledge of the glory of God in the face of Jesus Christ" (Heb. 2:9; 2 Cor. 4:6). In Christ, God *now* is revealed to the believer, while the kingdom promise to the pure in heart is that they *shall* see God. The kingdom promises continue: "He that walketh righteously, and speaketh uprightly. . . . Thine eyes shall see the king in his beauty" (Isa. 33:15-18). "Who shall ascend into the hill of the Lord? or who shall stand in his holy place? He that hath clean hands, and a pure heart" (Ps. 24:3, 4).

g. "Blessed are the peacemakers: for they shall

be called the children of God." *Peace* is one of the two great words in the kingdom. The King who is "the Prince of Peace," shall so reign that righteousness and peace shall cover the earth as waters cover the face of the deep (Cf Ps. 72:3, 7). In that kingdom there will be special distinction given to the one who promotes peace. "They shall be called the children of God." Under grace, no one is constituted a child of God by any works whatsoever. "For ye are all the children of God by faith in Christ Jesus" (Gal. 3:26).

h. "Blessed are they which are persecuted for righteousness' sake: for theirs is the kingdom of heaven." Again, the issue is *righteousness*. The Christian, on the contrary, suffers with Christ and for His sake, and his reward is in heaven. "But all these things will they do unto you for my name's sake" (John 15:21). "All that will live godly in Christ Jesus shall suffer persecution" (2 Tim. 3:12).

i. "Blessed are ye, when men shall revile you, and persecute you, and shall say all manner of evil against you falsely, for my sake. Rejoice, and be exceeding glad: for great is your reward in heaven: for so persecuted they the prophets which were before you." The believer is called to suffer for Christ's sake: "For unto you it is given in the behalf of Christ, not only to believe on him, but also to suffer for his sake" (Phil. 1:29). "If we suffer, we shall also reign with him" (2 Tim, 2:12). It should be noted that when the children of the kingdom are compared to any class of men in suffering, they are taken back to prophets which were before them, and not to the saints who comprise the body of Christ.

Concluding these observations concerning the nine beatitudes, attention should be given to the fact that, in contrast to the nine-fold, self-earned blessing of the kingdom, the believer under grace is to experience a nine-fold blessing which is produced *in* him by the direct power of the indwelling Spirit. A careful comparison should be made of the nine-fold blessing which is promised under the kingdom, with the nine-fold blessing which is prepared under grace. It will be seen that all that is *demanded* under the law of the kingdom as a condition of blessing, is, under grace, divinely *provided*. The two aspects of life which are represented by these two groups of characterizing words are most significant. The total of all the blessings in the kingdom is not comparable with the superabundant "fruit of the Spirit"—"love, joy, peace, longsuffering, gentleness, goodness, faith, meekness, temperance" (self-control, Gal. 5:22, 23). The very tense of the verb used is important. Under grace, the fruit of the Spirit *"is,"* which indicates the present possession of the blessing through pure grace; while under the kingdom, the blessing *"shall be"* to such as merit it by their own works.

2. *The similitudes of the righteous in the kingdom* (Mt. 5:13-16).

In this portion of Scripture the children of the kingdom are likened to the salt of the earth, and the light of the world. "Salt," as a figure, is not so used in the teachings of Moses or in the teachings of grace. However, the Christian is said to be "light in the Lord," and is exhorted to "walk" as a child of the light (Eph. 5:8). Again, "Ye are all the children of light, and the children of the day" (1 Thes. 5:5). But, concerning Israel in her coming kingdom blessing, it is said: "I the LORD have called thee in righteousness, and will hold thine hand, and will keep thee, and give thee for a covenant of the people, for a light to the Gentiles"; "I will also give thee for a light to the Gentiles, that thou mayest be my salvation unto the end of the earth"; "Then shall thy light break forth as the morning"; "And the Gentiles shall come to thy light, and kings to the brightness of thy rising"; "The LORD shall be thine everlasting light, and the days of thy mourning shall be ended" (Isa. 42:6; 49:6; 58:8; 60:3, 20). Still another contrast appears in this connection: The Christian is appointed to manifest Christ (1 Pet. 2:9); but the children of the kingdom are appointed to manifest their good works (Mt. 5:16).

3. *Christ interprets the law in its relation to the kingdom* (Mt. 5:17-48).

This Scripture declares that the law shall not pass until it is fulfilled. This has to do with observance, for it is added: "Whosoever therefore shall break one of these least commandments . . . shall be called the least in the kingdom of heaven." It is the law of Moses intensified. In so doing, Christ transfers the obligation from the outward act to the attitude of the heart. This intensifies, rather than relieves, its legal character. It carries with it the most scorching condemnation possible to law. The Christian is not under law. He has no "altar" other than Christ (Heb. 13:10). The altar is always related either to the Mosaic system, or to the coming kingdom, and is intensely legalistic in character. Concerning the kingdom it is said: "Their burnt-offerings and their sacrifices shall be accepted upon mine altar" (Isa. 56:7. Cf 60:7; Ezk. 43:13-27; Zech. 14:20). The child of the kingdom must agree with his adversary quickly, lest he be cast into prison where there is no degree of mercy available (5:25, 26). To the child of God it is said: "If it be possible, as much as lieth in you, live peaceably with all men" (Rom. 12:17-21). The high standard of generous submission is, in the kingdom teachings, substituted in place of the exact equity of the law of Moses (5:38-48). In place of the principle of "an eye for an eye, and a tooth for a tooth," the other cheek is to be turned, the cloak is to be added to the coat, the second mile is to be traveled, no goods are to be withheld from him that asketh, and enemies are to be loved. This is not to be done as an expression of a high position already received in grace: it is to be done *meritoriously* that "ye may be the children of your Father which is in heaven." Such relations between men will be required and practised in the day when the King shall reign in righteousness and Satan is bound. The teachings of grace concerning murder, adultery, divorce, and swearing, are all clearly stated in the Scriptures.

In this portion of the "Sermon on the Mount," the extreme legal penalty for wrong-doing is imposed (5:20-22, 29, 30). Is any child of God under grace in danger of judgment, or the awful penalty of hell fire? Argument is uncalled for in the light of the Scriptures: "Verily, verily, I say unto you,

He that heareth my word, and believeth on him that
sent me, hath everlasting life, and shall not come
into condemnation [judgment]; but is passed from
death unto life" (John 5:24); "And I give unto
them eternal life; and they shall never perish, neither
shall any man [created thing] pluck them out of my
hand" (John 10:28); "There is therefore now no
condemnation to them which are in Christ Jesus"
(Rom. 8:1).

It is quite true that believers will be judged by
Christ as to the character of their life and service,
that the Father chastens every son whom He receiveth, and that the Apostle Paul suggested that he
might visit a certain church with a rod; but how different is all this from the penalty of hell fire which
is unconditionally imposed on the children of the
kingdom because of their sin! How imperfectly believers realize, when they turn from grace, the awful
penalties of the law and the meaning of eternal damnation! How precious, too, that such ignorance of
the law does not change the abiding, divine covenant
of grace into which the believer has been brought
through faith in Christ!

4. *Mere externalism rebuked* (Mt. 6:1-7, 16-
18; 7:21-29).

In the kingdom, a spirit of vain show as the ac-
tuating motive in alms-giving, offering of prayer, and
professions of devotion, will be judged instantly. On
the other hand, these things, if done in secret, will
be rewarded "openly." Such recompense should not
be confused with the rewards for service which are
promised the Christian at the judgment seat of

Christ. Humble faithfulness in the kingdom will receive its *immediate* recognition from the King.

5. *Prayer for the kingdom, and in the kingdom* (Mt. 6:8-17; 7:7-11).

What is commonly called "The Lord's Prayer," but what is, in reality, the prayer that the Lord taught His disciples when contemplating the kingdom, is not intended to be a ritual prayer. He said: "After this manner therefore pray ye." The prayer is directly concerned with the issues of the coming kingdom. "Thy kingdom come. Thy will be done in earth, as it is in heaven." Of the great themes mentioned in this model kingdom prayer, but one is taken up for special comment and emphasis. It is as though the Spirit of God was seeking to save the reader from any confusion at this point. This special comment amplifies the one petition: "And forgive us our debts, as we forgive our debtors." The divine comment on this reads: "For if ye forgive men their trespasses, your heavenly Father will also forgive you: but if ye forgive not men their trespasses, neither will your Father forgive your trespasses." This, again, is purely legal. Forgiveness on the part of the Christian is enjoined; but it is enjoined in agreement with the exalted principle of grace: "Tenderhearted, forgiving one another, even as God for Christ's sake hath forgiven you"; "Even as Christ forgave you, so also do ye" (Eph. 4:32; Col. 3:13. Cf 1 John 1:9). The legal character of this great kingdom prayer should not be overlooked because of sentimental reasons growing out of early training.

Attempts have been made to relate this divine forgiveness, which is conditioned on a forgiving attitude of the sinner, with the Father's present forgiveness toward the believer who is under grace. Such an interpretation is as foreign to the precise relationships which belong to grace as it would be if the passage were said to teach the present divine forgiveness of the unsaved. Present forgiveness for both the unsaved and the saved is a matter of pure grace, and the divine conditions which are imposed are in perfect harmony with this fact. In this age, the unsaved are forgiven as a part of the entire accomplishment in salvation on the one condition that they *believe* (Eph. 4: 32), and the saved are forgiven on the one condition that they *confess* (1 John 1: 9). These two words do not represent meritorious works; they represent the simple adjustment of the heart to that which is already provided in the grace of God. The cross has changed things for all. A covenant purely of law-works is stated in the passage in question. Such a covenant is the very foundation of all kingdom teaching; but it is wholly foreign to the teachings of grace. Christ, as some claim, must not be presented as a stern, austere Ruler. The marvel is that He is ever anything else. God's holiness is not subject to gracious leniency toward sin. Apart from the cross where redemption's price has been fully paid, there could be nothing but the consuming fire of judgment; but, since God in infinite love has provided a Substitute, there is boundless grace. In this age, God is dealing with men on the ground of His grace as it is in Christ. His dealings with men in the coming age are based on a very different relationship. At that time, the King will rule with a rod of iron. There is no word of the cross, or of grace, in the kingdom teachings. This prayer is, by its own expression, a kingdom prayer.

The whole basis of appeal in this prayer, as in 7:7-11, is the faithfulness of the Father to His children in the kingdom. The basis of appeal in prayer during the days before Christ, or under Moses, was the faithfulness of Jehovah to His covenants. The basis of appeal in prayer under grace is that of the believer's present union and identification with Christ. Access is provided only through Christ (Heb. 10:19, 20), and the new argument of appeal in prayer is, in the name, and for the glory, of Christ. Long after He had taught His disciples the kingdom form of prayer, and after He had turned to the teachings of pure grace He said: "Hitherto have ye asked nothing in my name: ask, and ye shall receive, that your joy may be full" (John 16:24). The kingdom form of prayer omits every feature of the essential note of prevailing prayer under grace.

6. *The law governing riches in the kingdom* (Mt. 6:19-24).

The right use of riches, as under grace, will be rewarded in heaven, and there is no compromise: "Ye cannot serve God and mammon."

7. *The Father's care over the children of the kingdom* (Mt. 6:25-34).

This portion of the Scriptures is one of surpassing sweetness. As God clothes the lillies of the field, so will He clothe those who rest in Him by faith; but

here His care is only for such as seek first the kingdom of God and His righteousness: while, under
grace, His care is unconditioned by any human work
or merit: "Casting all your care upon him; for he
careth for you"; "Be careful for nothing" (1 Pet.
5:7; Phil. 4:6). The same principle of divine care
was presented under the law of Moses; but in the
form of pure law: "Cast thy burden upon the
Lord, and he shall sustain thee: he shall never
suffer the righteous to be moved" (Ps. 55:22).

8. *Warning against judgment of others* (Mt. 7:
1-6.).

This kingdom law is unyielding: "Judge not,
that ye be not judged. For with what judgment ye
judge, ye shall be judged: and with what measure
ye mete, it shall be measured to you again." One
under grace has passed beyond all judgment, by virtue of his acceptance in Christ who died for him
(John 5:24). He may be chastened by his Father,
which is a form of judgment (1 Cor. 11:27-32); but
such judgment is never said to be the return of his
own sin back upon his own head, as is prescribed
in this portion of the kingdom teaching.

9. *Warnings against false prophets* (Mt. 7:15-
20.).

"Beware of false prophets, which come to you in
sheep's clothing, but inwardly they are ravening
wolves. Ye shall know them by their fruits." The
warning here is against false prophets who are to be
discerned by the quality of their lives. The warning to the children of God under grace is against

false teachers who are to be discerned by their doctrine concerning Christ (2 Pet. 2:1; 2 John 7-11): never by their lives; for outwardly, false teachers are said to appear as the "ministers of Christ," and to be dirctly under the power of Satan who himself appears as an angel of light (2 Cor. 11:13-15). The attractive personality of the false teacher affords great advantage as a background for the appeal he makes for his doctrine.

10. *Three determining statements concerning the kingdom.*

a. "For I say unto you, That except your righteousness shall exceed the righteousness of the scribes and Pharisees, ye shall in no case enter into the kingdom of heaven" (Mt. 5:20). Exposition is unnecessary concerning this passage. It is the foundation of all the demands for entrance into the kingdom of heaven. It should in no wise be confused with the believer's entrance into heaven through the finished work of Christ: "Not by works of righteousness which we have done, but according to his mercy he saved us" (Tit. 3:5).

b. "Therefore all things whatsoever ye would that men should do to you, do ye even so to them: for this is the law and the prophets" (Mt. 7:12). This passage stands as a conclusion of the whole appeal of this kingdom teaching. It is as a key to all that has gone before. The legal principle, restated in this passage, is not said to be any part of the teachings of grace: it is rather "the law and the prophets."

c. "Enter ye in at the strait gate: for wide is

the gate, and broad is the way, that leadeth to destruction, and many there be which go in thereat: because strait is the gate, and narrow is the way, which leadeth unto life, and few there be that find it'' (Mt. 7: 13, 14). Under the conditions laid down in the kingdom teachings, life is entered by a personal faithfulness (Mt. 5: 29, 30; 18: 8, 9; Lk. 10: 25-28). When this same exhortation is stated in the Gospel by Luke (13: 24), it opens with the words, ''Strive to enter in at the strait gate.'' The word *strive* is a translation of *agonizomai,* which means to *agonize.* It suggests the uttermost expenditure of the athlete's strength in the contest. Such is the human condition that characterizes all the kingdom passages which offer entrance into life. An abrupt change is met when turning to the Gospel by John, which Gospel was written to announce the new message of grace, which is, that eternal life may be had through *believing.* No two words of Scripture more vividly express the great characterizing relationships in law and grace than *agonize,* and *believe.* Grace is the unfolding of the fact that One has agonized in our stead, and life is ''through his name,'' and not by any degree of human faithfulness, or merit.

There is a dangerous and entirely baseless sentiment abroad which assumes that every teaching of Christ must be binding during this age simply because Christ said it. The fact is forgotten that Christ, while living under, keeping, and applying the law of Moses, also taught the principles of His yet future kingdom, and, at the end of His ministry and in relation to His cross, He also anticipated the

teachings of grace. If this three-fold division of
the teachings of Christ is not recognized, there can
be nothing but confusion of mind and consequent
contradiction of truth.

Again, it is not unreasonable to recognize that
these kingdom teachings should directly apply to a
yet future age. The Bible is the one revelation from
God to all peoples of all the ages. It is not difficult
to understand that much of the Scripture applies to
conditions which are now wholly in the past; nor
should it be difficult to understand that some of the
Scripture applies to conditions which are wholly
of the future. How else shall we know of the future? Certain revelations are of the coming tribulation period and are in no sense applicable to the
present time. Who has ever prayed that his flight
should not be on a sabbath day? Yet Christ commanded that prayer to be prayed (Mt. 24:20).

In like manner, the use of the word *"whosoever"*
in Mt. 7:24 does not imply that all the people of all
the ages are addressed. It is more reasonable to
believe that it applies to the people living under the
conditions of the period which the passage describes.
The all-inclusive word *he* is used by Christ when
He said, "But he that shall endure unto the end, the
same shall be saved" (Mt. 24:13); but nothing could
be more contradictory to the teachings of grace than
the principle set forth in this passage. There will
be a salvation in the tribulation for those who endure
its trials to the end. Under grace, the believer
endures because he *is* saved. If the word *"whosoever"* in Mt. 7:24 includes those who are saved by

grace, then they have been thrust into the blasting covenant of works which that passage proposes, and grace is wholly sacrificed.

Thus it may be concluded that the teachings of the law, the teachings of grace, and the teachings of the kingdom, are separate and complete systems of divine rule which are perfectly adapted to the varied conditions in three great dispensations. The teachings of Moses and the teachings of the kingdom are purely legal, while the instructions to the believer of this dispensation are in conformity with pure grace. There is much that is held in common within all these rules for conduct; but this is no justification for their admixture. All that in the law appertains to life under grace is preserved and restated from the law in the great injunctions and beseechings of grace. To transgress these bounds, is to frustrate grace, and to complicate the individual with the system of law in such a manner as to make him a debtor to do the whole law. The law cannot be broken or divided. It stands as a unit. To undertake any part of it, is to be committed to it all. Nothing could be more unreasonable, or more unscriptural, than to borrow some portions from the law system, either that of Moses, or of the kingdom, and, at the same time, reject other portions. He who will choose the law must, to be consistent, do the whole law (Rom. 10:5), and if he shall break it at one point, he is guilty of all (Jas. 2:10). How precious are the riches of grace in Christ Jesus! How sweet and fitting to the child of God in grace are the heavenly beseechings of grace!

II. THE ORDER VARIES AS TO THE SEQUENCE OF THE DIVINE BLESSING AND THE HUMAN OBLIGATION.

The second major distinction between the teachings of law and the teachings of grace is seen in the varying order between the divine blessing and the human obligation. This variation is found to exist when the principle of grace is compared with the principle of law in any form of the law whatsoever. It is equally true of the law of Moses, the law of the kingdom, or, when legally stated, of the larger conception of the law as being the whole revealed will of God. When the human obligation is presented first, and the divine blessing is made to depend on the faithful discharge of that obligation, it is of and in conformity with pure law. When the divine blessing is presented first, and the human obligation follows, it is of and in conformity with pure grace. The varying orders under law and grace may be stated in the words "do and live": or "live and do." In the case of the law, it is *do* something with a view to being something; in the case of grace, it is be *made* something with a view to doing something. Is the Christian who is under grace saved and kept *by* good works, or is he saved and kept *unto* good works? The law said "If you will do good, I will bless you"; grace says, "I have blessed you, now do good." Under the law, man lives well to *become* accepted of God; under grace man lives well since it *becomes* one to live well who is already accepted. The law presents first a human work to be *done*: grace always presents first a divine work to be *be-*

lieved. Law begins with the question as to what man ought to *do;* grace begins with the question as to what God has already *done.* Every word of the law revelation is thus made to be a conditional covenant of *human* works: while every word of the grace revelation is made to be an unconditional covenant of *divine* works.

The instructions given to Israel under Moses, and the instructions proposed for the government of the yet future kingdom in the earth, are purely legal in their character. The farewell word of Moses to Israel as recorded in the closing chapters of Deuteronomy is the crystallization of the whole law of Moses. One passage is the heart of this message: "And it shall come to pass, if thou shalt hearken diligently unto the voice of the LORD thy God, to observe and to do all his commandments which I command thee this day, that the LORD thy God will set thee on high above all nations of the earth: and all these blessings shall come on thee, and overtake thee, if thou shalt hearken unto the voice of the LORD thy God. Blessed shalt thou be . . . But it shall come to pass, if thou wilt not hearken unto the voice of the LORD thy God, to observe to do all his commandments and his statutes which I command thee this day; that all these curses shall come upon thee, and overtake thee: Cursed shalt thou be". . . (Deut. 28:1-68).

Every teaching of the kingdom which contemplates the responsibility of the individual is, in like manner, based on a covenant of human works, and is, therefore, purely legal in character. This may be observed in all the kingdom teachings of the Old

Testament, and the kingdom teachings of the New Testament. Grace is extended to the *nation* when, apart from all merit, she is placed in her land, and restored to divine blessing; but the rule of the King will be on the basis of pure law, and the responsibility of the *individual* to that rule necessarily will be in conformity to the same. Beyond what has gone before in the discussion, this fact will need but a passing illustration from the kingdom teachings of the New Testament:

"Blessed are the meek: for they shall inherit the earth"; "Blessed are the merciful: for they shall obtain mercy"; "Except your righteousness shall exceed the righteousness of the scribes and Pharisees, ye shall in no case enter into the kingdom of heaven"; "For if ye forgive men their trespasses, your heavenly Father will also forgive you: but if ye forgive not men their trespasses, neither will your Father forgive your trespasses"; "Judge not, that ye be not judged. For with what judgment ye judge, ye shall be judged: and with what measure ye mete, it shall be measured to you again"; "Not every one that saith unto me, Lord, Lord, shall enter into the kingdom of heaven; but he that doeth the will of my Father which is in heaven . . . Therefore whosoever heareth these sayings of mine, and doeth them, I will liken him unto a wise man" (Mt. 5:5, 7, 20; 6:14, 15; 7:1, 2, 21-24). To this may be added all other kingdom teachings of the New Testament.

The kingdom teachings, likewise, are to be distinguished from the teachings of grace by the order which each presents between the divine blessing and the human obligation. The word of the kingdom is, he that heareth my words and *doeth* them shall be blessed (Mt. 7:24). The word of grace is, he that heareth my words and *believeth* them shall be blessed (John 5:24).

In the teachings of grace, the gracious, divine blessing always precedes, and is followed by the human obligation. This is the order maintained throughout the great doctrinal Epistles of the New Testament. These Epistles are therefore subject to a two-fold division. In the first division, the mighty undertakings of God for man are disclosed: while in the second division the saved one is besought and exhorted to live on the plane to which he has been brought in the exceeding grace of God. The first division of the Book of Romans is the unfolding of the saving grace of God toward sinners, which is extended to them on the sole condition that they *believe* (1:16; 3:22, 26; 4:5; 10:4); the second division is an appeal for a corresponding manner of daily life, which life is "reasonable" in view of the results which God has already achieved in sovereign grace. This appeal is stated in the first verse of the second section: "I beseech you therefore, brethren, by the mercies of God, that ye present your bodies a living sacrifice, holy, acceptable unto God, which is your reasonable service" (Rom. 12:1). The Book of Ephesians opens with three chapters in which there is not one requirement for human conduct; it is the unfolding of the marvelous grace of God in bringing the believer to the exalted heavenly positions which are his in Christ. The opening verse of the second section is a condensation of all that follows: "I therefore, the prisoner of the Lord, be-

seech you that ye walk worthy of the vocation [call-
ing] wherewith ye are called" (Eph. 4:1). So, in
like manner, the Book of Colossians opens with a
portion which is devoid of even a semblance of an
appeal in matters of conduct, since it is occupied
with the unfolding of the glory of Christ and the
fact of the perfect standing of the believer in Him.
The second portion is an appeal: not for the human
works which might induce God so to bless the sinner;
but for works which are consistent with the present,
God-wrought, glorious union with Christ: "If ye
then be risen with Christ, seek those things which
are above, where Christ sitteth on the right hand of
God" (Col. 3:1).

The grace order between the divine blessing and
the human obligation is preserved in every offer
of salvation to the sinner and in every purpose
looking toward the preservation of the saint. Since
this is the basis of the divine purpose in the ages and
the only hope of the sinner, or the saint, it should not
be questioned upon a superficial consideration of the
Scriptures. There is the widest possible difference
between the two replies of Christ to practically the
same question: "What shall I do to inherit eternal
life?" Answer:— "This do, and thou shalt live."
Again: "What shall we do, that we might work the
works of God?" Answer:—"This is the work of
God, that ye believe on Him whom he hath sent."
One answer is related to the law of the kingdom:
the other is related to grace, wherein Christ is seen
as the "living bread which came down from heaven:
if any man eat of this bread, he shall live for ever."

It is to be concluded, therefore, that the sinner

is saved by grace apart from every human demand
other than that he receive that grace as it is for him
in Christ, and that the saint is kept by grace *unto*
good works; but not *by* good works. The righteous
Father must *insist* on the good works in the life of
His child; but He does not make these works the condition of His faithfulness. This is the vital distinction, then, between the order relating divine blessing
with human obligation in the two systems—law and
grace. One is a covenant of pure works; the other is
a covenant of pure grace.[1]

Since the covenant of grace which is based on
human faith was established in the promises made
to Abraham, the covenant of the law, made four
hundred years later, and added only for a temporary
purpose, cannot disannul it. The reign of law, with
its covenant of works, ceased with the death of Christ.
Its purpose had been accomplished, and its appointed
time had expired. Thus the by-faith principle which
was announced in the Abrahamic covenant is
brought again into force through the death of Christ.
The divine blessing is now unto him that "worketh
not, but believeth on him that justifieth the ungodly." "Abraham believed God, and it was
counted unto him for righteousness." "Now it was
not written for his sake alone, that it was imputed to

[1] Consideration should be given to the fact that rewards,
which are bestowed in addition to the blessing of the saving grace of God, are offered to the saved one on the principle
of merit; and, on the other hand, grace was offered to the
people under the law, in addition to the demands of the
law, in the provisions of the sacrifices. In no case do
these added blessings condition the exact character of the
covenant of grace, on the one hand, or the covenant of
works, on the other hand.

him; but for us also, to whom it shall be imputed, if we believe on him that raised up Jesus our Lord from the dead; who was delivered for our offences, and was raised again for our justification'' (Rom. 4: 3, 5, 24, 25). By this Scripture it is announced that the by-faith principle of the Abrahamic covenant is continued and now offered through the sacrificial death of Christ. This fact is restated thus: ''So then they which be of faith are blessed with faithful Abraham. For as many as are of the works of the law are under the curse: for it is written, Cursed is every one that continueth not in all things which are written in the book of the law to do them. . . . The law is not of faith'' (Gal. 3: 9-12). The law was a covenant of works; but the works always failed through the weakness of the flesh, and the law then became, of necessity, a condemnation and curse. According to this same Scripture, the holy will of God is not ignored in grace: ''Christ hath redeemed us from the curse of the law, being made a curse for us'' (3: 13). This, it must be observed, was wrought under the one great purpose: ''That the blessing of Abraham [acceptance in the imputed righteousness of God] might come on the Gentiles through Jesus Christ'' (3: 14).

After declaring that the law has passed, either as the grounds of the justification of the sinner (Gal. 3: 24), or as the rule of life for the believer (Gal. 3: 25), the Apostle challenges the law-ridden Christians at Galatia to consider the fact and force of two great covenants which can in no wise co-exist. He therefore points out that one gave way to the other:

"Tell me, ye that desire to be under the law [and he is writing to Christians only, concerning the law as a rule of their lives], do ye not hear the law? For it is written, that Abraham had two sons, the one by a bondmaid, the other by a freewoman. But he who was of the bondwoman was born after the flesh; but he of the freewoman was by promise. Which things are an allegory: for these are the two covenants [the by-works covenant which would depend on the flesh and the by-faith covenant which would depend only on God]; the one from the mount Sinai, which gendereth to bondage, which is Agar [the bondmaid]. For this Agar is mount Sinai in Arabia [where the Mosaic law was given], and answereth to Jerusalem which now is, and is in bondage with her children [Israel]. But Jerusalem which is above is free, which is the mother of us all [typified by Sarah, who illustrates the by-faith principle which depends on God alone]. For it is written, Rejoice, thou barren that bearest not [suggesting the utter helplessness of the flesh before God]; break forth and cry, thou that travailest not: for the desolate hath many more children than she which hath an husband [or the arm of flesh on which one might depend]. Now we, brethren [Christians], as Isaac was, are the children of promise [we have been saved by faith]. But as then he that was born after the flesh persecuted him that was born after the Spirit, even so it is now. Nevertheless what saith the scripture? Cast out the bondwoman [not merely her offspring, but the whole by-works principle which she represents] and her son: for the son of the bondwoman shall not be heir with the son of the freewoman. So then, brethren, we are not children of the bond-woman, but of the free'' (Gal. 4:21-31).

It was concerning the promise of the supernatural birth of Isaac that Abraham believed God, and that belief was counted unto him for righteousness. Afterwards, Abraham turned to the flesh in the birth of Ishmael (Gen. 16:1-4). This two-fold fact illustrates, with all the perfection of the Word of God, the two covenants—one of faith, and the other of works. The lapse in Abraham's faith typified the intrusion of an age of law. So, also, the relationship with Agar represents what man can do in his effort to be accepted of God. The supernatural relationship with Sarah represents what God can do for one who will *believe*. The marvels of grace are indicated by the multitudinous offspring of Sarah: not that her physical seed, Israel, are the children of faith; but they, being more exalted than the children of Agar, typify the surpassing victory of God through grace. There can be no co-mingling, or compromising, of these two great covenants. ''What saith the Scripture?'' should be the end of discussion. The testimony is, ''Cast out the bondwoman and her son: for the son of the bondwoman shall not be heir with the son of the freewoman.'' The by-works principle of the law, and the by-faith principle of grace, cannot co-operate, or co-exist, either in the salvation of the sinner, or in the rule of life for the believer.

The by-works principle of the law is not limited to the fleshly effort to do the particular things found in the law of Moses, and the law of the kingdom.

It is the fleshly effort to do *anything* by which one seeks to become acceptable to God. Therefore, when the teachings of grace are attempted with a view to being accepted of God, they become purely legal in their character. In like manner, when the elements which are contained in the law and restated under grace are attempted in the power of the Spirit and on the basis that acceptance with God is already gained through Christ, these precepts become purely gracious in their character. This principle may be extended to the larger sphere of any and all self-imposed law, regardless of Bible injunctions. In which case it will be seen that the doing of any good works with a view to being accepted of God, is purely legal in character; contrawise, the doing of any good works because one believes himself to be accepted through Christ, is purely gracious in character. The legalist may thus enter the field of the teachings of grace and suppose himself to be subject to the whole Bible, when, in reality, he has no conception of the blessings and relationships in grace. A person either chooses to accept Christ in the confidence that Christ is *all* he will ever need to make himself acceptable to God, or he chooses to depend on the best that he can do for himself by good works. The latter is the normal bent of the natural mind. The proposition of becoming acceptable to God by being good, appeals to the fallen heart as the only reasonable thing to do, and, apart from that which it has pleased God to reveal concerning grace, it *is* the only reasonable thing to do. It therefore becomes a question of believing the *Record* God has given concerning His Son (1 John 5:10).

Since there is so much delusion in a counterfeit, the person most difficult to reach with the Gospel of divine grace is the person who is *trying* to do all that a Christian ought to do, but is doing it as a means of becoming accepted before God. His willing acknowledgment of the value of the Christian life his unquestioned reception into the fellowship of believers, and his real sincerity in all Christian activities, constitute his greatest hindrance. Such an one is more deluded than the person who acknowledges no relationship to God. Both fall short and are lost through their failure to believe on Christ as the all-sufficient Saviour; but, naturally, the person who has no false hope is more apt to become conscious of the fact that he is lost than is the person who believes he is a Christian. The law cannot save, and the one who transforms the teachings of grace into a legal system by attempting to do them in order that he may be right with God, is still unsaved.

Turning to meritorious works as a basis of salvation, be those works a precise counterfeit of a true Christian life, is to be under a by-works relation to God, and therefore to be under condemnation; for by the works of the law shall no flesh be justified in His sight. Turning to meritorious works as the basis of keeping after one is saved, or as a rule of life for the saved, is to return to a by-works relation to God, from which one has already been saved. It is to fall from grace, and to lose the liberty wherewith Christ has made us free. The by-works principle can no more avail for our keeping, than it can avail for our salvation. As God could provide Abraham with a seed under an unconditional covenant, so, under the same unconditional covenant, He could guarantee the future of that seed even to the time when their number shall exceed the stars of the heavens. Likewise, under the present unconditional covenant of grace made in the blood of Christ, God can guarantee the future security of every child of His under grace. Therefore it is of faith, that it might be by grace; to the end the promise might be *sure* (Rom. 4:16).

Lastly, the covenant of works is "cast out" because it is fulfilled and superseded by the fuller and more perfect covenant of faith. All that the covenant of works contemplated as a result of a lifetime of human struggle, is instantly accomplished in the power of God through the covenant of faith. By faith in Christ, the believer is *made* the righteousness of God in Him, and *made* accepted in the Beloved. This is a perfection of relationship with God to which no human works could ever attain, and to which human works can add nothing. Being related to God through the by-faith principle, the whole object of law-works is more than fulfilled. Thus the law is ended in the death of Christ. The bondwoman is cast out. Christ is the end of the law for righteousness to every one that *believeth*.

Amazing indeed, is the blindness of heart that is not instructed by the tragic experience of failure on the part of the countless millions who have been lost under the by-works covenant! Yet men are still turning to their own works, both moral and religious, in the vain hope that through them they may be accepted of God. To such He must ever be as unapproachable as the mountain of awful fire, thunder, lightning, and earthquake; but to the one who turns to the sufficiency which is in Christ, God becomes the Father of all mercies, and His power and grace are exercised in the behalf of that one for all time and eternity. The awful throne of God's holy judgments becomes a throne of infinite *grace*. To one thus saved, and whose security is guaranteed, the by-works covenant of the law is in no wise adapted as a rule of life; for that covenant looks beyond to a time of acceptance still future, when the flesh shall have completed its task. Only the teachings of grace are consistent for one who is saved by grace. Those teachings alone counsel him as to that manner of life which is in accord with his present position in grace.

The second major distinction between the rule of law and the rule of grace is, then, that these two systems are opposites in reference to the order between the divine blessing and the human obligation, and this holds true for any life or service whatsoever which may be undertaken.

III. BECAUSE OF DIFFERENT DEGREES OF DIFFICULTY AND DIFFERENT DEGREES OF DIVINE ENABLEMENT.

The three rules of life—the law of Moses, the law of the kingdom, and the teachings of grace—are widely different because of two facts: (1) The requirements of the manner of life under them are far from uniform, and (2) these systems differ in the degree of divine enablement which is provided in each. These two facts are so closely related with these governing systems that it is necessary to consider these two facts in their relation to each rule of life:

First, *The Law of Moses.*

In discussing the law as a regulation for human conduct, attention should be given,

1. *As to the measure of requirement which is imposed.*

The standard of conduct presented by the law of Moses was limited in its requirements to the extent that its demands were imposed on even unregenerate men. The Mosaic law was addressed to the natural man, and, it is evident, its requirements did not exceed his limitations; yet because of the weakness of the flesh, these demands were never actually fulfilled by any person other than Christ.

2. *As to the degree of divine enablement.*

There is no hint in connection with the proclamation of the law of Moses of any divine enablement being provided for the keeping of that law. God addressed those commandments to men, and the result was no more than the unaided flesh would produce. The law dispensation, extending over a period of fifteen hundred years, thus became a demonstration of the universal failure of man under the reign of pure law. Christ, through His death, became the end of the reign of law; as He, through His death, is the end of confidence in self-works for all who put their trust in Him.

Second. *The Law of the Kingdom.*

Again, attention should be given,

1. *As to the measure of requirement which is imposed.*

The standard of conduct which will be required under the law of the kingdom is, as has been seen, advanced and intensified in its demands beyond that which is presented under the law of Moses. In the kingdom rule, portions of the Mosaic law are extended beyond the overt act to include the very thought and intent of the heart. Added to this, there are entirely new requirements concerning matters of personal yieldedness and devotion to God which are foreign to the Mosaic system.

2. *As to the degree of divine enablement.*

The degree of divine enablement which will obtain under the rule of the kingdom is seen in three provisions: (a) The environment, (b) the inclined heart, and (c) the outpoured Spirit.

(a) The environment in the kingdom will be that of a purified, transformed earth; creation will be delivered from its present bondage and corruption; Satan will be bound and confined to the abyss; and the subjects in the kingdom will realize the immediate power and inspiration of the personal reign of the King, which will be extended over all the earth.

(b) Added to this is the revealed fact that the King will have inclined the hearts of His people to do His holy will. This great promise is made to Israel as a vital part of the new covenant under which Israel, during the reign of her Messiah King, will yet live in her own land (Cf Jer. 31: 33-37; Heb. 8: 7-12). These kingdom blessings will also be extended to the nations of the earth (Isa. 11: 10).

In the prophecy by Moses concerning the attitude of heart which Israel will experience when restored to her own land, we read: "And the LORD thy God will bring thee into the land which thy fathers possessed, and thou shalt possess it; and he will do thee good, and multiply thee above thy fathers. And the LORD thy God will circumcise thine heart, and the heart of thy seed, to love the LORD thy God with all thine heart, and with all thy soul, that thou mayest live. . . . And thou shalt return and obey the voice of the LORD, and do all his commandments which I command thee this day" (Deut. 30: 5-8. Cf Hos. 2: 14-23; Zeph. 3: 14-20; Rom. 11: 26, 27).

So, again, in the new covenant it is stated: "Behold, the days come, saith the LORD, that I will make a new covenant with the house of Israel, and with the house of Judah: not according to the covenant that I made with their fathers in the day that I took them by the hand to bring them out of the land of Egypt; which my covenant they brake, although I was an husband unto them, saith the LORD: but this shall be the covenant that I will make with the house of Israel; After those days, saith the LORD I will put my law in their inward parts, and write it in their hearts; and will be their God, and they shall be my people. And they shall teach no more every man his neighbour, and every man his brother, saying, Know the LORD: for they shall all know me, from the least of them unto the greatest of them, saith the LORD: for I will forgive their iniquity, and will remember their sin no more" (Jer. 31:31-34. Cf Heb. 8:8-12).

(c) The promise concerning "the last days" for Israel, according to Joel 2:28-32, is that the Spirit is to be poured out upon all flesh. He records further: "And your sons and your daughters shall prophesy, your old men shall dream dreams, your young men shall see visions: and also upon the servants and upon the handmaids in those days will I pour out my Spirit. And I will shew wonders in the heavens and in the earth, blood, and fire, and pillars of smoke. The sun shall be turned into darkness, and the moon into blood, before the great and the terrible day of the LORD come. And it shall come to pass, that whosoever shall call on the name of the LORD shall be delivered: for in mount Zion and in Jerusalem shall be deliverance, as the LORD hath said, and in the remnant whom the LORD shall call."

That this great promise began to be fulfilled at Pentecost, is explicitly stated by Peter in his sermon on that day. It must be borne in mind, however, that Peter's reference to Joel's prophecy concerning the kingdom was made in connection with the renewed appeal to Israel, extended at Pentecost, that she repent and receive her Messiah whom she had slain. As the Gospel was extended to Gentiles in the formation of the Church, the abiding ministries of the Spirit became evident, and the final outpouring of the Spirit which, according to Joel, is to characterize the inception of the kingdom in the earth, awaits the return and enthronement of the King.

Little is revealed as to the enabling power of the Spirit for the individual's life and conduct in the kingdom. Doubtless, to some extent, such power will be imparted. The particular emphasis falls on the national glory as suggested by the phrase "all flesh," and the individual is said to be moved to prophesy and to see visions and to dream dreams.

Thus will Israel be situated in the kingdom. She will have her added responsibilities in the larger demands of the kingdom law, and she will have the added advantage of the kingdom environment, the inclined heart to do the will of the King, and upon her the Spirit will be poured out.

Third, *The Teachings of Grace.*

The standard of conduct prescribed under the teachings of grace is immeasurably more difficult to maintain than that prescribed either by the law of Moses, or the law of the kingdom. It is as much higher than these as heaven is higher than the earth. Similarly, the divine enablement provided under grace is nothing less than the infinite power of the indwelling Spirit.

The teachings of grace are addressed only to the supernatural man who is both born of the Spirit and indwelt by the Spirit. These teachings are such as naturally belong to a citizen of heaven. Since the saving work of God places the believer in the heavenly positions in Christ, and transfers his citizenship from earth to heaven, it is only consistent that he should be required to walk as it becometh a citizen of heaven. This, it is evident must be a supernatural life. Turning to the Scriptures which reveal the position and responsibility of the child of God under grace, it is found that a *superhuman* manner of life is proposed and that a *supernatural* power is provided for its exact and perfect execution. These are two of the most vital facts concerning the teachings of grace and they should be observed with great care:

1. *As to the character of the requirements which are imposed.*

The manner of life which is enjoined under grace is superhuman. This aspect of the teachings of grace may be seen at every point. A very few passages will suffice by way of illustration:

"Casting down imaginations, and every high thing that exalteth itself against the knowledge of God, and bringing into captivity every thought to the obedience of Christ" (2 Cor. 10:5); "That ye should shew forth the praises [virtues] of him who hath called you out of darkness into his marvellous light" (1 Pet. 2:9); "Giving thanks always for all things unto God" (Eph. 5:20); "That ye walk worthy of the vocation wherewith ye are called" (Eph. 4:1); "Walk in the light" (1 John 1:7); "Walk in love" (Eph. 5:2); "Walk in the Spirit" (Gal. 5:16); "Grieve not the holy Spirit of God" (Eph. 4:30); "Quench not the Spirit" (1 Thes. 5:19).

There is no question as to the superhuman character of these injunctions. What human resource is able to reproduce the very virtues of Christ? Who is able to give thanks *always* for *all* things? Who will be able so to live that he will not grieve the *Holy*

Spirit, nor quench the Spirit? This demand is for a *superhuman* manner of life, and the passages quoted are only representative of the whole character of the teachings of grace. These teachings surpass the standards of the law of Moses in the measure in which infinity surpasses the finite. When unfolding the high character of the teachings of grace, Christ said: "A new commandment I give unto you, That ye love one another; as I have loved you, that ye also love one another"; "This is my commandment, That ye love one another, as I have loved you" (John 13:34; 15:12). The new commandment is in contrast to an old commandment of Moses: "Love thy neighbour as thyself." These Scriptures may be taken as a fair illustration of the difference between the standards of the law of Moses, and the standards of grace. Under the Mosaic system, love for others was to be in the degree in which one loved himself: under grace it is to be in the degree in which Christ has loved us and given His life for us (1 John 3:16).

The standards of the teachings of grace surpass the standards of the laws of the kingdom. The same example—of love one for another—will again illustrate. The requirement in the kingdom on this point is stated thus: "Ye have heard that it hath been said, Thou shalt love thy neighbour, and hate thine enemy. But I say unto you, Love your enemies, bless them that curse you, do good to them that hate you, and pray for them which despitefully use you, and persecute you; that ye may be the children of your Father which is in heaven: for he maketh his sun to rise on the evil and on the good, and sendeth rain on the just and on the unjust. For if ye love them which love you, what reward have ye? Do not even the publicans the same?" (Mt. 5:43-46).

This is a great advance over the standard of love demanded under the law of Moses. There love was required to a limited degree; but nothing was said concerning the necessary attitude toward the enemy. Christ implies that the law of Moses proposed love for the neighbour and hate for the enemy. The degree of love expected under the ideals of the kingdom is only such as might reasonably be expected from the heart that has been inclined to do the kingdom law. It bears no comparison to the standards of love which are proposed under grace. Consider, first, that love under grace is the "fruit of the Spirit" (Gal. 5:22). Literally, "the love of God is shed abroad [gushes forth] in our hearts by [out from] the Holy Ghost which is given unto us" (Rom. 5:5). This both guarantees the exact reproduction in the child of God of the love of Christ—"as I have loved you"—and destroys every ground of personal reward for such love. The believer is not said to be rewarded for those graces which are not his own, but which are produced in him by the indwelling Spirit. On the other hand, love, according to the standards of the kingdom is distinctly said to be a matter for personal reward. By such love for enemies, the children of the kingdom will be the children of their Father which is in heaven. This, it is evident, is made to depend on self-wrought conformity to the Father who Himself is benevolent to His enemies. In the "Sermon on the Mount," the Spirit is not once mentioned nor is any divine enablement suggested.

Consider, also, that love, as anticipated in the

teachings of grace, is the very heart of the Evangel and evangelism. By the imparted, divine compassion for the lost which brought Christ from heaven to earth and took Him to the cross to die, under grace, men are to be impelled to win souls. Such divine compassion for souls has been the dynamic of all soul-winning work from Pentecost until now. It was the experience of the Apostle Paul as disclosed in his testimony: "I say the truth in Christ, I lie not, my conscience also bearing me witness in the Holy Ghost, that I have great heaviness and continual sorrow in my heart. For I could wish that myself were accursed from Christ for my brethren, my kinsmen according to the flesh" (Rom. 9:1-3). There was no occasion for the Apostle to be accursed from Christ, nor did he expect to be; but he was *willing* to be. Thus was the love of Christ, who bore the sin of others, definitely reproduced in the one in whom the Spirit wrought. True passion for the salvation of men is not a manifestation of love springing out of human nature. It must be *imparted* from God. Therefore evangelism is neither expected nor required in either the law of Moses, or the law of the kingdom.

By this very partial treatment of the varying degrees of difficulty presented in these dissimilar rules of conduct, it may be seen that the standards under grace are infinitely higher than the standards of either the law of Moses, or the law of the kingdom. They are *superhuman*.

2. *As to the divine enablement.*

A supernatural power is provided for the exact and perfect execution of the superhuman rule of life under grace. There is no aspect of the teachings of grace which is more vital than this, or which so fully differentiates these teachings from every other rule of life in the Bible. Under grace, the all powerful, abiding, indwelling and sufficient Holy Spirit of God is given to every saved person. This statement is abundantly established by revelation (John 7: 37-39; Rom. 5: 5; 8: 9; 1 Cor. 2: 12; 6: 19; Gal. 3: 2; 1 Thes. 4: 8; 1 John 3: 24; 4: 13),[1] and is assumed in every teaching of grace. The superhuman manner of life under grace is not addressed to some spiritual company alone within the whole body of Christ; it is addressed to *all* believers alike. The imposition of this superhuman manner of life upon *all* believers alike, carries with it the revelation that *all* have the supernatural power by which to live according to the superhuman standards. This, it is evident, is according to the teaching of the Word of God.

The character of pure grace is destroyed when the reception of the Spirit into the individual heart is made to depend on any human merit, goodness, or personal consecration whatsoever. In 1 Cor. 6: 19, 20 we read: "What? know ye not that your body is the temple of the Holy Ghost which is in you, which ye have of God, and ye are not your own? For ye are bought with a price: therefore glorify God in your body, and in your spirit, which are God's." The law element is excluded here. Under the law, it would have been written: "Glorify God in your bodies and spirit and ye shall become temples of the

---

[1] Careful study will disclose the fact that Lk. 11: 13; Acts 5: 32; 8: 12-17; 19: 1-7; Eph. 1: 13 do not contradict this positive doctrine of Scripture.

Holy Spirit.'' Under grace, believers *are* temples of the Spirit without reference to merit, and this is true of every aspect of their salvation. The fact that they *are* temples of the indwelling Spirit is the basis of this appeal for a holy life. A consideration of 1 Cor. 5:1, 2, 13; 6:1-8 will give abundant evidence of the meritless condition of the Corinthian saints at the time the Spirit addressed this appeal to them through the Apostle Paul. The earnest supplication is for a daily life which corresponds to the wonderful fact that they are *already* temples of the Spirit.

There is an important distinction to be noted between the *indwelling* and the *infilling* with the Spirit. No Scripture asserts that all believers are *filled* with the Spirit. The filling with the Spirit, which is the requirement for an experience of blessing and the exercise of divine power, is an issue which should be considered wholly apart from the revelation concerning the indwelling Spirit.

The fact that the Spirit indwells every believer is peculiar to the age of grace. In the law dispensation, for particular divine purposes, certain individuals were, at times, filled with the Spirit; but there is no revelation stating that *every* Israelite, being under the law, was a temple of the Spirit. In like manner, under the law, there was no *abiding* character to the relationship between the Spirit and individuals upon whom He came (Ps. 51:11). The Spirit came upon them, or departed, according to the sovereign purpose of God. Under grace, the Spirit is not only given to *every* believer, but He never withdraws. This assurance is based on the unfailing prayer of Christ (John 14:16). This is in precise accordance with the conditions embodied in the covenant of grace. Should human merit determine His abiding presence, then, under that relationship, the basic principle of grace would be superseded by the principle of law-works. The entrance of the Spirit into the heart, and His abiding presence there, is a part of the saving and keeping power of God, which is by grace alone. The revelation of the New Testament with regard to the indwelling, abiding Spirit in every believer is in full agreement with the doctrine of pure grace.

When considering the question of the enabling power of the Spirit in the individual lives of the children of the kingdom, it will be seen from the Scriptures that, at the opening of that period at least, the Spirit is to come upon all flesh, and the individual will prophesy, dream dreams, and see visions (Joel 2:28-32; Acts 2:16-22); but there is no revelation to the effect that this will be an *abiding* presence and ministry, since it is related to mighty signs and wonders in nature which accompany the second advent of Messiah. And, in like manner, there is no revelation concerning the enabling power of the Spirit for conduct in the daily life of the individual in the kingdom. The kingdom teachings of the Scriptures do not emphasize the work of the Spirit. Any divine provision for personal enablement in daily life, it would seem from a careful examination of the Scriptures, is foreign to every aspect of law-rule; whether it be that of Moses, or that of the kingdom.

So vital is the fact that the enabling Spirit is now given to *every* believer as a part of salvation by grace, that it is presented as a fundamental characteristic of this age. This is the dispensation of the indwelling Spirit. We read: "But now we are delivered from the law, that being dead wherein we were held; that we should serve in newness of spirit [Spirit], and not in the oldness of the letter" (Rom. 7: 6). Thus the new enabling power of the Spirit characterizes this age, as the "oldness of the letter" characterized the age that is past. Likewise circumcision is now "of the heart," in the Spirit, and not in the "letter" (Rom. 2: 29), or as it was in the flesh under the law. Again, "Who also hath made us able ministers of the New Testament; not of the letter, but of the spirit [Spirit]: for the letter killeth, but the spirit [Spirit] giveth life" (2 Cor. 3: 6). Reference in this passage is not made to different methods of interpreting Scripture—a spiritualizing, or a literal method; but to two dispensations with their different methods of divine rule. "The letter killeth"—such is the inevitable ministry of the law; "But the spirit giveth life"—divine life, spiritual vitality, energy, and power is provided for the believer under grace, and for *every* believer alike. Thus it is revealed that the blessing of the indwelling Spirit is an essential characteristic of this age.

If the manner of life under grace is *superhuman*, so, also, the provided enablement is *supernatural*, and is as limitless as the infinite power of God. Since God has proposed a humanly impossible manner of life, He has, in full consistency, provided the Spirit who giveth life. Too much emphasis cannot be placed on the fact that, since God has proposed the impossible rule of life and provided the sufficient

Spirit, the believer's responsibility is thereby changed from being a *struggle* of the flesh to being a *reliance* on the Spirit. Grace thus introduces a new problem for the believer's life which is wholly foreign to every aspect of the law. It is the problem of the adjustment of the heart to the holy presence of the Spirit, and of maintaining the unbroken attitude of dependence on the Spirit. The new principle of achievement consists in getting things accomplished in the believer's daily life and service by trusting the power of Another, rather than by trusting the energy of the flesh. The revelation concerning this new problem of life under grace constitutes the major part of the teaching of the Epistles. Not only is the faith principle directly taught in the Epistles; it is implied and assumed in every injunction under grace. The unfolding of the precise relationship between the personality of the Spirit, and the personality of the believer, is not omitted. Experimentally, the believer, when empowered by the Spirit, will be conscious only of the exercise of his own faculties. The Spirit does not disclose His presence directly; His ministry is to reveal and glorify Christ. His presence will be evidenced, however, by the victory that is wrought, which victory could be wrought only by the Spirit.

Thus, either the by-works principle of the law, or the by-faith principle of grace, may be chosen by the believer as a method of achievement even within the deepest issues of Christian conduct and service. If these heaven-high demands are undertaken in the energy of the flesh, they become purely legal in character; if they are undertaken in full reliance on the provided energy of the Spirit, they are purely gracious in character. One is wholly within the scope of the covenant of the law, which covenant is based on works; the other is wholly within the scope of the covenant of grace, which covenant is based on faith. Thus the teachings of grace, when attempted in the energy of the flesh, become a legal code, the demands of which are the most impossible to meet. How very many Christians are under this aspect of law; even those who give some attention to the actual precepts of grace!

There are two inseparable revelations given in the grace teachings of the New Testament. Each one is the counterpart, complement, and supplement of the other, and untold violence is done to the whole revealed purpose of God in this age when either one of these themes is made to stand alone. One theme is presented in that body of Scripture which sets forth the character of conduct that is becoming to the one who is already saved and safe in the grace of God; the other theme is presented in that body of Scripture which sets forth the fact that the life in grace is to be lived in sole dependence on the enabling power of the indwelling Spirit. The latter body of Scripture includes all the details and instructions concerning the life of faith, and the walk in the Spirit. It is obviously imperative that these two revelations shall not be separated. Otherwise, on the one hand, the teachings of grace will seem to be an impossible law-code, or, on the other hand, the walk in the Spirit will seem to be an uncharted, aimless procedure.

In the grace teachings of the New Testament, these

two aspects of truth are never separated. In adducing proof of this, it is impossible in a work of this length to review every Scripture bearing upon this truth. Proceeding from the fact that the superhuman manner of life under grace is taught in all the New Testament books beginning with the Gospel by John, there is space for only one quotation from each of these up to, and including, the Epistle to the Colossians. This body of Scripture discloses the truth that the life in grace is to be lived only by the enabling power of God:

John 7:37-39. "In the last day, that great day of the feast, Jesus stood and cried, saying, If any man thirst, let him come unto me, and drink. He that believeth on me, as the scripture hath said, out of his belly shall flow rivers of living water. (But this spake he of the Spirit, which they that believe on him should receive: for the Holy Ghost was not yet given; because that Jesus was not yet glorified)." Here the superhuman outflow of rivers of living water is distinctly said to be the result of the energy of the Spirit.

Acts 1:8. "But ye shall receive power, after that the Holy Ghost is come upon you: and ye shall be witnesses unto me." The revelation here is that, apart from the power of the Spirit, there can be no vital witness unto Christ.

Rom. 6:14; 8:4. "For sin shall not have dominion over you: for ye are not under the law, but under grace." No enabling power was provided for the doing of the law; but such power is provided under grace. "That the righteousness of the law might be fulfilled in us, who walk not after the flesh, but after the Spirit.'' No passage in the teachings of grace is more decisive than this. ''The righteousness of the law,'' referred to, is evidently no less than the whole will of God for His child under grace. This divine will is to be fulfilled *in* the believer; but never *by* the believer.

I Cor. 12:4-7. ''Now there are diversities of gifts, but the same Spirit. And there are differences of administrations, but the same Lord. And there are diversities of operations, but it is the same God which worketh [energiseth] all in all. But the manifestation of the Spirit is given to every man [Christian] to profit withal.'' As all Christian service is by the exercise of a spiritual gift, these gifts are wholly realized by the energy of the power of God.

II Cor. 10:3-5. ''For though we walk in the flesh, we do not war after the flesh: (for the weapons of our warfare are not carnal [fleshly], but mighty through God to the pulling down of strong holds); casting down imaginations, and every high thing that exalteth itself against the knowledge of God, and bringing into captivity every thought to the obedience of Christ.'' For this superhuman manner of life, the believer is to be ''mighty through God.''

Gal. 5:16. ''This I say then, Walk in [by means of] the Spirit, and ye shall not fulfil the lust of the flesh.'' This promise is as sure as it is far-reaching.

Eph. 6:10, 11. ''Finally, my brethren, be strong in the Lord, and in the power of his might. Put on the whole armour of God, that ye may be able to stand against the wiles of the devil.'' True overcoming strength is none other than the imparted ''power of God.''

Phil. 2:13. "For it is God which worketh in you both to will and to do of his good pleasure." Here the divine enablement reaches to the very molding of the desires of the heart, and to the full accomplishment of those desires.

Col. 2:6. "As ye have therefore received Christ Jesus the Lord, so walk ye in him." In this Scripture the very same faith-principle, by which alone a soul can be saved, is continued as the principle by which alone he is to walk.

The whole aspect of grace, which provides a supernatural sufficiency for the superhuman, heavenly conduct, and which is the believer's reasonable life and service, is summed up in two great doctrines of the New Testament:

a. The superhuman manner of life is to be Christlike. He is the pattern: "Let this mind be in you, which was also in Christ Jesus" (Phil. 2:5); "As he is, so are we in this world" (1 John 4:17); "Christ also suffered for us, leaving us an example, that ye should follow his steps" (1 Pet. 2:21); "For to me to live is Christ" (Phil. 1:21). To be inlawed to Christ (1 Cor. 9:21) is to be committed to the very standard of which He is the ideal. Therefore the Christian's standard is superhuman, and beyond the power of human achievement.

b. It is the supreme purpose of the indwelling Spirit to reproduce Christlikeness in the believer. The most comprehensive statement of the reproduction of Christ in the believer is found in Gal. 5:22, 23: "But the fruit of the Spirit is love, joy, peace, longsuffering, gentleness, goodness, faith, meekness, temperance" (self-control). Every word, as here used, represents a superhuman quality of life. It is an exact description of the life of Christ; but Christ-likeness is never gained by the energy of the flesh. These virtues are not found in human nature; they are the "fruit of the Spirit." Under the law, that degree of love is required which is possible to the natural man; under grace, the divine love is wrought in the heart by the Holy Spirit. This is true of *all* the superhuman demands under grace. They are wrought into the life by the Spirit. The heavenly standard requires: "Rejoice in the Lord alway: and again I say, Rejoice" (Phil. 4:4). This is humanly impossible, but the fruit of the Spirit is "joy," and the Lord has said, "That they might have my joy fulfilled in themselves" (John 17:13). The standard of grace requires that "The peace of God" shall "rule in your hearts" (Col. 3:15). Man has never achieved this, but the fruit of the Spirit is "peace," and Christ has said: "My peace I give unto you" (John 14:27). The nine-fold fruit of the Spirit represents the true Christian graces, since under grace, this fruit is produced in the heart and life by the Spirit.

Likewise, Christian service is to be superhuman. It is the outflow of "rivers of living water"; but "this spake he of the Spirit" (John 7:37-39). It is the full proof of "that good, and acceptable, and perfect, will of God" (Rom. 12:2); but, "it is God which worketh in you both to will and to do of his good pleasure" (Phil. 2:13). It is all supernatur-ally wrought; for it is the exercise of a spiritual gift—a "manifestation of the Spirit" (1 Cor. 12:7). As Christian character is the composite of the inwrought graces, so Christian service is an imparted "grace." "But unto every one of us is given grace according to the measure of the gift of Christ" (Eph. 4:7); and, "But the manifestation of the Spirit is given to every man to profit withal" (1 Cor. 12:7).

Divine grace, inwrought and imparted by the indwelling Spirit, results in a manifestation of the very graciousness of God in and through the heart of the believer. It is in no sense an *imitation* of God's graciousness; it is a *reproduction* by the indwelling Spirit of that graciousness in the life and service of the believer. This truth is one of the most extensive doctrines of the New Testament (Cf Rom. 12:3-6; 15:15; 1 Cor. 1:4; 3:10; 15:10; 2 Cor. 1:12; 4:15; 6:1-3; 8:1, 6, 7, 9; 9:8, 14; 12:9; Gal. 2:9; Eph. 3:2-8; 4:7, 29; Phil. 1:7; Col. 3:16; 4:6; 2 Thes. 1:12; 2 Tim. 2:1; Heb. 4:16; 12:15; Jas. 4:6; and 2 Pet. 3:18).

It may be concluded, then, that there are three major distinctions between law and grace: (1) They are unlike because they impose separate and sufficient rules of life, which are, in their character, either wholly legal or wholly gracious; (2) They are unlike because there are in these systems opposite orders between the human obligation and the divine blessing; and (3) They are unlike because the requirements of these systems of divine rule differ, with corresponding revelations concerning divine enablement provided in each.

SECTION FIVE

THE LAW DONE AWAY

Since law and grace are opposed to each other at every point, it is impossible for them to co-exist, either as the ground of acceptance before God or as the rule of life. Of necessity, therefore, the Scriptures of the New Testament which present the facts and scope of grace, both assume and directly teach that the law is done away. Consequently, it is not in force in the present age in any sense whatsoever. This present nullification of the law applies not only to the legal code of the Mosaic system and the law of the kingdom, but to every possible application of the principle of law. The larger conception of the law, as before defined, is three-fold: (1) The actual written instructions of both the teachings of Moses and the teachings of the kingdom; (2) The law covenant of works in all of its applications, which conditions blessing and acceptance with God on the ground of personal merit; And, (3) the law principle of dependence on the energy of the flesh, in place of the faith principle of a dependence on the power of the indwelling Spirit. It will also be seen that (4) Judaism is done away.

That the law, in the widest three-fold meaning of

the term, is now set aside, is revealed as a fundamental fact in the divine economy of grace. That the law has now ceased, even in its widest meaning, should be considered with unprejudiced attention.

I. THE ACTUAL WRITTEN INSTRUCTIONS OF BOTH THE TEACHINGS OF THE LAW OF MOSES AND THE KINGDOM ARE DONE AWAY.

These actual written commandments, either of Moses or the kingdom, are not the rule of the believer's life under grace, any more than these systems are the basis of his salvation. The complete withdrawl of the authority of these two systems of law will now be considered:

First, *The Passing of the Law of Moses is the Explicit Teaching of the New Testament Scriptures.*

An important and determining feature of this truth is found in the difference which is revealed between the abiding, eternal character of the Abrahamic covenant and the temporal, limited character of the law covenant of Sinai. The Abrahamic covenant anticipated both the earthly seed through Israel, and the spiritual seed that would stand related to God on the principle of faith. This covenant, being without human condition, simply declares the unchanging purpose of Jehovah. It will be achieved in pure grace, apart from every human factor, and its accomplishments are eternal. On the one hand, the covenant of the Mosaic law was a temporary, *ad interim*, dealing with God, which was deliberately chosen by the nation Israel, and which applied to them only. It was plainly designed to govern that people in their land, and for such time as might intervene between their acceptance of that covenant, and the coming of the promised Seed. The Seed is Christ. The coming of Christ into the world was the realization of the hope contained in the Abrahamic covenant, and, of necessity, the termination of the *ad interim* reign of the law. We read: "For the promise, that he should be the heir of the world, was not to Abraham, or to his seed, through law, but through the righteousness of faith. For if they which are of the law be heirs, faith is made void, and the promise [the Abrahamic covenant] made of none effect: because the law worketh wrath: for where no law is, there is no transgression [though there is sin]. Therefore it [the promise through Abraham] is of faith, that it might be by grace; to the end the promise might be sure to all the seed; not to that only which is of the law [believing Israelites], but to that also which is of the faith [even believing Gentiles] of Abraham; who is the father [on a faith principle] of us all. . . . And therefore it [the faith] was imputed to him for righteousness. Now it was not written for his sake alone, that it was imputed to him; but for us also, to whom it shall be imputed, if we believe on him that raised up Jesus our Lord from the dead" (Rom. 4:13-24). Thus it is demonstrated that the law has no place in the divine dealings under grace. We read again:

The law "was added . . . till the seed should come" (Gal. 3:19); but when the Seed did come, the authority of the Mosaic law was no longer required, or even possible, as a principle of divine rule. It was the purpose of God to close every door of access to Himself, but one. This fact is next stated in the argument from the Scriptures: "But the scripture hath concluded all [both Jew and Gentile] under sin" (Gal. 3:22). This, it has been seen, is more than a declaration that men are sinners by nature and by practice, and therefore subject to divine displeasure; it is a universal, judicial decree which places the whole race absolutely without merit before God. From that position there is no escape other than through the exercise of pure grace on the part of God. The divine motive in the universal sentence of the race under sin is declared to be, according to that which follows in the text: "That the promise by faith of Jesus Christ might be given to them that believe" (Gal. 3:22). Thus the *ad interim* reign of the law is completely annulled, and the divine blessing is now centered in Christ as the sole object of *faith,* being promised to them that *believe.* The law principle is not retained as a possible optional relationship to God: "There is none other name under heaven given among men, whereby we must be saved" (Acts 4:12).

It is important to observe, however, that, while God has completely terminated the reign of law by the death of Christ, so far as His relation to man is concerned, man is free to reject or distort the truth of God, and to impose the law obligation upon himself. In such a case, it does not follow that God accepts, or even recognizes, any self-imposed legalism. He could not do so. It does follow, however, that the self-constituted legalist, to be consistent with his own choice, should any part of the law be accepted as binding, must observe the whole of the law to do it. The law was a unit. He that offendeth in one point is guilty of all; whatsoever the law saith, it saith to them that are under the law, and, he is a debtor to do the whole law. Since the law is done away, these statements can only apply to the one who, without divine sanction or recognition, has *assumed* the obligation of the law.

The following Scriptures disclose the fact that the law was never given to any people other than Israel: "Hear, O Israel" (Deut. 5:1); "Who are Israelites; to whom pertaineth the adoption, and the glory, and the covenants, and the giving of the law" (Rom. 9:4); "For when the Gentiles, which have not the law, do by nature [practice] the things contained in the law, these, having not the law, are a law unto themselves" (Rom. 2:14); "Then said Pilate unto them, Take ye him, and judge him according to your law" (John 18:31); "Gallio said unto the Jews, If it were a matter of wrong or wicked lewdness, O ye Jews, reason would that I should bear with you: but if it be a question of words and names, and of your law, look ye to it; for I will be no judge of such matters" (Acts 18:14, 15). The chief captain of the Roman army wrote of Paul, "Whom I perceived to be accused of questions of their law" (Acts 23:29). Paul answered for himself: "Neither against the law of the Jews, neither against the temple, nor yet against Caesar, have I offended any thing at all" (Acts 25:8); "But this cometh to pass, that the word might be fulfilled that is written in their [not your] law" (John 15:25).

There is no record of any assumption of the law

on the part of Gentiles before the death of Christ. At the cross, it will be seen, the divine application of the law ceased even for the Jews, and *all*—Jew and Gentile—were shut up to grace alone; but the Jews, because of unbelief, still persist in the observance of the law which was given to them from God by the hand of Moses; while Gentiles, because of failure to recognize the meaning of the death of Christ and the essential character of pure grace, are assuming the law obligation. This many are doing, some as a means unto justification before God, and some who are saved by faith in Christ, as a rule of life. These two errors—that of the Jew and that of the Gentile—are clearly set forth in Scripture. Of Israel it is said: "But even unto this day, when Moses is read, the vail is upon their heart." But in the case of an individual Jew receiving Christ it is said: "Nevertheless when it [the heart of a Jew] shall turn to the Lord, the vail shall be taken away" (2 Cor. 3:15, 16).

Turning to the Gentiles, there are two aspects of their assumption of the law: (1) With reference to the certainty of divine judgments on the Gentiles before the cross, or during the period in which the law was divinely imposed on Israel, it is said: "For as many as have sinned without law shall also perish without law." Then it is added concerning Israel, "And as many as have sinned in the law shall be judged by the law" (Rom. 2:12). It is impossible that this Scripture offers an optional choice between justification by the law, and justification which is by faith alone; for the word is final relative to God's dealing in this age: "By the deeds of the

law there shall no flesh be justified in his sight''
(Rom. 3:20). Reference here is, without question,
to conditions which did obtain when the law was in
force. (2) Regarding assumption of the law by Gentiles it is said: ''For when the Gentiles, which have
not the law, do by nature, [practise] the things
contained in the law, these, having not the law, are
a law unto themselves: which shew the work of the
law written in their hearts, their conscience also bearing witness, and their thoughts the meanwhile ac-
cusing or else excusing one another'' (Rom. 2:14,
15). Thus the anticipation of assumption of the
law by Gentiles is revealed, and the precise effect
of the law upon them. The conscience is molded
and they stand before a self-imposed condemnation.
To such there is no blessing. All that the legal
conscience can do is to *accuse* or *excuse* for failure.
Let it never be supposed that, because of self-imposed legality and misguided conscience, there is
any divine recognition of Gentiles as being under the
law. God must be true to His eternal purpose as
revealed in His Word, and men stand, or fall, before Him now on the sole basis of their attitude toward His saving grace in Christ. Those who are now
lost may honestly suppose that they do the will of
God in perpetuating the principle of the law with
its blasting curse; but they are lost notwithstanding,
apart from Christ. It is the people of a past age
who will be judged by the law. The Gentiles who
now practise the things contained in the law are not
said to be subject to divine judgment because of
broken law: they are, by that self-imposed law,
either self-accused, or self-excused, according as they

have created a conscience in regard to the law. The law produces the effect only of discomfort, misdirection, confusion, and limitation of their own conscience.

Before turning to the positive teaching of the Scripture relative to the passing of the law, it may be important to restate the three major aspects of the law, which are yet to be considered in this connection more at length:

1. Both the commandments and requirements of the Mosaic system, and the commandments and requirements of the kingdom, are wholly legal in their character, and, together, comprise the written statement of the law; which law, it will be seen, is set aside during the present reign of grace.

2. Every human work, be it even the impossible, heaven-high beseeching of grace, which is wrought with a view to meriting acceptance with God, is of the nature of a legal covenant of works, and, therefore, belongs only to the law. Through the finished work of Christ, acceptance with God is perfectly secured; but that acceptance can be experienced only through a faith which turns from dependence on merit, and rests in Christ as the sufficient Saviour. In like manner, it will be seen, the whole proposition of legal, meritorious acceptance with God has passed during the reign of grace.

3. Again, any manner of life, or service, which is lived in dependence on the flesh, rather than in dependence on the Spirit, is legal in character and has passed during the present period in which grace reigns. It is written: "If ye be led of the Spirit, ye are not under the law" (Gal. 5:18). The law

made its appeal only to the flesh, and, therefore, to turn to the flesh, is to turn to the sphere of the law.

The law, though wholly superseded by grace, may now be self-imposed. This may be done by turning for a rule of life to the written legal code of Moses, or of the kingdom; it may be done by turning to self-works as the basis of acceptance with God; or it may be done by depending on the energy of the flesh for power to live well-pleasing to God. Self-imposed law, of whatever kind, is not acceptable to God; but it, like all human sin, may be chosen by the free will of man, and may be practised in opposition to the revealed will of God.

In view of the positive Biblical statements relative to the passing of the law, question may be raised as to the meaning of certain passages:

Gal. 3:23. "But before faith came we were kept under the law." This is in no sense the present experience of the unsaved before they accept Christ. The Apostle is here speaking as a Jew, and of those circumstances which could have existed only for the Jew of the early church who had lived under both the dispensation of Moses, and the dispensation of grace. Nevertheless, in the wider meaning of the law before stated, all humanity was delivered by the death of Christ from the obligation of meritorious works, and from the necessity of depending on the flesh. "For as many as are of the works of the law are under the curse: for it is written, Cursed is every one that continueth not in all things which are written in the book of the law to do them"; "Christ hath redeemed us from the curse of the law"; "God sending his own Son . . . condemned sin in the flesh: that the righteousness of the law might be fulfilled in us" (Gal. 3:10, 13; Rom. 8:3, 4).

1 Cor. 9:20. The Apostle said that he became "to them that are under the law, as under the law, that I might gain them that are under the law." This is plainly a consideration of the whole class of people who have imposed the law upon themselves in any aspect of the law whatsoever (Note Gal. 4:21).

Rom. 4:14. "For if they which are of the law be heirs, faith is made void, and the promise made of none effect." This is equally true of all humanity when the larger aspects of the law are in view; but, it should also be pointed out that, the age-long designation of the Jews as being "of the law," in contrast to Gentiles to whom no law was ever given, still obtained in the early church (Cf Rom. 2:23; 4:16).

Rom. 2:13. "For not the hearers of the law are just before God, but the doers of the law shall be justified." This is to state an inherent principle of the law. It was an absolute covenant of works. No one is now to be justified by the law (Cf Rom. 3:20; Gal. 3:11). Again, "As it is written. For circumcision verily profiteth, if thou keep the law: but if thou be a breaker of the law, thy circumcision is made uncircumcision" (Rom. 2:24, 25). This, likewise, is a principle which belonged to the law. Failure to keep the law was a discredit to God, and an insult to His righteousness (Cf Isa. 52:5). The same principle is a warning to all who attempt, or even contemplate, the keeping of the law (See, also Jas. 2:10).

Rom. 3:31. "Do we then make void the law through faith? God forbid: yea, we establish the law." The law has never been kept by those who tried to keep it. It is kept, however, by those who humbly acknowledge their helplessness to do anything well-pleasing to God, and who turn and find shelter in Christ who has met every demand of the law for them. Such, and only such have ever vindicated the holy law of God. The people who attempt to keep the law have always outraged the law.

Rom. 7:16. "If then I do that which I would not, I consent unto the law that it is good." The use of the word "law" throughout this whole context (7:15 to 8:13) is clearly of the wider sphere of the whole will of God, rather than the limited commandments of Moses. Not once is Moses mentioned; but "the law of God" is three times referred to (7:22, 25; 8:7).

The complete passing, through the death of Christ, of the reign of the Mosaic law, even for Israel, is the extended testimony of Scripture. A few important passages which declare the fact of the passing of the law here given:

John 1:16, 17. "And of his fulness have all we received, and grace for [added to] grace. For the law was given by Moses, but grace and truth came by Jesus Christ." According to this passage, the whole Mosaic system was fulfilled, superseded, and terminated in the first advent of Christ.

Gal. 3:19-25. "Wherefore then serveth the law? It was added because of transgressions, till the seed should come to whom the promise was made . . . that the promise by faith of Jesus Christ might be given to them that believe. But before faith came, we [Jews] were kept under the law, shut up unto the faith which should afterward be revealed. Wherefore the law was our schoolmaster [child-conductor] to bring us unto Christ, that we might be justified by faith. But after that faith is come, we [Jews] are no longer under a schoolmaster" (the law). Comment is unnecessary concerning this unconditional declaration as to the passing of the Mosaic system.

Rom. 6:14. "For sin shall not have dominion over you: for ye are not under the law, but under grace." While the direct message of this passage is of the enablement that is provided for the life under grace, which was never provided under the law, the positive statement is made, *"Ye are not under the law."*

Rom. 7:2-6. "For the woman which hath an husband is bound by the law to her husband so long as he liveth; but if the husband be dead, she is loosed from the law of her husband. So then if, while her husband liveth, she be married to another man, she shall be called an adulteress: but if her husband be dead, she is free from that law; so that she is no adulteress, though she be married to another man. Wherefore, my brethren, ye also are become dead to the law by the body of Christ; that ye should be married to another, even to him who is raised from the dead, that we should bring forth fruit unto God. For when we were in the flesh, the motions of sins, which were by the law, did work in our members to bring forth fruit unto death. But now we are delivered from the law, that being dead wherein we were held; that we should serve in newness of spirit [Spirit], and not in the oldness of the letter."

Several important revelations are given in this passage. The relation of one who had been under the law (which was true of the Apostle Paul) to the teachings of grace was that of a wife to her second husband. The law, or obligation, of the wife to her husband ceases with his death. Should she be married to a second husband, she is then under an entirely new obligation. The sacrificial death of Christ was the ending of the reign of the law, which law is likened to the first husband. "Wherefore, my brethren, ye also are become dead to the law by the body of Christ; that ye should be married to another, even to him who is raised from the dead." Nothing could be clearer than this. The Christian is now under obligation to Christ. He is "inlawed" to Christ. He has only to fulfil "the law of Christ." Certainly it is most unreasonable to propose that a woman should try to be obligated to two husbands at the same time: yet this is the divine illustration of the error of co-mingling the teachings of law and the teachings of grace. Spiritual polyandry is offensive to God.

In the new union which is formed with Christ, there is to be the bringing forth of fruit unto God. This is a reference to the fact that the Christian's life and service is to be enabled by the power of God and therefore is superhuman. The Christian, it is clearly stated, is not only "dead to the law," but is "delivered from the law," and every aspect of the law, that he should serve in "the newness of the

Spirit"; for the teachings of grace are particularly characterized by the fact that they are to be wrought by the enabling power of the Spirit. The Christian is *not* to live and serve in "the oldness of the letter," which is the law. It is by vital union in the body of Christ as a living member that the believer is both absolved from every other relationship, and is made to be centered only in that which belongs to the living Head. Thus positively is it indicated that the opposing principles of law and grace cannot co-exist as rules of conduct.

2 Cor. 3:7-13. "But if the ministration of death, written and engraven in stones, was glorious, so that the children of Israel could not steadfastly behold the face of Moses for the glory of his countenance; which glory was to be done away: how shall not the ministration of the spirit [Spirit] be rather glorious? For if the ministration of condemnation be glory, much more doth the ministration of righteousness exceed in glory. For even that which was made glorious had no glory in this respect, by reason of the glory that excelleth. For if that which is done away was glorious, much more that which remaineth is glorious. Seeing then that we have such hope, we use great plainness of speech: and not as Moses, which put a vail over his face, that the children of Israel could not steadfastly look to the end of that which is abolished."

It is the law as crystallized in the Ten Commandments which is in view; for that law alone was "written and engraven in stones." In the midst of the strongest possible contrasts between the reign of the teachings of the law and the teachings of grace, it is declared that these commandments were "done away," and "abolished." It should be recognized that the old was abolished to make place for the new, which far excels in glory. The passing of the law is not, therefore, a loss; it is rather an inestimable gain. The striking contrasts which are presented in this whole context are here arranged in parallels:

The Teachings of the Law	*The Teachings of Grace*
1. Written with ink.	1. Written with the Spirit of the living God.
2. In tables of stone.	2. In fleshy tables of the heart.
3. The letter killeth.	3. The Spirit giveth life.
4. The ministration of death.	4. The ministration of the Spirit.
5. Was glorious.	5. Is rather glorious.
6. Done away.	6. Remaineth.
7. Abolished.	7. We have such hope.

Gal. 5:18. "But if ye be led of the Spirit, ye are not under the law." There is no place left for the law, and hence no occasion for its recognition. To be led of the Spirit is to realize a manner of life which surpasses and more than fulfills every ideal of the law.

Eph. 2:15. "Having abolished in his flesh the enmity, even the law of commandments contained in ordinances."

Col. 2:14. "Blotting out the handwriting of ordinances that was against us, which was contrary to us, and took it out of the way, nailing it to his cross."

John 15:25. "But this cometh to pass, that the word might be fulfilled that is written in their law." This one and only reference in the upper-room discourse to the law of Moses is most significant. As has been shown, Christ, in this discourse, has taken His followers beyond the cross and is unfolding to them the very foundations of the new teachings of grace. These men were Jews; but in this teaching Christ does not speak to them as though the law of Moses was binding on them. He says "their law"; not "your law," thus indicating that these Jews who had come under grace were no longer under the reign of the law of Moses.

By this Scripture not only is the whole law system definitely declared to be done away during the dispensation of grace; but it is noticeable that the law, as law, is never once applied to the believer as the regulating principle of his life under grace. This is not an accidental omission; it is the expression of the mind and will of God.

Thus it may be concluded that the written law of Moses is not intended to be the rule of the believer's life under grace. Yet, on the other hand, the abiding principles of the law which are adaptable to grace, are carried forward and restated under the teachings of grace; not as law, but reformed to the mold of infinite grace. This great fact is aptly illustrated by the experience of an American citizen who was in Germany at the breaking out of the recent war. Fleeing through Holland, he reached England with his pocket filled with German gold coin. This coin, bearing the German stamp, was of no value as currency in England; but, when melted and restamped in the mints of England, it bore all the value of coin in that realm. Thus the intrinsic value of the gold of the law is preserved and reappears bearing the stamp of the new teachings of grace.

In applying the teachings of grace it is legitimate to point out that a similar principle obtained under the law of Moses, thus to demonstrate that the precept in question represents the unchangeable character of God; but it is both unscriptural and unreasonable to apply the teachings of the Mosaic system directly to the children of grace. Since both the law of Moses and the teachings of grace are complete in themselves, neither one requires the addition of the other, and to combine them is to sacrifice all that is vital in each. Great importance should be given therefore to the positive, unvarying message to the believer which is stated in the words, *"Ye are not under the law, but under grace."*

Second. *The Error of Co-mingling the Law of the Kingdom with the Teachings of Grace.*

If it be accepted that the Messianic, earthly kingdom, with Israel restored to her land in the full realization of all her covenants, under the reign of Christ sitting on the throne of David, has not been established, and there is now no semblance in the light of present world conditions of that kingdom on earth, then it follows that the laws and principles which are to govern in the kingdom, and which could apply only to conditions within that kingdom, are not yet applied by God to the affairs of men in the earth. It is not a question, as in the case of the law of Moses, of discontinuing that which has once been in force under the sanction of God; it is rather a question as to whether the kingdom laws, which have their application of necessity in the future earthly kingdom of Messiah, should be imposed now on the children of God under grace. Definite proofs are needed to establish the fact that there are kingdom laws presented in the Scriptures. These proofs have already been offered. Having granted that the kingdom laws are found in the Scriptures, should they be considered as any part of the divine instruction now governing the daily life of the Christian? Certainly it is no more difficult to believe that Scripture reveals a rule of life which is not yet in force because belonging to a yet future age, than it is to believe that Scripture reveals a rule of life which is not now in force because belonging to an age which is wholly past. In considering the question as to whether the laws of the kingdom are to be applied to the Christian in this age, the fact that there is a complete system of kingdom ruling, and that this ruling is strictly legal in its character, is assumed on the basis of proofs already given. Certain vital issues, though already mentioned, should not be forgotten at this point:

1. *The two systems cannot co-exist.*

The laws of the kingdom, being legal in their character, introduce those principles of relationships to God which can never co-exist with the relationships which obtain under grace. By such co-mingling of opposing principles, all that is vital in each system is sacrificed. On the one hand, the sharp edge of the law, which constitutes its sole effectiveness, is dulled by an admixture of supposed divine leniency; on the other hand, the truth concerning the absolute graciousness of God is corrupted by being commercialized, conditioned on the merit of man, and made subject to the persuasion of man. The principle of pure grace demands that God shall in no wise recognize human merit, and that He invariably shall be graciously disposed toward man, and therefore needing at no time to be persuaded by man. God is never reluctant in the exercise of grace: instead, He seeks, draws, and entreats man. The principles of law and grace are mutually destructive, and doctrinal confusion follows the intrusion of any legal principle into the reign of grace. When law is thus intruded, not only is the clear responsibility of the believer under grace obscured, but the priceless attitude of God in grace, which He purchased at the infinite cost of the death of His Son, is wholly misrepresented.

Since the kingdom rule is purely legal, and since the believer is not under law, it follows that he is not under the injunctions of the kingdom.

2. *It is not necessary to combine them.*

The laws of the kingdom are not required to be combined with the teachings of grace, since every item within those laws, which could have any present application, is exactly and amply stated in the teachings of grace. It is not necessary, then, for the believer to assume any law obligation whatsoever.

When it is shown by Scriptural exposition that the laws of the kingdom are not applicable to the Christian under grace, opposition is sometimes aroused which is based on wrong personal training, habits of misinterpretation, and prejudice. The cost of unteachableness should be weighed with much care; for the sacrifice of the liberty and blessing which belongs to uncomplicated grace is a loss too great for computation. By the right division of the Scriptures, the truth will be clearly seen that grace reigns uncomplicated and undiminished by law.

The kingdom law is a complete and indivisible system in itself. It is therefore unscriptural, illogical, and unreasonable to appropriate convenient and pleasing portions of this law, and to neglect the remainder. It should be considered that, as in the Mosaic system, to adopt some portions of the law is to be committed logically to *all* its teachings. "For Moses describeth the righteousness which is of the law, That the man which doeth those things shall live by them"; "Cursed is every one that continueth not in all things which are written in the book of the law to do them"; "And the law is not of faith: but, The man that doeth them shall live in them" (Rom. 10:5; Gal. 3:10, 12. Cf Lev. 18:5); "Now we know that what things soever the law saith, it saith to them who are under the law" (Rom. 3:19); "For I testify again to every man that is circumcised, that he is a debtor to do the whole law" (Gal. 5:3). Not only are some aspects of the kingdom law never attempted by Christians (Cf Mt. 5:42); but its whole character, being legal, is opposed to grace.

The law of Moses is interrelated and wholly dependent on the sacrifices and ritual provided for Israel in the land. The laws of the kingdom are only related to the yet future kingdom conditions which shall be in the earth under the power and presence of the King when Satan is bound, creation delivered, and all shall know the Lord from the least unto the greatest. All harmony of truth is shattered when there is the slightest co-mingling of the principles of law and grace. Grace alone now reigns through Christ to the glory of God the Father, the Son, and the Holy Spirit.

II. THE LAW COVENANT OF WORKS, IN ALL OF ITS APPLICATION, WHICH CONDITIONS BLESSING AND ACCEPTANCE WITH GOD ON PERSONAL MERIT, IS DONE AWAY.

Under this conception of law, its scope is extended beyond the actual writings of the Mosaic system and the law of the kingdom, and includes, as well, any human action, whether in conformity to a precept of Scripture or not, which is attempted with a view to securing favor with God. The law formula is, "If you will do good, I will bless you." It matters nothing what is undertaken as an obligation. It may be the highest ideal of heavenly conduct belonging to the teachings of grace, or it may be the simplest choice of moral action in daily life; but if it is attempted with a view to securing favor with God, such relationship to God is self-imposed, since it ignores His attitude of grace, and such attempt is purely legal in character and result. Let it be restated that the basic principle of grace is the fact that *all* blessings originate with God, and are offered to man *graciously*. The formula of grace is, "I have blessed you, therefore be good." Thus it is revealed that the motive for right conduct under grace is not to secure the favor of God, which already exists toward saved and unsaved to an infinite degree through Christ; it is rather a matter of consistent action in view of such divine grace. The unsaved are not urged to secure salvation by meritorious conduct, or even to influence God in their behalf by asking for salvation. Since God is revealed as standing with out-stretched hands, offering His greatest possible blessings in grace, and is moved to do so by His unchanging, infinite love, it illy becomes a sinner to fall before Him in an attitude of coaxing and beseeching, as though he were hoping to move God to be merciful and good. The message of grace is: "But as many as received him, to them gave he the power [right] to become the sons of God" (John 1:12). The eternal saving grace of God is offered to all who will *believe*. Moreover, the saved do not return to divine fellowship after a relapse into sin because they plead for divine forgiveness; their restoration is conditional on *confession*. They do not abide in divine fellowship because they seek, or merit, the light; they are istructed to "walk in the light" which is all theirs through riches of grace. In no case are divine blessings to be secured by human merit, or by pleading; they await the faith that will appropriate them. Every gift of divine love is provided and bestowed in pure grace; and not of necessity, nor as a payment, nor a recognition of human merit. Such lavishings of grace create a superhuman obligation for that manner of life which is consistent with the heavenly blessing and position which grace bestows; but the heavenly blessing and position is never earned by even a super-human manner of life.

The determining character of pure law is seen in the fact that it is a covenant of works wherein the divine blessing is conditioned on human merit. No semblance of this principle is to be found under grace, except that rewards are to be bestowed for faithful service upon those who have already entered into every present position and possession provided in grace. It therefore follows that, not only the written rules of the law, but the very principle of the law covenant of works, has been done away in this age of grace.

III. THE LAW PRINCIPLE OF DEPENDENCE ON THE ENERGY OF THE FLESH, IN PLACE OF THE GRACE PRINCIPLE OF DEPENDENCE ON THE POWER OF THE INDWELLING SPIRIT, IS DONE AWAY.

The third and last major distinction between law and grace is seen in the attitude of heart-dependence which is maintained in view of any and all obligation toward God. The law, being a covenant of works and providing no enablement, addressed itself to the limitations of the natural man. No more was expected or secured in return to its commands than the natural man in his environment could produce. The requirements under the law are, therefore, on the plane of the limited ability of the flesh. On the other hand, grace, being a covenant of faith, and providing the limitless enablement of the power of the indwelling Spirit, addresses itself to the unlimited resources of the supernatural man. The requirements to be met under grace are, therefore, on the plane of the unlimited ability of the Spirit. There is no divine injunction addressed to the unregenerate concerning his daily life. The Gospel of the saving grace of God alone is offered to him. The only divine injunctions now in force in the world are addressed to those who *are* saved, and these heaven-high standards are to be realized on the principle of faith toward the sufficiency of the indwelling Spirit, and never by dependence on the energy of the flesh.

Thus, it may be seen, that any aspect of life, or conduct, which is undertaken in dependence on the energy and ability of the flesh is, to that extent, purely legal in its character; whether it be the whole revealed will of God, the actual written commandments contained in the law, the exhortations of grace, or any activity whatsoever in which the believer may engage. Dependence on the arm of the flesh is consistent only with pure law; dependence on the power of God is demanded under pure grace. Since there is no provision for the flesh in the plan of God for a life under grace, the law is done away.

IV. JUDAISM IS DONE AWAY.

It is often inferred that Christianity is an outgrowth or product of Judaism. In reality these two systems are as independent of each other as the two opposing principles of law and grace. Being thus so widely different in their essential elements, they are, like the principles which they embody, as far removed the one from the other as heaven is higher than the earth.   One is of the earth, the old creation, and the flesh; the other is of heaven, of the new creation, and the Spirit.   As there are elements and threads of truth which run throughout the entire Bible, so certain features which belong to Judaism are seen to reappear in Christianity; but this obvious fact should not be made the basis of a supposition that these systems are the same, or that one was merged into the other.   God, holiness, Satan, man, sin, redemption, and the issues of eternity, are not only relevant facts of both Judaism and Christianity, but they are essential facts of all time, from its beginning to its end.   It is true that the same God is the God of the Gentile as well as of the Jew, and that the Jew anticipated the value of Christ's death by sacrifices, as we realize the value of His death through faith; but it does not therefore follow that God's purposes and ways are the same with Israel as with the Church.

When these two systems are confused, it is because the differentiating essentials which constitute the Jewish religion and Christianity are ignored.

First. *Considering Them as Rules of Life.*

The Old Testament system of law is absolutely superseded by the new system under grace.   Christians are not under law either for justification or for sanctification.   When Christ said, "I came not to destroy, but to fulfil," and that nothing should pass from the law until all was fulfilled (Mt. 5: 17, 18), He was dealing with Israel while Judaism was still in force, and anticipating the Messianic Kingdom which, it is revealed, will be purely legal in its character.

Second. *Considering Them under Their Respective Aspects.*

In the matter of service, there is nothing but contrast between Judaism and Christianity. Israel, under Judaism, went in to perform a sacrifice; we go out to proclaim a sacrifice. Judaism had its ritual, its forms, and its ceremonies which were typical. Christianity could incorporate none of these since it provides a living union to Christ who is Substance and Antitype of all that Judaism prefigured.

Third. *Considering Them in Respect to Personal Relationship to God.*

Under Judaism, the nation was related to Him by the covenant of Sinai, the Abrahamic covenant being temporarily set aside until Christ should come (Gal. 3:19), and individual Israelites were spiritually renewed through their personal faith, though the exact character of their salvation is not revealed. But, under grace, all the positions and possessions of the believer in relation to God transcend the earthly promises of Israel.

The message of Ephesians 2:18 to 3:10 does not teach that the Church is being built on the prophets of the Old Testament; reference is only to the prophets and apostles of the New Testament (Cf 4: 11). In like manner, the "mystery" (3:6) is the formation of a new humanity—the Church—out of both Jews and Gentiles, and not a combining of Old Testament saints with New Testament saints. The theological term, *The Old Testament Church,* has no Scriptural warrant (Acts 7 : 38 is no exception, being merely a reference to an assembly of people). The true Church began at Pentecost, and was made possible through the new outflow of grace in Christ Jesus,—by His death, resurrection, and ascension,—and the descent of the Holy Spirit. Similarly, Gentile branches are not grafted into Judaism, but into Christ (Rom. 11 : 17). He is the Vine.

Judaism speaks of an earthly people and an earthly walk in the flesh. Christianity speaks of a heavenly people and of a heavenly walk in the Spirit. Since one is of the old creation, its people are under the curse of the First Adam, and its history closes in failure. Since the other is of the new creation, its people are ensphered in the resurrected Christ, and its history will be the consummation of the glory of divine grace. Christianity is indebted to Israel for the humanity of Christ and for the Oracles of God; but Israel, the people, must be distinguished from Judaism, the law system. Israel abides to the present hour, while Judaism, so far as divine recognition goes, ceased with the death of Christ. Israel, like all the nations, was, as a whole, in Adam, lost and undone. While for Israel there was healing for sin and mercy from God, no one under Judaism had any clear vision or revelation of the new life and relationship under grace, which more than all else distinguishes Christianity.

The new life and relationship which characterizes Christianity is Christ as the sphere of the new creation. CHRISTIANITY IS CHRIST. It is the unlimited, unrestrained love of God in Christ and its final result will be the unveiling of the glory of His grace in the ages to come. Judaism, through the nation Israel, purposed the highest glory in the earth. Christianity, through the Church, purposes the highest glory in heaven. One is of the "first man" who is "of the earth, earthy." The other is of the second Man, who is "the Lord from heaven."

Judaism was based on the law and, like the law, applied only to Israel and passed out of force with the death of Christ. So, likewise, Israel alone was delivered from the written commandments of Moses through the death of Christ. However, both Jew and Gentile were delivered by that death from the hopeless principle of human merit, and from the useless struggle of the flesh.

The exalted quality of the law is never questioned. It is the expression of the very character of God. "Wherefore the law is holy, and the commandment holy, and just, and good" (Rom. 7:12). The law did not die; it was a race that died unto the law in Christ the Substitute. The holy demands of infinite righteousness can never change or pass away; but man may be changed in his exact responsibility to God and to certain particulars of His holy demands.

The sanctity of the law is never preserved by those who attempt to keep it. The holy will of God was never wrought by any person other than Christ. The effort of man has universally failed. The supposition that God will be pleased and honored by any fleshly attempt to do His will, is a delusion as old as the race. Those who *try* to keep the law, or *try* by their own effort to do the whole will of God, outrage the law at every step by their absolute failure.

On the other hand, those who, in recognition of the righteous character of the law, bow before those holy demands, acknowledging their utter failure and inability to fulfil them, and who flee to Christ that they may stand in His redemption and partake of the very righteousness of God in Him and be sheltered under the cross whereon He met every demand of the law for them, are the only ones who really uphold the law, or keep it. "Do we then make void the law through faith? God forbid: yea, we establish the law" (Rom. 3:31).

We may conclude, then, that every aspect of the reign of the law has ceased with the death of Christ and the introduction of the reign of grace. There is no longer any obligation to do the things which are written in the law, only as they have been transferred and restated under the teachings of grace; there is no longer any obligation to secure favor with God by human merit; and there is no longer any yoke of bondage, or impossible burden to do what no flesh has ever been able to do. There is perfect liberty and victory in the priceless provisons of grace; "For ye are not under the law but under grace."

SECTION SIX

THE SABBATH, A TEST QUESTION.

The distinction between the reign of law and the reign of grace is at no point more sharply drawn than in the question of the observance of the seventh day of the week or the first day of the week; for these two days are symbolical of the dispensations to which they are related. Likewise, at no point is personal religious prejudice, which is born of early training and sentiment, more assertive than on the sabbath question. It was His liberal teaching on the observance of the sabbath which, more than aught else, provoked the wrath of the Jewish leaders against Christ, and, it may be observed, there is no religious subject to-day which so draws out personal convictions and opinions. The reason is evident. Few have really comprehended the exact character and principle of grace. To many, Christianity is a system of human works and character building from which merit accrues. And the observance of a sabbath day presents extraordinary opportunities for the exercise of meritorious works. The question is a far deeper one than the observance, or the manner of observance, of a day. It is the fundamental question whether grace is to reign supreme in place of law, or whether it is to be co-mingled with law. The roots of this problem reach down to the bed-rock issue which forms the very structure of the two opposing principles of pure law and pure grace. For its solution, the question demands more than a superficial opinion. Truly the choice of a particular day and the manner of its observance is a test question as to the individual's intelligent adjustment to the whole grace revelation. As there can be no proper co-mingling of the reign of law and the reign of grace, there can be no proper co-mingling of elements which, according to the Scriptures, are the essential features of these widely different days. A "Christian Sabbath" is a mis-nomer, and the very use of the term indicates inexcusable inattention to Bible terms, and an unchallenged freedom of mind and heart which is willing to sacrifice the richest treasures of grace by co-mingling them with law. It is not a problem of interpretation; it is a question of whether personal sentiment, prejudice, or ignorance, shall blindly override the very foundation of the right divisions of Scripture.

These two days, typical of two opposing governing principles and two great dispensations, are absolutely unrelated. Of the whole Decalogue, it is the sabbath-day commandment only which is *not* carried forward in any manner whatsoever into the reign of grace, nor could it be. Failure to base the distinction between these age-representing days upon the essential character of their respective relationships—pure law and pure grace—is resulting in an almost universal confusion of mind on the subject among Christians, and this, in turn, provides the opportunity for present-day legalists to promote their Christ-rejecting heresies.

Intelligent comprehension of pure law is clarifying to the mind, for its very oppositeness to pure grace safeguards a clear comprehension of grace. On the other hand, the greatest foe of such clear comprehension of pure grace and its issues is the confusing, soul-wrecking and unscriptural *admixture* of these opposing principles. This admixture is ruinous at every point; but at no point is it more destructive of Scriptural distinctions than in the confusion of a Jewish sabbath with the Christian's day—the Lord's day, or Sunday.

Consideration at length might be given to many vital differences between the law obligations and the obligations under grace, such as circumcision, tithing, and sacrifices; but unlike the sabbath question, these issues are self-adjusting when the glory of grace in some measure is comprehended. To many, on the other hand, the sabbath question bulks largest as an essential of their religion. It, therefore, demands particular consideration.

The reasons for this discussion are four: (1) It vitally determines the individual's conception of, and blessing in, grace. (2) It, of necessity, determines the character of the believer's conduct and measure of comprehension of his Scriptural obligation to God. (3) It is the central issue of a misleading heresy. And, (4) it is now urged as a national reform, in which it is proposed to legislate a Jewish sabbath on a Christ-rejecting world.

This consideration of the Sabbath question is based on the preceding analysis of the principles of law and grace and this discussion cannot be followed clearly apart from an understanding of what has gone before. So, also, in so far as an earnest appeal may avail, the reader is besought to leave prejudice behind, and to stand on the uncompromised *"Thus saith the Lord."*

Two major aspects of this subject are here considered. (1) The Biblical testimony regarding the Jewish sabbath, and (2) The Biblical testimony concerning the Christian's "Lord's day." To this is added (3) A consideration of certain current errors.

I. THE BIBLICAL TESTIMONY REGARDING THE JEWISH SABBATH

This theme is to be taken up in sub-divisions in which the Jewish sabbath is considered as related to various periods of time:

First. *The Period from Adam to Moses.*

Two theories obtain concering the question of sabbath observance during this period. There are those who contend that the sabbath was committed to man in Eden, and there are those who contend that the sabbath was given to Israel only, at the hand of Moses.

The first theory is usually advanced with a view to applying the institution of the sabbath to *all* men before the law even was given, in order that the sabbath law may be treated as now applicable to *all* men, even after the termination of the Mosaic law in the cross. This form of argument is not restricted to the Seventh-Day legalists; it is employed by many writers and religious leaders who are attempting to transfer the Biblical authority concerning the Jewish sabbath to the observance of the Lord's day. These, by Judaizing Christianity, are obscuring the truth about grace.

When it is claimed that the sabbath obtained from Adam to Moses it is said: "The sabbath was divinely sanctified at creation." This sanctification, it is true, is clearly stated in Gen. 2:1-3: "Thus the heavens and the earth were finished, and all the host of them. And on the seventh day God ended his work which he had made; and he rested on the seventh day from all his work which he had made. And God blessed the seventh day, and sanctified it: because that in it he had rested from all his work which God created and made."

When it is assumed that the sabbath was imposed on man at Eden, it is based on the supposition that this passage so teaches; which, however, the passage does not necessarily imply. And it should also be remembered that Genesis was not written until Moses' time, and, when seeking for Biblical evidence regarding the pre-Mosaic observance of the seventh day it will be found that, unlike other religious activities, such as prayer, circumcision (Cf John 7:22), and sacrifices the observance of which is recorded of that period, there is no mention of a sabbath observance from creation to Moses.

It is incredible that this great institution of the sabbath could have existed during all these centuries and there be no mention of it in the Scriptures dealing with that time. The words of Job, who lived five hundred years and more before Moses, offer an illustration. His experience discloses the spiritual life of the pre-Mosaic saint, having no written Scriptures, and striving to know his whole duty to God. Job and his friends refer to creation, the flood, and many details of human obligation to God; but not once do they mention the sabbath. Again, it is impossible that this great institution, with all that it contemplated of relationship between God and man, could have existed at that time and not have been mentioned in any portion of the argument of the book of Job.

There is little force in the contention that a seven-day week was recognized as early as Jacob's time, and therefore a sabbath day must have existed which marked off the week. The seven-day week is the natural fourth part of a lunar month and does not necessarily demand a sabbath day with religious significance for its measurement. Likewise, there is little force in the suggestion that Chinese history hints at the observance of one sacred day in every week. Such argument, even if true, should not be set over against the positive testimony of the Scriptures.

There is one passage which determines this question beyond all discussion. The following quotation from the confession of the priests and Levites under Nehemiah definitely fixes the time of the institution of the sabbath: "Thou camest down also upon Mount Sinai, and spakest with them from heaven, and gavest them right judgments, and true laws, good statutes and commandments: and madest known unto them thy holy sabbath, and commandedst them precepts, statutes, and laws, by the hand of Moses thy servant'' (Neh. 9:13, 14). The sabbath given to Israel as a *sign* (Ex. 31:12-17), was never given to Gentiles. There is no record that Gentiles ever recognized the sabbath, either between Adam and Moses, or between Moses and Christ. The sabbath is of the law; but the law did not begin to reign until Moses (Rom. 5:12-14).

It is to be concluded, then, that the sabbath was imposed upon Israel only and as a part of the law as given by Moses.

Second, *The Period from Moses to Christ.*

The sabbath began to be observed by Israel from the time of its institution through Moses. Invested with the character of a *sign* between Jehovah and the nation Israel, it was in no sense extended to Gentiles. These facts are disclosed in the following Scriptures:

"The LORD spake unto Moses, saying, Speak thou also unto the children of Israel, saying, Verily my sabbaths ye shall keep: for it is a sign between me and you throughout your generations; that ye may know that I am the LORD that doth sanctify you. Ye shall keep the sabbath therefore; for it is holy unto you: every one that defileth it shall surely be put to death: for whosoever doeth any work therein, that soul shall be cut off from among his people. Six days may work be done; but in the seventh is the sabbath of rest, holy to the LORD: whosoever doeth any work in the sabbath day, he shall surely be put to death. Wherefore the children of Israel shall keep the sabbath, to observe the sabbath throughout their generations, for a perpetual covenant. It is a sign between me and the children of Israel for ever: for in six days the LORD made heaven and earth, and on the seventh day he rested, and was refreshed'' (Ex. 31: 12-17).

Nothing but blind prejudice could apply this or any other Old Testament Scripture concerning the sabbath, to the Gentiles. The sabbath was a part of Israel's law, and it was the possession of that law which distinguished that nation from all other peoples of the earth.

It is equally erroneous to insist that the sabbath was always celebrated on the last day of the week. The sabbath, but for necessary exceptions, was the seventh in a series of seven, whether days or years. Of necessity it often fell on other days of the week as as well as on Saturday. There were at least fifteen sabbaths which were *fixed* dates in their given month, and these sabbaths fell on those particular dates regardless of the day of the week.[1] In one instance, seven sabbaths were counted from the fifteenth day of the month, and the day following that last sabbath of the seven, was Pentecost (Lev. 23: 15, 16). These seven sabbaths, it is evident, became pre-determined dates by arbitrary reckoning from the first sabbath. So, likewise, the day that Christ was in the tomb was a

---

[1] From Lev. 23: 37, 38, it has been claimed by some that these fixed sabbaths were extra sabbaths which were added to the regular sabbaths. This claim, however, is not supported by Num. 28: 9, 10. The comparison of these important Scriptures reveals the fact that the word *"besides"* of Lev. 23: 37, 38, does not indicate *more* sabbaths; but rather refers to additional *offerings* to be made over and above the regular sabbath offerings.

fixed sabbath. It was the fifteenth of Abid, which by divine arrangement in that particular year fell on a Saturday. That this was a fixed sabbath is proven by the fact that the day before was "preparation" day (Mk. 15:42), which day was determined for the fourteenth of that month (Ex. 12:2, 6). Again, certain working days were established days. The lamb must be taken on the tenth day of the first month and be killed, roasted with fire, and eaten on the fourteenth day of the month. Likewise, Abid sixteenth could in no wise have been a sabbath for that date was appointed as the beginning of harvest (Deut. 16:9. Cf Lev. 23:15). All these labors would have been direct violations of the sabbath law; yet these ceremonies were appointed for certain pre-determined dates, and from time to time must inevitably have been in conflict with the pre-determined sabbaths.

By all of this it is evident that the sacred character of the day belonged to its relative place in a series of seven days, and not to a particular day of the week.

During the period from Moses to Christ in which the sabbath obtained under the direct sanction of God, it was, as the word *sabbath* indicates, a day of physical rest. It was binding on the whole nation Israel, and death was the penalty for its violation. No fire was to be kindled, no food prepared, no journey undertaken, no buying or selling permitted, and no burden to be borne. Even the land was to have its sabbaths (Ex. 31:12-17; 35:3; 16:22-26; Neh. 10:31; 13:15-21; Lev. 25:4; 2 Chron. 36:21). The sabbath law, like all of the law, was so poorly observed that Jehovah finally carried the nation into captivity with the declared purpose that the land might enjoy its sabbaths.

The sabbath was inter-related with the law, just as it is embedded in the heart of the Decalogue. The exact manner of its observance is revealed only in the teachings of Moses, and since the law was a covenant of human works, the sabbath was the divine provision for rest under that covenant. The modern conception of a sabbath, isolated from the laws which governed it, and adapted to the Christian dispensation as the day of religious activity, public meetings, Christian service, and worship, is entirely out of harmony with every Scripture bearing on the sabbath. It is taught by some that although the laws which conditioned the manner of sabbath observance have ceased, the recognition of the day, whether it be Saturday, or Sunday, remains as a binding obligation. The result of such teaching is the imposition of the observance of a day without any exact instruction as to the manner of such observance. This teaching is both inconsistent and unscriptural. Moreover, the unscriptural inconsistency is greatly increased when the celebration of the sabbath is changed from Saturday to Sunday, and is imposed on Gentiles.

The sabbath was a vital institution under the reign of the law. It depended on the entire law system for its proper observance, and the law system depended on the sabbath for its normal action. The complete legal system stands, or falls, together. The Mosaic age was given over to the uncomplicated functioning of the entire law system; but that age, and all that characterized it, was, when Christ died, superseded by the reign of grace.

Third.   *The Period Represented by the Gospels.*

Much confusion concerning the sabbath is due to a failure to recognize the peculiar character of the period represented by the Gospels. It should be remembered that Christ was first a "minister of the circumcision"; He was "made under the law"; and He lived and wrought under the law. The law did not pass at His birth. It passed at His death. During the days of His ministry, He recognized, kept, and enforced the sabbath as an integral part of the whole Mosaic system. True, He insisted that the Mosaic system, and the sabbath in particular, be delivered from the encrusted teachings of men which had been superimposed on the law of Moses. These man-made additions to the law were held by the Jews to be as binding and sacred as the very Word of God. Because He ignored all else but the Word of God, Christ appeared as a liberalist on the question of the sabbath. He also claimed to be "Lord of the sabbath," which He was, and by virtue of that position, He had authority to change the sabbath, or, if He chose, to abolish it forever. A greater than Moses, through whom the law came, was in their midst. It is certain that He purposed to rescue the sabbath from being an enslaving institution and to restore its functions as a benefit to man. This He announced when He said: "The sabbath was made for man, and not man for the sabbath." That is, man was not made to be sacrificed for a day; but the day was made for the blessing of man.

Before His death, the sabbath was one of the most important issues in the experience and ministry of

Christ. However, it is both obvious and suggestive that He never mentioned that day in the upper-room discourse, nor is that day once mentioned as an obligation in all of His post-resurrection ministry. It is inconceivable that the sabbath, which was so vital a part of the Mosaic system, should be omitted from these great age-characterizing teachings of Christ, if it was the purpose of God that this Jewish day should have any place in the present reign of grace.

It has also been claimed that Christ extended the sabbath-keeping obligation to all men, when He said: "The sabbath was made for man, and not man for the sabbath." This issue turns on the exact meaning of the word *man* as here used. Did Christ signify by this statement that the Jewish sabbath was by His authority extended to *all* men? Or did He use the word *man* in its more limited sense as applying only to the nation Israel? Two facts determine the answer: (1) The sabbath is *never* by any subsequent Scripture applied to Gentiles, and (2) the word *man* is used in the Old Testament no less than 336 times, when referring to Israel alone, and many times in the New Testament when referring only to Christians. It is said: "Christ is the head of every man"; the Spirit "is given to every man"; "If any man build on this foundation"; "Every man shall have praise"; "That we may present every man perfect in Christ Jesus." In all these Scriptures the word *man* has only the limited meaning. It is therefore evident that Christ said, in harmony with all Scripture, that the sabbath was made for Israel; for there is no Biblical evidence that Christ ever imposed the Jewish sabbath on either Gentiles or Christians; but true to the law, He did recognize its important place and obligation in relation to Israel until the reign of the law should be terminated through His death.

Fourth. *The Period Represented by the Acts and the Epistles.*

In considering the sabbath question, great importance must be attributed to the exact character of those teachings of the New Testament which come after the founding of Christianity through the death and resurrection of Christ, and by the advent of the Spirit on Pentecost.

It should be observed first that the law, as a rule of conduct, is not once applied to the Christian, and that these Scriptures by overwhelming revelation, assert that the law has passed, through the death of Christ. They assert that the law has ceased both as a means of justification, and as a rule of life for the one who is justified (John 1: 16, 17; Rom. 6: 14; 7: 1-6; 2 Cor. 3: 1-18; Eph. 2: 15; Col. 2: 14; Gal. 3: 19-25). If it is claimed that the Decalogue, in which the sabbath is embedded, was not of the law, and therefore was not terminated with the death of Christ, this contention is disposed of completely by the reference in Rom. 7: 7-14 to the last of the commandments, in which Scripture this commandment is explicitly mentioned as *"the law."* So, also, according to 2 Cor. 3: 7-14, that which was "written and engraven in stones"— the Decalogue, including the sabbath day—is *"done away"* and *"abolished."*

It should be observed next that, if an issue so vital as was the sabbath under the law, is imposed on the

Church, it is incredible (1) that the early Christians would not be reported as having at some time discharged their personal obligation to the sabbath, or (2) that the necessity of recognizing the sabbath would not be somewhere incorporated in the new teachings of grace. Turning to these Scriptures we discover:

1. *The sabbath in the Book of The Acts.*

The word *sabbath* is used nine times in the Acts, and wherever it is referred to as a day which is observed, it is related only to the unbelieving Jews, who, as would be expected, perpetuated, and who still perpetuate, the observance of the sabbath day. Not once in this Book is it stated, or even implied, that Christians kept a sabbath day. It is said that the Apostle Paul went into the synagogue of the Jews and reasoned with them every sabbath; but this can imply nothing more than that he took advantage of their gathering together on that day in order that he might preach to them. Such may be the experience of any missionary to the Jews to-day.

2. *The sabbath in the Epistles.*

Turning to the Epistles, it will be seen in this portion of the Scriptures, as in the Book of Acts, that no Christian is said to have observed a sabbath day. It is highly probable that some in the early church who were drawn into the observance of the law were also complicated with issues of sabbath keeping; but the Spirit of God has omitted every such incident, if such there was, from the pages of Scripture. Thus the

Inspired Record does not reveal the complication of
one believer with the Jewish sabbath, even as an error
in conduct; nor are sinners termed Sabbath breakers.

Upon examination of the direct injunctions and
doctrinal teachings of the Epistles, it is discovered
that the word *sabbath* is used but once, the term
seventh day mentioned in one passage only, and the
legalistic observance of a *day* is referred to but once.
These passages deserve particular attention:

Col. 2 : 16, 17.   In the context in which this Scripture is found, the Apostle warns believers against any
complicity with the law, or works-covenant, since they
have been transferred to a position under grace.   The
passage states that they have been made "complete"
in Christ, to which estate nothing could ever be added;
hence for the one who is "in Christ," the objective of
all meritorious works is already gained, and the legal
obligation to do good works is forever met (v. 10).
The believer is also said to be "circumcised with the
circumcision made without hands, in putting off the
body of the sins of the flesh by the circumcision of
Christ."   Therefore, since the flesh, the one thing the
law proposed to control, is, in the sight of God, put
away, there is no need of the law.   The Jewish child
was circumcised on the eighth day, which was the first
day of a new week following the passing of a completed week.   The circumcision on the eighth day, or
first day of a new week, typified the deliverance from
the old creation which would be accomplished for
believers through the resurrection of Christ from the
dead; for in that death He bore all the curse of the
old creation.   For this reason the believer under grace
is not called upon to celebrate any aspect of

the old creation which was represented by the sabbath (v. 11). The one who is saved has been "buried
with him in baptism, wherein [the baptism] also ye
are risen with him through the faith of the operation
of God [his own faith in God's power], who hath
raised him from the dead." The use of the *aorist*
tense in connection with the reference to a burial with
Him in baptism, places that burial as being contem-
poraneous with the circumcision just mentioned.
Therefore it is evident that the baptism with the
Spirit which vitally relates the believer to Christ is in
view (1 Cor. 12:13. Cf Gal. 3:27). In that baptism, as in no other, the Christian partakes of all that
Christ is, and all that Christ has done. He shares in
Christ's crucifixion, death, burial, and resurrection
(Rom. 6:1-10). With the old creation thus buried
in the tomb of Christ, the believer is in no wise obligated to any observance related to the old creation
(v. 12). Again, the believer has been delivered from
the law by no less an undertaking than the nailing
of the law with its handwritings and ordinances to
the cross. After this great transaction, how can the
child of God reasonably recognize the law in any
respect whatsoever (v. 14)? To the one who is thus
complete in Christ, *circumcised* in Christ, *buried* with
Christ, and *delivered* from the authority of all handwritings and ordinances, the Apostle writes: "Let no
man therefore judge you in meat, or in drink, or in
respect of an holyday, or of the new moon, or of the
sabbath days [day]: which are a shadow of things to
come; but the body [substance] is Christ." All these
were essential features of the law (1 Chron. 23:31;
2 Chron. 2:4; 31:3), and as such were to cease in

the present age of Israel's chastisement (Hos. 2:11), and are to be reinstated in the coming kingdom (Ezk. 45:17). They were but shadows of the Substance— Christ. Having the Substance, the believer is warned against turning to the mere shadow. According to this Scripture, the law, which included the sabbath day, is abolished. If it is objected that the reference in this passage is to extra ceremonial sabbaths, the contention cannot be sustained; for the words here used are *ton sabbaton*, which are the exact words that are invariably used to designate the regular Jewish sabbath.

It is significant, then, that in all the Epistles, wherein the believer's obligation under grace is set forth, the only use of the word *sabbath* is under absolute prohibition concerning its observance, and that it is there held to be in conflict with the most vital and superseding elements of grace.

Heb. 4:4. In this passage the one reference in all the Epistles to the *seventh day* is found. We read: "For he spake in a certain place of the seventh day on this wise, And God did rest the seventh day from all his works." As before, the occasion for this reference to a seventh day is explicit in the context. In the whole passage (4:1-13) Hebrew Christians are warned lest, as their fathers failed to enter into rest under Joshua (v. 8), they themselves should fail to enter, experimentally, into the rest provided in the finished work of Christ, of whom Joshua was but a type. In the application of this passage, it may be noted that the rest under Christ is not for one day in the week, nor is it that sabbath-rest which was due after a six-day strain of meritorious works. It is rather the abiding rest of faith in Another who, as Substitute, has wrought all the "works of God." This blessed rest is promised "to him that worketh not." Likewise, it is in no sense the rest of death. It is rather the rest of Christ's imparted, resurrection life, and that life is ceaselessly active. The extent and character of the activity of the new life in Christ is a violation of every commandment which enjoins a sabbath day of rest.

Gal. 4:9, 10. At this point in this Epistle, the Apostle chides the Galatian believers for observing "*days*" which are borrowed from the law, and tells them that by the keeping of legal days they have turned from grace to the law: "But now, after that ye have known God, or rather are known of God, how turn ye again to the weak and beggarly elements, whereunto ye desire again to be in bondage? Ye observe days, and months, and times, and years." The phrase, "*weak and beggarly elements*," is a description of the character of the law. As a means of securing moral and spiritual conduct, the law was "weak" since its correct observance was impossible through the "weakness of the flesh" (Rom. 8:3). As a source of heart-blessing, the law was "beggarly" (lit. poverty stricken) as compared to the riches of grace in Christ Jesus.

From this consideration of the Scriptures which describe and define the life of the believer *after* the cross, it is notable that in these Scriptures there is no example of the observance of a sabbath day by any believer, and no injunction for such observance. On the other hand, there is the most conclusive teaching concerning the complete ending of the law by the death of Christ, and the most faithful warnings lest the believer shall become ensnared by complicity with sabbath-day observance.

Fifth. *The Sabbath in Prophecy.*

There are two distinct aspects of the sabbath in prophecy: (1) Concerning its cessation in this age of Israel's chastisement, and (2) concerning its reestablishment when the present purpose in the Church is accomplished.

1. *The cessation of the sabbath.*

It is clear from Hos. 2:11 that the chastisement which was to fall on Israel, and which she is now experiencing, would be characterized by the cessation of *all* her solemn feasts and sabbaths: "I will also cause all her mirth to cease, her feast days, her new moons, and her sabbaths, and all her solemn feasts." Such is the unalterable decree of God, and had one word of this prophecy failed, He would have been proven untrue. These Jewish observances which were to cease included *all* her sabbaths. They ceased at the beginning of this age of grace, so far as any recognition from God is concerned. Otherwise, when will this prophecy be fulfilled? Uninstructed people may impose a solemn feast, or a Jewish sabbath, upon themselves; but this will accomplish no more than the creation of an abnormal conscience which either accuses or excuses but never satisfies the heart. Such is the invariable effect of self-imposed law (Rom. 2:14, 15).

2. *The reestablishment of the sabbath.*

Upon the completion of the present divine purpose in the Church, Israel's sabbaths will be reinstated. This is assured both for the great tribulation which must precede the glorious coming of Christ, and for the kingdom age which follows that coming. Concerning the great tribulation it is said: "But pray ye that your flight be not in the winter, neither on the sabbath day" (Mt. 24:20). No Christian has ever been inclined to offer this prayer. The time of its fulfillment does not concern him, nor does he have any relation to a sabbath day. It will be in the "time of Jacob's trouble," and Israel's sabbaths will then be observed again. Concerning the kingdom age we read: "And it shall come to pass, that from one new moon to another, and from one sabbath to another, shall all flesh come to worship before me, saith the LORD" (Isa. 66:23); "Thus saith the LORD GOD; The gate of the inner court that looketh toward the east shall be shut the six working days; but on the sabbath it shall be opened, and in the day of the new moon it shall be opened" (Ezk. 46:1). This is according to all prophecy concerning the kingdom. It is then that Israel shall "do all his commandments," including the sabbath (Deut. 30:8). The sabbath must be reinstated; for it is a "perpetual covenant" and sign between Jehovah and Israel, except for such time as He shall cause it to cease in His chastisement of that people (Ex. 31:16).

Sixth. *The Exact Day.*

The supposition that an *exact* continuation of weekly sabbaths is now being kept by all who observe the seventh day, is without foundation. It should be noted: (a) No day is holy in itself. From the natural standpoint, all days are alike and are equally subject to the same physical conditions. A day is holy by divine decree, and that decree is subject to change at the appointment of God. By no means did the day always fall on Saturday, nor were the sabbaths always separated by six full working days. (b) The sabbath was to begin with sunset and end with sunset. This was simple enough when ordered for Israel in the small geographical boundaries of Palestine. It is far different when applied to the whole earth, and, as some dare to claim, to heaven as well. No uniformity of the observance of an exact day is possible over the whole earth. While some are keeping Saturday on one hemisphere, others are keeping Sunday (as sabbath) on the other. Should two persons start from a given point to go around the earth in opposite directions, and both observe each sabbath from sundown to sundown, upon their return to the starting point, one would be observing Friday and the other Sunday. The question of observing an exact day from sunset is even more perplexing in the far North. The sun sets there but once in six months. In that region, to be Biblical and exact, there must be a twelve-month sabbath, and a week of seven years. (c) The exact day in which God finished creation and rested is quite unknown. He rested on the seventh day; but it could hardly be proven that sundown on Friday night at a given place on the earth is the perpetuation of the exact moment when God began to rest from His work of creation. Who can trace the exact moment, day, or year, through Eden, the flood, the bondage in Egypt, and the dark ages? Yet apart from the assurance that Saturday at a given place on the earth is the exact day in rotation of weeks from creation, there is no basis for the claim to the sacredness of the exact time to be observed. Ignorant people are too often encouraged in the belief that they are actually celebrating the rest of God in creation when they observe the hours as they fall on Saturday in the locality where they chance to live.

It is therefore the *manner* of the observance of the day, and not the exact time, which is in question. Shall it be the seventh day, or the first day? It must be one or the other; for there is nothing more unreasonable, illogical, and unbiblical, than the observance of the seventh day with confusion of Christian issues of worship and service, which is the practice of every sabbatarian, or the observance of the first day with confusion of the sabbath law, which is the present practice of Christendom. There would be little occasion for discussion of the question if the simple distinctions between law and grace were recognized.

II. THE BIBLICAL TESTIMONY CONCERNING THE LORD'S DAY.

This aspect of truth will be considered under two general divisions: (1) The reason for the observance of the day, and (2) The manner of observance of the day.

First, *The Reason for the Observance of the New Day.*

Even a cursory reading of those portions of Scripture which condition the daily life of the Christian will reveal the fact that, while every other fundamental principle of righteousness found in the Decalogue is restated in the teachings of grace, the sabbath is not once imposed upon the believer. On the contrary, as before shown, there is explicit warning against the observance of a sabbath day. This is a fact of revelation which should not be overlooked.

Throughout the history of the church, a new day has been observed which superseded the Jewish sabbath, and this change of days has not been contrary to the teaching of the Scriptures, as some insist; it has, rather, been according to the revealed plan and purpose of God. There are certain Biblical reasons for this change:

1. *The Mosaic system has ceased.*

The whole Mosaic system, including its sabbath day, has given way to the reign of grace. To this important truth sufficient proof has already been presented, but in spite of the clearest Biblical statement on this subject, there are two groups of professing Christians who evidently do not receive this divine testimony. (a) Those who persist in the observance of the seventh day; and (b) those who observe the first day, but who invest it with the character of the Jewish sabbath, and observe it on the authority of the law which was given to Israel by Moses. The position of these two classes should be considered separately:

(a) Those who persist in the observance of the seventh day, do so on the claim that, while the law passed away in the death of Christ, the Decalogue is not a part of the law and therefore it, with its sabbath day, has not been abolished. The answer to this subtle argument is clear and conclusive. Not only is the Decalogue included and embedded in the Old Testament statement of the law, but, in the New Testament, the Decalogue, as has already been shown, is distinctly said to be "the law." In Rom. 7: 7, the Apostle Paul has written of the tendency of his own heart toward sin. He states: "I had not known sin, but by the law: for I had not known lust, except the law had said, Thou shalt not covet." Thus he refers to the Tenth Commandment as "the law."

Furthermore, it is impossible now for any Jew or Gentile to keep the Ceremonial law of Moses, and thus it is evident that the New Testament warnings against law observance could not be a warning against an observance of the Ceremonial law. The Ceremonial law required for its observance the presence of Jehovah in the holy of holies, an altar, a priesthood and a temple in Jerusalem. All these prerequisites for the observance of the Ceremonial law were withdrawn at the beginning of the present age. The church of Rome, in its attempt to continue the law system, proposed to meet this difficulty by creating its own altar, temple service, and priesthood, and alleges that the Lord is present in the consecrated bread. The warnings which are found under grace against the keeping of the law are of necessity applicable only to the Decalogue, and not to the Ceremonial law.

The Ceremonial law governed the precise manner

of the observance of the sabbath and there is great unreasonableness, with attending confusion, when the attempt is now made to keep the Jewish sabbath apart from the Ceremonial law. The class of legalists who now try to observe the seventh day, having no way to introduce the Ceremonial law, borrow the features of the new day of grace. They hold services, worship, and do much religious work on the seventh day, which, being strictly a day of rest, was never designed to be a day of activity, religious or otherwise, nor was such activity ever allowed on this day during the reign of the law.

(b) There is even greater inconsistency in the position of those who recognize the first day of the week, but invest that day with the character of the sabbath, and keep the day on the authority of the law of Moses. Not only has the whole Mosaic system ceased with its sabbath and every requirement related to that day; but there could be no consistency in borrowing even one of the features of the Jewish sabbath. This error of borrowing certain features of the Jewish sabbath is committed by both of these classes of legalists. The law of Moses was never subject to a *partial* observance. It is a unit; for "what things soever the law saith, it saith to them who are under the law;" and, "the man which doeth those things shall live by them;" and again, "cursed, is every one that continueth not in all things which are written in the book of law to do them." There is no Scriptural warrant for a partial acceptance of the law, or a partial recognition of its sabbath day. The observance of the day with all its requirements must be *perfectly* kept, or *not at all*. The slightest recognition of the least of all the features of the sabbath commits a person who attempts it to keep the whole law. It therefore follows that the Christian who, while keeping the first day of the week, is influenced in the slightest degree by the law of Moses concerning a sabbath day, is, both by Scripture and reason, committed to keep every feature of the Jewish sabbath, as well as the whole Mosaic system. For example, the person who adopts even one feature of sabbath observance on the ground that it is enjoined by the law, is bound by that same sabbath law to stone to death every person who fails to keep any feature of that law. In fact, if he himself had been so guilty as to observe the first day of the week in place of the seventh, he must bow to the death penalty, in vindication of the righteous judgments of God. This death penalty is the uncompromising provision made in God's Word for sabbath breakers.

The original heresy of the church was the attempted admixture of law and grace teachings. It is one of the most destructive heresies of the present hour, and at no point of contact do the opposing principles of law and grace become more clearly crystallized than in the question of the exact day which is to be observed. There is no *"Christian Sabbath."* The new day which belongs to grace is in no way related to the sabbath. Observance must be either of one day or the other. To co-mingle them, as every legalist does, is to frustrate grace.

2. *A new day is divinely appointed under grace.*

This new day is also a particular day of the week and has been given a name which is in accordance

with its character. Its divine appointment is first
recorded in a prophetic message: "The stone which
the builders refused is become the head stone of the
corner. This is the LORD's doing; it is marvellous in
our eyes. This is the day which the LORD hath made;
we will rejoice and be glad in it (Ps. 118: 22-24).

In this Scripture, both the death and the resurrection of Christ are in view. He was the rejected
Stone, and His Father, through the resurrection, has
made Him the Head Stone of the Corner. The resurrection was appointed to take place on a certain day
which the Lord had determined, and that day was by
divine intention to be celebrated with joy and glad-
ness. The divine commentary on this passage is
given through the Apostle Peter as recorded in Acts
4: 10, 11: "Be it known unto you all, and to all the
people of Israel, that by the name of Jesus Christ of
Nazareth, whom ye crucified, whom God raised from
the dead, even by him doth this man stand here before
you whole. This is the stone which was set at nought
of you builders, which is become the head of the
corner."

Therefore the day which the Lord had appointed
when the rejected Stone would become the Head Stone
of the Corner, is the day of His resurrection. This
is the " day which the LORD hath made." It is therefore the Lord's day. In that day we are to "rejoice
and be glad." This new day is the day to which the
Apostle John makes reference when he said, "I was
in the Spirit on the Lord's day" (Rev. 1: 10). These
words of John were written fully sixty years after
the death of Christ and at a time when the new day

had become the accepted day among all believers.

The Lord's day should in no wise be confused with "The Day of the LORD." One is the first day of every week, which is observed as a commemoration of the resurrection of Christ. The other is a prophetic period, which is still future, and which concerns Israel and the whole creation.

The first Lord's day was the pattern of all the Lord's days that should follow. It began "very early in the morning," when the risen Lord said, "All Hail" (lit. rejoice)! It continued with His precious fellowship, and closed with His benediction of peace. From that early morning to its close it was a day of worship, activity, and joy. The sabbath, on the other hand, with no less symbolical significance, began with the setting sun, which spoke of complete cessation of activity, and of perfect rest.

The Christian has an unchangeable day. He may extend its observance to all days, but He cannot change the one day, which is divinely appointed, any more than Israel, or any one else, could change the divinely appointed seventh day. A change of the first day to another breaks the symbolic meaning of the day as it represents the true relationships under grace. It results in robbing Christ of that glory which is His alone. This is one of the wrongs committed by all those who persist in an attempted seventh-day observance. The two days do not present an optional choice to the Christian. The choice between these days is one which carries either acceptance or rejection of the most vital relationships between Christ and the believer under grace.

3. *A new day is indicated by important events.*

Beginning with the resurrection, and following it, every event recorded in the New Testament which had important religious significance fell on the first day of the week, or the Lord's day. No greater emphasis through events could be given to this new day than that found in the teachings of grace, and, added to this, is the fact that in these same Scriptures the sabbath day is wholly set aside. If it be claimed that there is no direct commandment for the keeping of the Lord's day, it should be observed that there is explicit command *against* the observance of the sabbath day, and that the lack of commandments concerning the Lord's day is both in accordance with the character of the new day, and the entire order of grace which it represents and to which it is related. Mention should be made of the great events which fell on the first day of the week.

a. On the first day of the week Christ arose from the dead. His resurrection is vitally related to the ages past, to the fulfillment of all prophecy, to the values of His death, to the Church, to Israel, to creation, to the purposes of God in grace which reach beyond to the ages to come, and to the eternal glory of God. Fulfillment of the eternal purposes related to all of these was dependent upon the coming forth of the Son of God from that tomb. He arose from the dead, and the greatness of that event is indicated by the importance of its place in Christian doctrine. Had not Christ arisen—He by whom all things were created, that are in heaven, and that are in earth, visible and invisible, whether they be thrones, or dominions, or principalities, or powers, He for whom things were created, who is before all things, and by whom all things consist (hold together) —every divine purpose and blessing would have failed, yea, the very universe and the throne of God would have dissolved and would have been dismissed forever. All life, light, and hope would have ceased. Death, darkness, and despair would have reigned. Though the spiritual powers of darkness might have continued, the last hope for a ruined world would have been banished eternally. It is impossible for the mind to grasp the mighty issues which were at stake at the moment when Christ came forth from the tomb. At no moment of time, however, were these great issues in jeopardy. The consummation of His resurrection was sure, for omnipotent power was engaged to bring it to pass. Every feature of the Christian's salvation, position, and hope was dependent on the resurrection of his Lord. Very much depended on the death of Christ, but every value of that death would have been sacrificed apart from the resurrection. When Christ arose from the dead, Christianity was born, and the new creation was brought into existence. There is nothing in the old order for the believer. He stands on resurrection ground. He belongs only to the new creation. God is faithful to all that He has wrought in Christ and He, according to His Word, will not suffer the child of the new creation to go back and celebrate the beginning of the old and fallen creation from which His child has been saved through infinite riches of grace. If the children of grace persist in relating themselves to the old creation by the observance of the sabbath, it is evidence of their limitations in the knowledge of the Word and will of God; it is to fall from grace.

Since the day of Christ's resurrection is the day in which the new creation was formed, and all that enters into the Christian's life and hope was brought into being, both according to Scripture and according to reason, the Christian can celebrate no other day than the Lord's day.

b. On the first day of the week Christ met His disciples in the new power and fellowship of His resurrection life.

c. On the first day of the week Christ symbolized the new resurrection fellowship by breaking bread with His disciples.

d. On the first day of the week He gave them instructions in their new resurrection ministry and life for Him.

e. On the first day of the week He commanded the disciples to preach the new message to all the world.

f. On the first day of the week Christ ascended into heaven as the "Wave Sheaf." In fulfilling the Old Testament type and the eternal purpose of God, it was necessary that He should appear in heaven as the earnest of the mighty harvest of souls whom He had redeemed and who came out of that tomb with Him to share His eternal life and glory. So, also, He must, having accomplished the sacrifice for sin, present His own blood in heaven (Lev. 16:1-34; Heb. 9:16-28). Having not yet ascended, He said to Mary, "Touch me not; for I am not yet ascended to my Father: but go to my brethren and say unto them, I ascend unto my father, and your

Father; and to my God, and your God" (John 20:17). How little the mighty import of this message from Christ was understood then, and how little it is understood even now! That He ascended on that day is evident; for He said unto them at evening of that day, "Behold my hands and my feet, that it is I myself: handle me, and see" (Lk. 24:39). He had ascended to heaven, accomplished His work there, and returned to earth to complete His post-resurrection ministry.

g. On the first day of the week He breathed on His disciples and imparted the Holy Spirit to them.

h. On the first day of the week the Spirit descended to take up His age-characterizing ministries in the world.

i. On the first day of the week the Apostle Paul preached to the assembled believers at Troas. The Spirit of God has distinctly emphasized the fact that the Apostle was in Troas *seven days*. Of necessity, then, the stay in that city included both a seventh day and a first day of the week. The Apostle was thus free to choose either day for his public ministry to the assembled saints. The record reads: "We . . . came unto them to Troas . . . where we abode seven days. And upon the first day of the week, when the disciples came together to break bread, Paul preached unto them" (Acts 20:6, 7).

j. The Apostle commanded the Corinthian believer to "lay by him in store," on the first day of the week, "as God hath prospered him" (1 Cor. 16:2).

k. On the first day of the week Christ appeared to John on Patmos in that revelation of Himself in all His present resurrection, heavenly glory. He appeared to John on the Lord's day.

4. *The new day typifies the new creation.*

The rite of circumcision, being accomplished on the eighth day, was a suggestion of the spiritual circumcision of the flesh which Christ wrought by His death and resurrection. The eighth day was the first day following a completed week. It is thus a picture of that new order which came through the death and resurreqtion of Christ. The Apostle writes: "In whom also ye are circumcised with the circumcision made without hands, in putting off the body of the sins of the flesh by the circumcision of Christ" (Col. 2:11). Not only has the old nature been judged in the crucifixion, death, and burial of the Son of God, and the new victory in the resurrection life of Christ been made possible; but, for the believer, the old creation went into that tomb and a new creation with its heavenly power and glory came out. The old creation was abolished and with it the sabbath which commemorated it. Only a new standing in the resurrected Christ abides and this both demands and provides a new day. That new day is the eighth day, or the first day following the ending of the old creation.

5. *The new day is typical of unmerited grace.*

The first day of the week is a type of the facts and relationships which are under grace; while the seventh day is a type of the facts and relationships which are under the law. On the seventh day man rested from all his work. This is in harmony with the law covenant of works, which required a man to do good in order that he might receive the blessing of God. Under the law, six days of faithful labor are followed by one day of absolute rest. On the other hand, the observance of the first day of the week is typical of the believer's position under unmerited grace. He begins with a day of blessing before any works are wrought, and then he is expected to live the following six days in the power and blessing he has received on that day. This is the order of the grace covenant of faith in which all saving grace is first bestowed as a gift from God, and is then followed by a life which is lived in the power of that new relationship with God. A day of rest belonged to a people who were related to God by works which were to be accomplished. A day of ceaseless worship and service belongs to a people who are related to God by the finished work of Christ. The seventh day was governed by an unyielding, ironclad law. The first day is characterized by the latitude and liberty belonging to grace. The seventh day was observed with the hope that by it one might be accepted of God. The first day is observed with the assurance that one is already accepted of God. The keeping of the seventh day was wrought by the flesh. The keeping of the first day is to be wrought by the indwelling Spirit.

6. *The new day began to be observed with the resurrection of Christ.*

It is claimed by a certain group of sabbatarians that the sabbath was kept by the early church until the day was changed by the Emperor Constantine in the year 321 A. D., or even later by the Pope of Rome. There is no ground for this erroneous and misleading teaching. The sabbath was never changed. It could not be. A new and far different day in significance, which alone could belong to this age of grace, superseded it. When this age is completed and law reigns again in the earth, the sabbath will be observed; but in no wise will man have changed the day. There is conclusive evidence that the first day of the week has been observed by the church from the very resurrection of Christ. This evidence is found both (a) in the Scriptures and (b) in the writings of the early fathers:

(a) Turning to the Epistles of the New Testament, wherein is conditioned the believer's life under grace, we discover that there is prohibition against the observance of a sabbath day, and that there is not one record that any Christian kept a sabbath day, even in error. On the other hand, there is abundant evidence, as has been seen, that the first day of the week was observed in the manner consistent with its significance.

(b) The testimony from the early fathers is also conclusive.[1]

Eusebius, 315 A. D., says: "The churches throughout the rest of the world observe the practice that has prevailed from Apostolic tradition until the present time so that it would not be proper to terminate our fast on any other day but the resurrection day of our Saviour. Hence there were synods and

---

[1] These quotations from the early fathers are taken from Bowman's *Historical Evidence of the New Testament*, Pgs. 130-135; *The Encylopedia Britannica* under *"Sunday;"* and Mosheim's *"Ecclesiastical History,"* Vol. I. Pg. 135.

convocations of our Bishops on this question and all unanimously drew up an ecclesiastical decree which they communicated to churches in all places—that the mystery of the Lord's resurrection should be celebrated on no other than the Lord's Day."

Peter, Bishop of Alexandria, 300 A. D., says: "We keep the Lord's Day as a day of joy because of him who rose thereon."

Cyprian, Bishop of Carthage, 253 A. D., says: "The Lord's Day is both the 1st, and the 8th day."

Tertullian, of Carthage, 200 A. D., says, speaking of the "sun-worshippers": "Though we share with them Sunday, we are not apprehensive lest we seem to be heathen."

Clement of Alexandria, 194 A. D., says: "The old sabbath day has become nothing more than a working day."

Irenaeus, Bishop of Lyons, 178 A. D., says: "The mystery of the Lord's resurrection may not be celebrated on any other day than the Lord's Day."

Bardesanes, 160 A. D., says: "Wherever we be, all of us are called by the one name of the Messiah, namely Christians, and upon one day, which is the first day of the week, we assemble ourselves together and on the appointed days we abstain from food."

Justin Martyr, 135 A. D., says: "Sunday is the day upon which we all hold our communion assembly, because it is the first day on which God having wrought a change in the darkness and matter made the world and Jesus Christ our Saviour, on that day, rose from the dead and on the day called Sunday all who live in cities or in the country gather together in one place and the memoirs of the Apostles, or the writings of the prophets are read as long as time permits." "On the Lord's Day all Christians in the city or country meet together because that is the day of our Lord's resurrection; and then we read the apostles and prophets. This being done, the president makes an oration to the assembly exhorting them to imitate and to practice the things which they have heard, and then we all join in prayer, and after that we celebrate the Lord's Supper."

Ignatius, Bishop of Antioch, 110 A. D., says: "If then those who walked in the ancient practices attain unto newness of hope no longer observing sabbaths, but fashioning their lives after the Lord's Day, on which our life also arose through him, that we may be found disciples of Jesus Christ, our only teacher."

Barnabas, one of the Apostolic fathers, writing 70 A. D., says: "Finally He saith, 'Your present sabbaths are not acceptable to me. I shall make a new beginning of the eighth day, that is the beginning of another world,' wherefore also we keep the Lord's Day with joyfulness, the day also on which Jesus rose from the dead."

Also, the "Didache of the Apostles" 70 A. D., says: "On the Lord's own Day gather yourselves together and break bread and give thanks."

By this line of unbroken testimony the evidence concerning the observance of the Lord's day is carried back to the days of the writings of the New Testament. It is quite true that Emperors and Popes have made decrees regarding the first day of the week. Everything was done that could be done to persecute the Jew, and to abolish Jewish practices; but the Jewish sabbath passed, and the new day came to be, not by the decree of man, but by the resurrection of Christ which brought in all that the Lord's day signifies.

7. *The new day has been blessed of God*

Christians have observed the Lord's day under the evident blessing of God for nearly 2000 years. Among them have been the most devout believers, the martyrs, the missionaries, and a countless throng of those who would have passed through any trial or persecution to know and do the will of God. It is a very serious charge to say that all these faithful saints have been disobedient, or as some sabbatarians now call all Christians who do not keep sabbath, "heretics," "deceivers," "having the mark of the Beast," and "blinded by Satan." The Gospel of grace is by these people substituted by "another gospel" which is to the effect that only those who keep the sabbath will be saved, and they also teach that God has "forsaken His church" and that she is "abandoned to Satan who rules her." In spite of the fact that God has never once imposed the sabbath upon the age of grace, they make the preaching of the sabbath their major theme, and in seeming bitterness, do not hesitate to hinder the good works of all who love and keep the Lord's day. Along with the error of preaching the law in place of the Gospel, these sabbatarians hold and teach other misleading heresies and unbiblical doctrines. Being so much in error concerning many fundamental doctrines of the Bible, it is not strange that they persist in sabbath legality.

The reasons for keeping the Lord's day, or the first

day of the week, are clear and sufficient to those who will receive the teachings of God's Word without prejudice.

Second. *The Biblical Observance of the Lord's Day.*

The manner in which the first day of the week should be observed is clearly indicated by the very name which is given to it in the Scriptures. Being the *Lord's day*, it is to be lived in that manner which will most honor and glorify the Lord. Whatever enters into the present relationship between the believer and his Lord, such as prayer, joyful worship, and service, will naturally characterize the observance of the day. Particular care should be exercised that no element of a Jewish sabbath be incorporated into the manner of the keeping of the Lord's day. Not only does such an intrusion create confusion in the mind as to the meaning and purpose of the day, but it is a co-mingling of the elements of law and grace, and this, it is certain, is not according to the mind of God. The two days are similar only in one respect: they both sustain the ratio of one particular day in seven. There is not the slightest reason for any combination of their respective features. Should this exhortation to watchfulness lest these days be confused seem to be extreme, it should be remembered that only thus can a believer stand fast in the liberty wherewith Christ has made him free, and not be entangled again in a yoke of bondage. Only thus can he be saved from violating the most precious aspect of his own relation to God under grace, and from disregarding the most vital injunctions of those Scriptures which condition his life under grace. Christians have been saved from the *curse* of the law by the death of Christ (Gal. 3:13). This marvelous deliverance has cost the sacrifice of the Son of God, and it cannot be an unimportant issue in the mind of God. The believer who would really keep the day in conformity to the revealed will of his Lord, should duly consider the fact that every aspect of sabbath observance is purely legal, and related only to law, and that Christ has died to save him from any complicity with the law. The observance of the Lord's day as recorded in the New Testament, is free from every relationship to the Jewish sabbath.

When contemplating the Scriptural observance of the Lord's day, three considerations arise: (1) It belongs to a particular people; (2) it is not subject to rules; and (3) its observance is not limited to one day.

1. *The Lord's day belongs to a particular people.*

As the sabbath under the law belonged only to the nation Israel, so, in like manner, the new day in grace belongs only to those who are regenerated by the Spirit. In arriving at the full force of this statement, it should be noted:

a. *The Lord's day, like every other aspect of grace, is an appeal to the individual believer only.*

As men are now saved by a *personal* faith, and afterwards their service is in the power of an *individual* gift by the Spirit, they walk *alone* in the Spirit, and they receive *their own* reward for faithfulness to God. In conformity with this truth, therefore, the observance of the day is to be *personal*. The exact manner of its observance is a matter between the individual believer and his Lord. The Scriptures presuppose that the believer is a normal Christian to the extent that he is yielded to God and walking in the Spirit, that it will be his delight to do the will of God, and to rejoice above all else in the larger freedom which the Lord's day affords for worship and service. If perchance he is not thus yielded to God, no forced, outward observance of the day will correct his carnal heart, nor would such an observance of a day be pleasing to God.

No day has been committed to the Church as a body. Apart from the two exceptions that the believer is to consider his possible influence upon a weaker brother, and his own conduct in the light of expediency, the day is to be observed by the individual out of the fullness of his own heart. Beyond this there are no rules, nor could there be; for apart from this there is no possibility of continuing in those exact relationships which belong to grace. Concerning the observance of the Lord's day the Apostle said: "Let every man [Christian] be fully persuaded in his own mind" (Rom. 14:5).

b. *The Lord's day is not for the unregenerate.*

The unsaved sustain no relation to the Lord's day, since that day belongs only to the new creation, and therefore the pressing of the observance of a religious day upon the individual who is unsaved, is misleading in the extreme; for it tends to the utter confusion of the Gospel of grace. God is not calling on the unsaved to keep a day to which they could in no

way be related. The issue between God and the sinner
is the one issue which the new Gospel of grace has
raised and imposed. It is a question as to whether he
will *believe* on the Lord Jesus Christ unto forgiveness
and eternal life. The person who observes a day
while rejecting Christ as Saviour, is no nearer salvation or acceptance with God than he would otherwise
be. That supposed merit, gained by keeping a day,
may be the one thing that hinders him from discovering Christ as the Saviour for a meritless sinner. Men
are not saved by any works whatsoever, and any
teaching which misdirects them at this point is
"another gospel" and subject to the anathema of
God (Gal. 1:8). If the motive in pressing the religious observance of a day upon the unregenerate be
for the moral and civic good of the community, the
question should be answered as to whether the moral
and civic betterment of the world is more important
than the salvation of men.

c. *The Lord's day is not a national day.*

When a day is imposed upon the nation it is, without exception, upon the authority of the Jewish sabbath of rest, and not on the authority of anything
which obtains in the new creation. The error of this
legalism needs no further exposition. God is certainly
not imposing a legal sabbath on any nation, or the
world, when He has given His Son to remove that
whole law-curse and to place men where they might
be saved apart from works of their own. In this age
God is represented as dealing with the individual
only. In matters of human government, it is the
"times of the Gentiles," with all that is involved, and

no individual or nation is now accepted of God on the basis of human works.

It is most imperative that a day of rest for man and beast be maintained by civic authority. No intelligent person could vote otherwise; but the day should be enforced as all other humanitarian laws and other portions of the Decalogue are enforced, and not as a meritorious religious observance. At any cost the sabbath-observance stumbling-stone should be kept from the path of the unsaved.

d. *The Lord's day and the children.*

The question often arises in the Christian home as to the manner in which the Lord's day should be observed by children. Upon this subject a suggestion may be advanced: Until he is of age, the child is properly under the direction of the parents and the government of the home. He should live in conformity to the wishes and customs of the parents, but it is vitally important that the child should be brought to know Christ as a Saviour at the earliest possible moment. Then the Lord's day becomes to him a matter of his own privilege and personal delight, and not a law prescribed by the parents. Care should be taken, as well, that the day of grace should not become a subject of dislike and prejudice in the mind of the child.

2. *The Lord's day is not subject to rules.*

Such is the character of all the teachings of grace, and at this point the grace teachings are wholly in contrast to the teachings of all law. The law contemplated the people to whom it was addressed as being

children and thus subject to "tutors and governors."
Every detail of their prescribed life was a matter of
explicit *law*. The flesh was in no way depended upon
to direct itself. The believer under grace is an *adult
son* in the Father's house, with the wider latitude
which belongs to the full-grown, self-responsible man.
Therefore the teachings of grace are not explicit as to
detail. They anticipate the immediate inner judgment by the indwelling Spirit. Under grace, great
principles are announced, but the outworking of those
principles is to be according to the leading of the
Spirit in the individual. Liberality is enjoined, but
the object and amount of the gift is a matter of
prayerful dependence on the Spirit. As to service,
every Christian is to be instant in season and out of
season, but the gifts for service and the manner and
place of their exercise is "as he will." Prayer is to
be offered without ceasing, but we know not what to
pray for as we ought. However in this again, the
Spirit helpeth our infirmities and He maketh intercession for us according to the mind of God. The
believer's life under grace is a "walk in the Spirit."
Step by step, every detail is to be wrought in the
heart by the Spirit, and there are no more detail-
rules for the observance of the Lord's day than for
the outworking of any other responsibility or privilege under grace. The flesh is not now to be controlled
by laws; but by the Lordship of the Spirit. Not having specific rules for the keeping of the Christian's
day, and not duly considering the divine provision
for a spiritual life in the power of the Spirit, men,
hoping to keep control of the flesh, have turned to the
Jewish sabbath laws and forced them onto the Lord's

day. In so doing, they have repudiated one of the
most vital accomplishments of the death of Christ,
they have robbed believers of their liberty in grace,
and, so far as their influence goes, they have degraded
the full-grown sons of God to the level of mere children who are under "tutors and governors."

The real question is not, How shall we preserve the
sacredness of the day unless we have laws and enforce
them? It is rather, can the believer, to whom the
day belongs, be trusted, when filled with the Spirit, to
glorify God on the Lord's day? Evidently there will
be no failure to observe the day on the part of the
Spirit-filled believer. But what of the great company
of carnal Christians? Should they not be held by
laws to the keeping of the day? In reply to this important question it should be stated: The position of
a carnal Christian is different from that of the unsaved. The Lord's day belongs to the Christian, but
it does not belong to the unregenerate. The Christian
alone faces the problem related to the Lord's day.
The problem, therefore, resolves itself into this: Is
God satisfied when the Christian's life is merely a
forced, outward conformity to unpleasant ideals?
The answer is obvious. One of the essential glories
of grace is that God-honoring manner of life which
is an outflow and overflow of the heart. No painful
observance of law will ever correct a carnal heart.
The cure is found only in the right adjustment of the
heart to the Spirit. Too often the Christian life is
presented as being a matter of observing certain rules
and sustaining a superficial outward conduct, to the
neglect of the divinely provided, victorious, overflowing life in the Spirit. Notwithstanding the conster-

nation of the untaught legalist who proposes to regulate Christian conduct by precept, the truth stands that the Lord's day imposes no rules, and yields to no law. True to grace, there are, however, certain well-defined principles to be stated:

a. *It, being the Lord's day, is to be lived well-pleasing to Him.*

This principle is the embodiment of all other principles related to the keeping of the Lord's day; but the detail of this heaven-high ideal, as has been seen, cannot be determined by rules, nor can it ever be wrought by the flesh. There is but one exception: It has pleased the Lord to give minute instruction as to the manner of the observance of His memorial supper.

b. *The Lord's day celebrates the resurrection of Christ.*

If this be true, then all obligation to observe the day of rest, which is related to the old creation, is excluded. The day is to be celebrated in the new life and service of the resurrected Christ.

c. *The Lord's day yields to no law.*

Like all law, the law of a certain day has been kept and fulfilled for the believer by Christ. There remains for the believer only overflowing praise and joyful service. The element of *necessity* has likewise passed. Men are not compelled to keep a day to be accepted of God. They, if saved, are already accepted "in the beloved." The day should be kept *because of* perfection in Christ, and not *unto* perfection in Christ.

d. *It is a day of personal delight.*

When the Lord's day becomes a burden to the individual, to him it is no longer a day of grace. It is characterized by that attitude of heart which *delights* to do the will of God. When this day was prophetically announced, it was said: "This is the day which the LORD hath made; we will rejoice and be glad in it." So, also, the first word from the lips of the resurrected Christ on the morning of His resurrection was, "All hail!" (The word here is *chairo,* and means *rejoice,* or, *O joy!.*) The Lord's day should be celebrated in the fullest experience of the "joy of the Lord."

e. *The Lord's day is a day for the largest Christian activity.*

The risen Lord revealed the character of the day on that same early morning when He said: "Go tell." This is the obligation toward the new evangel, the giving of which is to occupy every believer. As the Old Testament priests went *in* to perform a sacrifice, the New Testament priests,—all believers under grace,— are to go *out* to the ends of the earth to tell of the sacrifice which has been performed. The Lord's day is not a day for selfish entertainment or amusement. It is not a day for idleness and rest. Its privileges should be, and will be, preserved by all who delight to do His will. It becomes an opportunity for many who are held by secular work during the days of the week, to offer the fuller service of prayer, worship, and testimony which belongs to their Lord. The instructed Christian no longer labors to be accepted of

God, which was the obligation under the law; but he, being accepted in grace, labors to glorify his Lord who saves him. He has ceased from his *own* works, and though ceaselessly active, is working in the power and energy of the Spirit. His activity is not limited to one day, or to six days: it is "in season and out of season" according to the mind and will of the Spirit. Spirit-filled believers have always violated every feature of a strict Jewish sabbath of rest when serving as "able ministers of the new convenant." If led of the Spirit thus to serve, the resulting violation of the sabbath is in reality the work of the Spirit. It would be a herculean task, indeed, to attempt to prove that *all* Christian service and activity exercised on the first day of the week for nineteen centuries has been offensive to God because it violated the demands of a sabbath of rest, or that the neglect of the seventh day by **all** the believers of the Christian era, has, in the mind of God, merited the penalty of death. Yet this is the logical charge to be made against all these believers unless it be admitted that they had individually entered, as a prerequisite to service, into the sabbath rest of that which is finished forever in the cross.

f. *The Lord's day observance is to be governed by the law of expediency, and the law of love.*

The law of expediency permits the undertaking on the Lord's day of only those things which are advisable, advantageous, and suitable. Judgment in these things should be formed only in view of the Biblical teachings concerning the Lord's day responsibility,— not the Jewish sabbath,—and in view of the need of others, and the possible influence which any particular action might have upon others. The Christian objective is not a slavish conformity to certain laws governing a day. It is concerned rather with the question as to what will most glorify Christ and advance the cause of His saving grace in the earth.

When adjusted to the law of love, the Christian will not exercise his own liberty in such a manner as to hinder and offend a weaker brother who through false teaching has developed a conscience toward a Jewish sabbath, nor will he rob others of the exercise of their own worship and service. Such issues have to be given due consideration when dealing with all questions of travel and of relationship to those who serve.

3. *The manner of the observance of the Lord's day may be extended to all days.*

The Lord's day observance alone is capable of being extended to all days; for in no wise could a Jewish sabbath be thus extended. It is evident, therefore, that the Apostle's reference to the keeping of a day, as found in Rom. 14: 1-12, is a reference to the Lord's day and not to a sabbath day. He writes: "Who art thou that judgest another man's servant? to his own master he standeth or falleth. Yea, he shall be holden up: for God is able to make him stand. One man esteemeth one day above another: another esteemeth every day alike. Let every man be fully persuaded in his own mind. He that regardeth the day, regardeth it unto the Lord; and he that regardeth not the day, to the Lord he doth not regard it. . . . For we shall all stand before the judgment seat of

Christ. . . . So then every one of us shall give an account of himself to God.''

The primary teaching of this passage puts the emphasis on the fact that Christian conduct is largely a matter to be settled between the believer and his Lord. There need be no fear; ''God is able to make him stand.'' The passage might be understood as presenting a contrast between a man who keeps one day, and a man who keeps no day at all. In such a case, God will deal with the wrong in His child, if wrong there be. In attempting to adjust such a situation, men might compel the erring one to observe a day, or, as a penalty for failure, exclude him from their fellowship. The divine method is to change the heart. This God alone can do.

But in this particular instance it will be observed that concerning the man of whom it is said that he does not regard the day, it is also said that ''unto the Lord he doth not regard it.'' It is as much a matter of devotion to God in the case of the one man as it is in the case of the other. It is therefore probable that the contrast is between the man who keeps *one* day as unto the Lord, and another man who keeps *all* days as unto the Lord. There must be sufficient room in the Christian fellowship for these two equally sincere men to live in joyful companionship in Christ. It would be quite human for each of these men to form mutually exclusive denominations for the conservation of his own peculiar convictions. This, however, would not be in harmony with the life under grace. The man who esteems all days alike, extends the joyous worship, praise, and service belonging to the Lord's day into every day. This leads to the consideration of the fact that there is (a) a true sabbath under grace, and (b) there is yet to be a millennial sabbath in the earth.

a. *The true sabbath under grace.*

The sabbath under the law was a *day*. The sabbath under grace is a *life*. The law, even of the sabbath, was but "a shadow of good things to come," but Christ is now the Substance. The sabbath under grace knows no shadow. It is radiant with the glory of the resurrected Christ.

In Hebrews 4: 1-16 there is full revelation concerning the sabbath under grace. This whole message is gathered up in one brief portion of the passage: "There remaineth therefore a rest to the people of God. For he that is entered into his rest, he also hath ceased from his own works, as God did from His" (vs. 9, 10). There is no reference in this Scripture to the rest into which the Christian enters at death. It is rather, "For we which have believed do enter into rest" (v. 3). It is the rest of "him that worketh not, but believeth on him that justifieth the ungodly" (Rom. 4: 5), and the rest of the one who, "walking in the Spirit," discovers that he does not fulfill the lust of the flesh, and who enters into the realization of the provision through the indwelling Spirit that the whole will of God is to be fulfilled *in* him, rather than *by* him. This great blessing is not restricted to a sabbath day; it is an unbroken sabbath life. The sabbath of the law was, then, a *day* of absolute rest; the sabbath under grace is a *life* which is delivered from all works of the flesh since Christ has wrought, and is free from every dependence on the flesh since the Spirit has been given. No burden was allowed to be borne on the sabbath under the law; every burden is to be cast on the Lord in the sabbath of grace. The sabbath of the law was a day of rest *for* self; the sabbath of grace is a rest *from* self. It is a life which is to be lived to the glory and praise of Another. In the sabbath under the law, man was to cease from doing his own will for one day in seven; in the sabbath under grace the believer is to be constantly and wholly yielded to God.[1]

Every vestige of the system which provided for the giving of one-seventh of the time in conformity to the

[1] There is significance in the fact that the Greek word for *week* is *sabbaton*, which also means *sabbath*. Thus in Mt. 28: 1, referring to the day of Christ's resurrection, we have the possible literal reading: "At the end of the sabbath as it began to dawn on the first day of sabbaths" (Cf Mk. 16: 2, 9; Lk. 24: 1; John 20: 1, 19; Acts 13: 14; 16: 13). At least three expositions of this passage are possible.

1. That there is no significance in the fact that the resurrection day is called *sabbath* since it is the same Greek word for *week*. This is evidently the position taken by translators generally. The one passage, "I fast twice in the week" (Lk. 18: 12) would be difficult under a sabbath interpretation unless it be taken to mean, "I fast twice on the sabbath."

2. That the use of the word *sabbaton* in connection with the day of resurrection warrants the use of the phrase, *Christian Sabbath*, but the strong objection to this usage is the absolute prohibition in the Epistles against the sabbath day under any form whatsoever.

3. That the resurrection morning was the first day of all the days which were to enter into the age of grace, and that age, so far as a sabbath is concerned, is a period in which the believer has entered into rest. Under this interpretation, the resurrection day was the *first day of sabbaths*, which series was to include every succeeding day until the Lord returns.

will of God, is removed, and in its place the every-day, unchanging experience of that good, and accept-able, and perfect will of God has been substituted. It is inconceivable that Christ was more devoted to His Father on one day than on another. To intrude the legal sabbath into the present order of fellowship with God, is to rob Him of six-sevenths of His glory in grace.

It is true that the Christian has a day which is given to him from God, and this day is to be observed; but its observance is never a matter of greater piety, devotion, or yieldedness to God than of any other day. Its observance consists in a larger freedom, because of the cessation of temporal cares, to do all that his heart is yearning to do all the days. The sabbath in grace is, therefore, an experience of all that enters into the highest ideals of the Christian's life and de-votion to God. Blessed indeed are the children of God who learn to turn from holy days, from lenten seasons, and from all mere forms, if these even suggest the thought of fitfulness in fellowship and service with Christ. Doubtless, in spite of the glory of the true sabbath under grace, there will always be those who will continue to give their tenth, in place of giv-ing themselves and all that they are and have, and who will give a mere fraction of their time for devo-tion to God, rather than their lives. The true sabbath under grace is well stated in these words: ''Whether therefore ye eat, or drink, or whatsoever ye do, do all to the glory of God'' (1 Cor. 10: 31) ; ''Be instant in season, out of season'' (2 Tim. 4: 2) ; ''Pray without ceasing'' (1 Thes. 5: 17) ; ''Giving thanks always for all things'' (Eph. 5:20); "Rejoice evermore" (1 Thes. 5:16); and, "Be ye steadfast, unmoveable, always abounding in the work of the Lord" (1 Cor. 15:58).

b. *The millennial sabbath.*

The sabbath, as a type, will have its final earthly fulfillment in the coming kingdom-reign of Christ. It seems probable that it will be at the end of its six thousand years of labor and oppression under the power of sin and Satan, that the earth will celebrate its predicted thousand-year, jubilee sabbath of rest. During that period the Church will be reigning with the King as His Bride, and Israel will again keep her seventh-day sabbath, but in the new enabling power which is to be provided in that age of the divine glory in the earth. Of that kingdom-age it is written: "And it shall come to pass, that from one new moon to another, and from one sabbath to another, shall all flesh come to worship before me, saith the LORD" (Isa. 66:23).

III. CERTAIN CURRENT ERRORS.

A brief recapitulation of what has already been covered of the current errors on the sabbath question is here given in conclusion of this aspect of the teachings of grace.

First. *That the Sabbath Obtains from Creation to the End of Time.*

There is no Scripture upon which this claim may

be based, either for the period from Adam to the giving of the law, or from the death of Christ until the end of the present age of grace.

Second. *That the Sabbath was Ever Given to Gentiles.*

The disastrous results of the prevalent custom of borrowing certain features from Judaism, including its sabbath, and intruding them into Christianity cannot be too strongly emphasized. This error carries with it the obligation to keep the law in its totality, disregards one of the most vital accomplishments of Christ in His death, and creates a condition of hopeless confusion in all matters related to the right divisions of the Scriptures.

The whole seventh-day error is a logical outcome of an assumed freedom to apply Jewish Scriptures to the Church of God.

Third. *That the Decalogue was Never a part of the Law, and Therefore the Sabbath of the Decalogue is Now Binding Though the Law is Done Away.*

This claim is silenced by the Scriptures. The Decalogue is included, incorporated, and embedded in the Old Testament statement of the law; and in the New Testament, the decalogue is explicitly declared to be "THE LAW" (Rom. 7:7).

Fourth. *That the Jewish Sabbath was Changed to the Lord's Day.*

Emperors, Popes, church councils, and creeds have declared the obligation to observe the first day of the week as the sabbath. Such decrees have never changed the sabbath to the Lord's day. The sabbath could not be changed. An entirely different day has been established by God Himself. This new day belongs to the transcendent realities of the new creation which was brought into existence through the resurrection of Christ. The Lord's day is different from the sabbath in every consideration but one, namely, like the Jewish sabbath, it is a reservation of one particular day in seven.

Fifth. *That the Lord's Day Should be Called the Christian Sabbath.*

The practice of speaking of the Lord's day as the Christian sabbath is wholly without Scriptural warrant, and is no doubt more often the result of careless habit, or lack of due consideration of the Bible teachings, than of unbelief.

Sixth. *The Practice of Adopting Rules from the Jewish Sabbath Law to Supplement the Precious Absence of Rules for the Lord's Day.*

This blasting error should be judged without mercy, for it, in effect, drives every grace-aspect of the Lord's day from the field, and induces one "to tempt God" (Cf Acts 15:10). The toleration of this error not only reveals a total misconception of the glories of grace, but it darkens counsel, and complicates the saving Gospel of Christ.

Seventh. *That the Universal Observance of a Sabbath, or Lord's Day, Should be Required by Legislation of a Town, a State, or a Nation.*

This teaching, likewise, is foreign to Scripture. Let those who are pursuing this idea pause to consider whether their energy might not be employed in a manner which is more pleasing to Christ by heeding His last command to go into all the world and preach the Gospel, rather than to attempt to compel unwilling, Christ-rejecting hearts into a mere religious formality which only develops self-righteous Pharisees who are as surely doomed without Christ as though they had never heard of a holy day.

There is probably no word of Scripture which more clearly defines the essential fact concerning the Christian than the phrase, *"In Christ,"* and as the Christian is the most important fact of all creation, there has never been a word uttered which was so far-reaching in its implication, or which is fraught with greater meaning to humanity than the phrase, *"In Christ."* This phrase, with its equivalents, "In Christ Jesus," "In Him," "In the Beloved," "By Him," "Through Him," and "With Him," appears in the grace teachings of the New Testament no less than 130 times. This most unusual emphasis upon one particular truth is arresting, and its import must not be slighted. Over against the emphasis which is given to this truth in the teachings of grace, is the corresponding fact that there is no hint of a possible position *in Christ* in any teaching of the law or of the kingdom. The believer's present position in Christ was not seen even in type or prophecy. In the ages past it was a secret hid in the mind and heart of God. He who *hath* blessed us with all spiritual blessings in Christ, "hath chosen us in him before the foundation of the world, that we should be holy and without

301

blame before him in love: having predestinated us
unto the adoption of children by Jesus Christ to himself, according to the good pleasure of his will, to the
praise of the glory of his grace, wherein he hath made
us accepted in the beloved. In whom we have redemption through his blood, the forgiveness of sins,
according to the riches of his grace; wherein he hath
abounded toward us in all wisdom and prudence;
having made known unto us the mystery [sacred
secret] of his will, according to his good pleasure
which he hath purposed in himself: that in the dispensation of the fulness of time he might gather together in one all things in Christ, both which are in
heaven, and which are on earth; even in him: in whom
also we have obtained an inheritance, being predestinated according to the purpose of him who worketh
all things after the counsel of his own will: that we
should be to the praise of his glory, who first trusted
in Christ.''

Who can comprehend the full scope of these eternal
wonders? Knowing the limitation of the human
heart, at this point the Apostle breaks forth into
prayer: ''Wherefore I also, after I heard of your
faith in the Lord Jesus, and love unto all the saints,
cease not to give thanks for you, making mention of
you in my prayers; that the God of our Lord Jesus
Christ, the Father of glory, may give unto you the
spirit of wisdom and revelation in the knowledge of
him: the eyes of your understanding [heart] being
enlightened; that ye may know what is the hope of
his calling, and what the riches of the glory of his inheritance in the saints.''

Having thus prayed that the Christian may *know*

by divine illumination the hope of his calling and the riches of the glory of the inheritance which God now has in the saints, he continues to pray that they may also know by the same divine revelation, "the exceeding greatness of his power to us-ward who believe, according to the working of his mighty power, which he wrought in Christ, when he raised him from the dead, and set him at his own right hand in the heavenly places, far above all principality, and power, and might, and dominion, and every name that is named, not only in this world, but also in that which is to come: and hath put all things under his feet, and gave him to be head over all things to the church, which is his body, the fulness of him that filleth all in all" (Eph. 1:2-23).

Growing out of this glorious relationship *in Christ*, is a most natural responsibility to walk worthy of the calling; but the issues of a daily life and the character of the conduct which should enter into it, though important in their place, are lost and forgotten in the blaze of the eternal glory of that unchangeable grace which has brought the believer into the new creation *in Christ Jesus*.

To be *in Christ* is to be in the sphere of His own infinite Person, power, and glory. He surrounds, He protects, He separates from all else, and He indwells the one *in Him*. He also supplies in Himself *all* that a soul will ever need in time or eternity.

The union which is formed *in Christ* is deeper than any relationship the human mind has ever conceived. In His priestly prayer, in which He had advanced onto resurrection ground, and where He contemplated the glory of His finished work as having been already accomplished (Cf John 17:11), Christ spoke of three unities within the sphere of one relationship: (1) The unity within the Persons of the Blessed Trinity, (2) the unity between the Persons of the Trinity and all believers, and (3) the unity between the believers themselves, since they are *in Him*. We read: "Neither pray I for these alone, but for them also which shall believe on me through their word; that they all may be one; as thou, Father, art in me, and I in thee, that they also may be one in us. . . . I in them, and thou in me, that they may be made perfect in one" (John 17:20-23). Who can fathom the depths of the revelation that the believer is related to Christ on the very plane of that oneness which exists between the Father and the Son?

Again, Christ likens the union which exists between Himself and the believer to the vital, organic relation that exists between the vine and its living branch. The branch is *in* the vine and the life of the vine is *in* the branch; but the branch possesses no independent life in itself. It cannot exist apart from the vine. The human child may outgrow dependence upon its parents and, in turn, support and sustain them; but the branch can never become independent of the vine. In like manner, the fruit and every manifestation of life in the branch is due to the ceaseless inflow of the vitality of the vine. The fruit is as much the fruit of the vine as it is the fruit of the branch (Cf John 15:5; Rom. 7:4; Gal. 5:22, 23). Thus it is with the one who is *in Christ*.

Considering the same fact of unity, the Apostle Paul likens Christ to the head and the believers to members in a body. This figure illustrates the same vital, dependent relationship. The member in the body partakes of the merit and honor of the head, and the life and power of the head is imparted to the member. So perfect is this unity between the Head and the members of the body, that it is probable that Christ will never be seen in glory apart from His body, and the body will never be seen apart from Him (Cf 1 Cor. 12:12).

From these illustrative Scriptures it will be observed that the unity between Christ and the believer is two-fold: The believer is *in Christ*, and Christ is *in* the believer. The believer is *in Christ* as to positions, possessions, safe-keeping, and association; and Christ is *in* the believer giving life, character and dynamic for conduct.

It has already been pointed out that the upper-room conversation, recorded in John, chapters 13 to 16, presents the grace teachings of Christ, and is the germ of all the truth that is found in the Epistles, which, in turn, contain the revelation of the essential fact of the new creation and the resulting obligation as to daily life. The doctrinal truth of the Epistles, which is the doctrinal truth of grace, is subject to the same two-fold division—what the saved one is *in Christ*, and the character and power of the daily life that will be experienced when the victorious energy of the indwelling Christ is imparted.

At one point in the midst of the upper-room discourse, Christ compressed the whole doctrinal structure of grace into one brief phrase. This phrase is notable because it is the key to all the facts and relationships under grace, and because of its simplicity and brevity of language:

"Ye in me, and I in you" (John 14:20).

These two aspects of the truth under grace will be considered separately. (1) "Ye in me," (2) "I in you."

1. "Ye In Me."

Every child of God is vitally united to Christ. He is placed *in Christ* by the baptism with the Spirit, which ministry of the Spirit is not only a part of salvation and therefore already accomplished for all who are saved, but it is distinctly said to be a ministry that is wrought for *all* who believe on Christ. The Scriptures state: "For by one Spirit are we all baptized into one body, whether we be Jews or Gentiles, whether we be bond or free; and have been all made to drink into one Spirit" (1 Cor. 12:13). This is the one passage in the Word of God which reveals the precise meaning and objective of the baptism with the Spirit. Since its meaning is clear, there is no excuse for the prevalent errors connected with this truth. Being accomplished for *"all,"* the baptism with the Spirit includes the one who has just been saved. Thus the *time* of its accomplishment is revealed. It is, of necessity, synchronous with salvation itself, and therefore a part of it. Likewise, the same passage presents the divine objective which is accomplished by the Spirit's baptism. It is "into one body," and that believers may be "made to drink into one Spirit." There was a time when the individual was not *in Christ,* which is the present estate of all who are unsaved. There follows a time when the individual, being saved, is *in*

Christ. This great change consists in the fact that he has been placed in that vital organic union with Christ by the baptism with the Spirit. By the Spirit he has been baptized into the very body of Christ, and this ministry of the Spirit, likewise, unites all who are saved into a unity of their own; for they are "made to drink into one Spirit."

There is no other work of God for the individual which seems to accomplish so much as the baptism with the Spirit; for by it the living union with Christ is established forever, and by virtue of that union the believer has entered the sphere of all heavenly *positions* and all eternal *possessions* which in grace are provided for him *in Christ*. To the Christian, Christ has become, in the divine reckoning, the sphere of his being, and this reckoning contemplates all that the Christian *is* and all that he *does*. Certain aspects of this truth, among many, are to be noted:

First, *Christ is the Sphere of the Believer's Positions.*

A sphere is that which surrounds an object on every side and may even penetrate that object. To be within a sphere is to partake of all that it is and all that it imparts. Thus the bird is in the air and the air is in the bird; the fish is in the water and the water is in the fish; the iron is in the fire and the fire is in the iron. Likewise, in the spiritual realm, Christ is the sphere of the believer's position. He encompasses, surrounds, encloses, and indwells the believer. The believer is *in Christ,* and Christ is *in the believer.* Through the baptism with the

Spirit, the Christian has become as much an organic part of Christ as the branch is a part of the vine, or the member is a part of the body. Being thus conjoined to Christ, the Father sees the saved one only *in Christ,* or as a living part of His own Son, and loves him as He loves His Son (Eph. 1:6; John 17:23).

As an accompanying result of this vital union *in Christ* certain facts of relationship are created which are the believer's new positions *in Christ,* and are the consequence of the work of God in grace. To present fully *all* the new positions into which the Christian is brought *in Christ,* would necessitate an analysis of all the great doctrinal portions of the Epistles. By way of illustration, a brief selection from these positions is here presented.[1] Of the saved one it is said that he is:

Elect and *called* of God (1 Thes. 1:4; 5:24).

Redeemed by God through the blood of His Son (Col. 1:14).

Reconciled to God by the death of His Son (2 Cor. 5:19).

Sheltered eternally under the propitiation made in the blood of Christ (1 John 2:2).

Forgiven all trespasses, past, present, and future (Col. 2:13).

Condemned no more forever (Rom. 8:1).

Justified freely by His grace (Rom. 3:24).

Sanctified positionally, or *set apart* unto God *in Christ* (1 Cor. 1:30).

Perfected for ever (Heb. 10:14).

[1] A more complete analysis of the believer's positions will be found in the author's book *Salvation.*

Made meet to be a partaker of the inheritance of the saints in light (Col. 1:12).

Made accepted in the Beloved (Eph. 1:6).

Made the righteousness of God in Him (2 Cor. 5:21).

Made nigh to God in Christ Jesus (Eph. 2:13).

A child and *son* of God (John 1:12; 1 John 3:3).

Free from the law and *dead* to the law (Rom. 7:4, 6).

Delivered from the power of darkness (Col. 1:13).

Translated into the kingdom of God's dear Son (Col. 1:13).

Founded on the Rock Christ Jesus (1 Cor. 3:11).

God's gift to Christ (John 17:11, 12, 20; 10:29).

Circumcised in Christ (Col. 2:11).

An holy priest, chosen and peculiar (1 Pet. 2:5, 9).

Object of divine love, grace, power, faithfulness, peace, consolation (Eph. 2:4, 8; 1:9; Heb. 13:5; Col. 3:15; 2 Thes. 2:16).

Object of Christ's intercession (Heb. 7:25).

His inheritance (Eph. 1:18).

Seated in the heavenly in Christ (Eph. 2:6).

A citizen of heaven (Phil. 3:20 R. V.).

Of the family and *household* of God (Eph. 2:19; 3:15).

Light in the Lord (Eph. 5:8).

In God, in Christ, and *in the Spirit* (1 Thes. 1:1; John 14:20; Rom. 8:9).

Possessed with the *first fruits* of the Spirit. Born (John 3:6), baptized (1 Cor. 12:13), indwelt (1 Cor. 6:19), and sealed (Eph. 4:30).

Glorified (Rom. 8:30).

Complete in Him (Col, 2:10).

Possessing every spiritual blessing (Eph. 1:3).

Of these and all other positions which are the present possession of the child of God through his vital union with Christ, it may be said that they are:

1. *Invisible.*

The believer's positions, like all things related to the Spirit, are invisible; but as is true of spiritual things, they are more real and abiding than visible things. "For the things which are seen are temporal; but the things which are not seen are eternal" (2 Cor. 4:18), and, "Whom having not seen, ye love" (1 Pet. 1:8. Cf 1 Tim. 1:17; 6:16; Heb. 11:27; 1 John 4:12). Even the present revelation by the Spirit is such as "Eye hath not seen."

2. *Unexperienced.*

The positions *in Christ* are never subject to human experience. They produce no sensation by which they may be identified. They are taken by faith, and joyous appreciation may come as a result of believing.

3. *Apprehended by faith.*

Faith is the new and effectual faculty of the spiritual life. By it what is said in the Word of God is received as true. Such apprehension is, at best, only partial; but, notwithstanding the limitations of human knowledge, the positions are all perfect through Christ. Of this perfection, "the half has never been told."

4. *Contested.*

Scripture presents the warfare of Satan as being waged in the sphere of "the heavenly." There is abundant assurance that Satan's power can never spoil any aspect of the believer's actual positions *in Christ;* but Satan is able, except as the believer lays hold by faith of the power of God, to hinder the life of blessing which should flow out of that vital union with Christ.

5. *Unmerited.*

Human merit, as in all the operations of grace, is excluded from the divine reckoning concerning these positions *in Christ.* They rest on the perfect merit of Christ. This is the very heart of the new standing before God. "In Christ Jesus ye who sometimes were far off are made nigh by the blood of Christ" (Eph. 2:13).

6. *Unchangeable.*

The standing and position of the child of God *in Christ* cannot be increased or decreased. It abides as He is, "the same yesterday, and to day, and for ever" (Heb. 13:8).

7. *Eternal.*

Finally, since these positions *in Christ* are related to, and depend only on Christ, they will endure as long as He endures: "Wherefore he is able also to save them to the uttermost [without end] that come unto God by him" (Heb. 7:25).

These great positions and relationships *in Christ* are the result of the unrestrained outflow of the exceeding grace of God. They, therefore, do not appear in any teaching of the law of Moses or of the kingdom. These positions could not be gained by law-works or by any human merit. Correspondingly, the manner of life which they propose cannot be lived according to the law in the energy of the flesh. The whole system of grace is both inter-related and complete within itself and cannot yield to the principle of the law at any point whatsoever.

Second, *Christ is the Sphere of the Believer's Possessions.*

Again the enumeration must be partial:

1. *A new standing in Christ.*

The new standing *in Christ* includes *all* the positions under grace, a portion of which have just been enumerated. These positions are "the riches of grace in Christ Jesus." The possession for a day even of one of these glories of grace would be well worth the trials and struggles of a lifetime. But in contrast to such a valuation, they are *all* gained, and *all* retained without struggle or trial; they are God's *gift* in grace. Such wealth cannot be comprehended by the unaided human mind. The Apostle prayed: "The eyes of your understanding [heart] being enlightened; that ye may know what is the hope of his calling, and what the riches of the glory of his inheritance in the saints" (Eph. 1:18); "And to know the love of Christ, which passeth knowledge, that ye might be filled with all the fulness of God" (Eph. 3:19); "That ye might be filled with the knowledge of his will in all wisdom and spiritual understanding" (Col. 1:9). There are no limits to be placed on the possibility of the illumination of the mind by the Spirit.

2. *A new life in Christ.*

The Scriptures lay great emphasis upon the fact that the Christian possesses a new life from God. That life is *imparted.* Christ said: "I am come that they might have life, and that they might have it more abundantly" (John 10:10). The satanic counterfeit of this fundamental truth is the teaching that the new life consists in a new *manner* of life,— a new *standard* or *ideal.* A new life imparted will naturally result in a new manner of life; but no manner of life, old or new, constitutes the means through which the imparted life is gained. "The gift of God is eternal life through Jesus Christ our Lord" (Rom. 6:23); and, "I give unto them eternal life; and they shall never perish" (John 10:28). Life from God is bestowed through a new birth, results in sonship, and secures the Fatherhood of God.

3. *The new presence and power of the Spirit.*

It is stated in Rom. 5:5 that "the Spirit is given unto us." This is true of every person who is saved. The Spirit is the birth-right in the new life. By Him alone can the character and service that belongs to the normal daily life of the Christian be realized. The Spirit is the "All-Sufficient One." Every victory in the new life is gained by His strength, and every reward in glory will be won only as a result of His enabling power.

4. *A new inheritance.*

The inheritance of the old creation in Adam was beyond description in its horror. It was to be "without Christ . . . having no hope, and without God in the world" (Eph. 2:12). With Christ, God hath freely given us all things else (Rom. 8:32). The Christian's inheritance is nothing short of "all things"; for he is an heir of God, and a joint heir with Christ (Rom. 8:17). Peter writes: "Blessed be the God and Father of our Lord Jesus Christ, which according to his abundant mercy hath begotten us again unto a lively hope by the resurrection of Jesus Christ from the dead, to an inheritance incorruptible, and undefiled, and that fadeth not away, reserved in heaven for you" (1 Pet. 1:3, 4). The present blessings of the presence and power of the Spirit are but an "earnest of our inheritance" (Eph. 1:14. Cf Acts 20:32; 26:18; Col. 1:12; Heb. 9:15). This inheritance is a present possession which is sealed to the child of God under grace. In addition to the "all things" of Christ, it includes the "all things of the Father" (John 16:12-15), and these are to be revealed to the heart *now* by the Spirit (1 Cor. 2:9, 10); "The living God, who giveth us richly all things to enjoy" (1 Tim. 6:17); "Therefore let no man glory in men. For all things are yours; whether Paul, or Apollos, or Cephas, or the world, or life, or death, or things present, or things to come; all are yours; and ye are Christ's; and Christ is God's" (1 Cor. 3:21-23).

5. *A new enemy.*

To be *in Christ* is to experience the same enmity and opposition from Satan which he entertains toward Christ. There is no enmity on Satan's part toward the unsaved. They form a part of his world-system and are said to be under his power (Eph. 2:2; Col. 1:13; 1 John 5:19, R. V.; 2 Cor 4:3, 4). Satan's enmity is against God and against the people of God because God, by His divine nature, is in them, and they are *in Christ*. We read: "Finally, be strong in the Lord, and the strength of his might. Put on the whole armour of God, that ye may be able to stand against the wiles of the devil. For our wrestling is not against flesh and blood, but against the principalities, against the powers, against the world-rulers of this darkness, against the spiritual hosts of wickedness in the heavenly places" (Eph. 6:10-12. R. V.).

6. *Access to God.*

A mediator is required between God and man since God is holy and man is unholy. Job, who lived many centuries before Moses, gave utterance to his own sense of need of a mediator. Speaking of God he said: "For he is not a man, as I am, that I should answer him, and we should come together in judgment. Neither is there any daysman betwixt us, that might lay his hand upon us both" (Job. 9:32, 33). There could be none to mediate between God and man unless God Himself should provide. This He did in the Person of His Son. It is written: "Now a mediator is not a mediator of one, but God

is one" (Gal. 3:20). A mediator must stand between two parties; for there is no occasion that he
mediate for one. The teaching of the Scriptures is
that God mediated His own case. That is to say,
He stood between Himself and sinful man. "God
was in Christ, reconciling the world unto himself,
not imputing their trespasses unto them" (2 Cor.
5:19). God undertook through the death of His
Son to protect the sacredness of His own holy standards and law which had been outraged by sinful man,
and at the same time to secure the welfare of the
offender. This is the work of a mediator. Every
demand of His holiness was met in Christ who, as
Substitute, bore the judgment which God in righteousness must impose, and every interest of the sinner was provided for in the marvels of saving grace
which were set free through the death and resurrection of Christ. Christ has thus become the one and
only ground of meeting between God and man. "He
is the propitiation for our sins: and not for ours
only, but also for the sins of the whole world" (1
John 2:2).

The present wide-spread tendency to slight the
fact of the holy demands of God against sin and to
assume that the sinner is free to come to God on
the basis of divine goodness and mercy, is not only
a gross misrepresentation of the truth of God's
Word, it is a satanic device to keep men from the
salvation that is in Christ. The goodness and mercy
of God can never be questioned, but that goodness
and mercy has been exercised to the last degree of
divine ability in the provision of a Mediator who is
mighty to save. Christ said: "I am the light,"

"I am the door," "I am the way, the truth, and the life: no man cometh unto the Father, but by me." There is, therefore, no approach to God for saint or sinner other than through the Mediator whom God has provided. All the types of the Old Testament which forshadowed the work of Christ for man were equally clear on this great truth. As the shed-blood of the animal sacrifices typified the efficacious blood of Christ, no individual of the Old Testament dispensation was permitted to come into the presence of God apart from the shedding and sprinkling of blood. Christ is the Mediator of a new and better covenant. His shed-blood is the antitype of all that was required in the sacrifices of the Old Testament; but in the present relation between God and man, the truth takes on an added reality and intensity which is beyond estimation. No man is now free to thrust himself into the presence of God simply because he wills to do so. Every door is closed but One. If God does not destroy the offender as He did in the old dispensation, it is not because the offense is any less worthy of death; it is because of His present attitude of longsuffering through grace. So much the more is man now obligated to respect the unchangeable truth that Christ is the only way to God. "For there is one God, and one mediator between God and men, the man Christ Jesus" (1 Tim. 2: 5). This mediation of the Son of God is seen in certain aspects:

a. *Access into the grace of God.*

It is through Christ and Him alone that we have access into the grace of God. "By whom also we

have access into this grace" (Rom. 5:2). This is
as true for the saved as it is for the unsaved. The
unsaved are saved only through the grace which is in
Christ Jesus. Likewise, the saved are kept and stand
only through Christ, and all their relationship to
God is through Christ alone.

b. *Access into fellowship with God.*

All communion and fellowship with God is on the
basis alone of the Person and work of Christ. As
the high priest of the old order went into the holy
of holies once a year and communed with God, likewise, the priest of the new order—the child of God—
is free to enter the presence of God and there to
abide. But as the priest of the old order was received before God only because he was under the
sprinkled blood, with the same divine discrimination,
the priest of the new order is received only because
he is under the precious blood of Christ. God receives His children into fellowship on the sole basis
of the efficacious blood of Christ whether they understand this fact or not. How vitally important it is,
however, that they should understand and give continual heart-acknowledgment of all that Christ is to
them! "Having therefore, brethren, boldness to
enter into the holiest by the blood of Jesus, by a new
and living way, which he hath consecrated for us,
through the veil, that is to say, his flesh; and having
an high priest over the house of God; let us draw
near with a true heart in full assurance of faith,
having our hearts sprinkled from an evil conscience,

and our bodies washed with pure water" (Heb. 10:19-22).

c. *Access to God in prayer.*

Christ is the only access to God in prayer. How misleading is the supposition that any one can reach the ear of God who will simply speak to Him! Apart from the Mediator Christ Jesus, there is no access to God in prayer and there can be no real prayer. The new basis of prayer in the present relationship to God is that, prayer is to be made in the Name of Christ. This is revealed by Christ in the upper room and is a part of His unfolding of the glories of grace. "If ye shall ask anything in my name, I will do it"; "And in that day ye shall ask me nothing. Verily, verily, I say unto you, Whatsoever ye shall ask the Father in my name, he will give it you. Hitherto have ye asked nothing in my name: ask, and ye shall receive, that your joy may be full" (John 14:14; 16:23, 24). God receives all His children when they pray; but He receives them in Christ, and their prayer is effectual and prevailing only as it is in the Name that is above every name, and on the ground of the blood that has been shed. How important, again, that the saved one understand this truth and that he come to God with full heart-acknowledgment of the Mediator—Christ!

The unsaved have no access to God in prayer. "But," it is often asked, "how then can they be saved, if they cannot ask God to save them?" The answer is simple: No person is ever saved because he asks God to do it. He is saved through grace only when he *believes*. God is offering salvation to men. He does not need to be implored or moved in their behalf. He has been moved to give His Son to die. What more could He do? This marvelous gift of His grace is for all who will *believe*.

7. *The Word of God.*

The written Word of God is one of the priceless possessions of the child of God *in Christ*. It is the unfolding of all the revelation concerning the majesty and grace of the Father, the salvation and glory that is in the Son, and the power and blessing that is in the Spirit, the facts about heaven and earth, about sin and salvation, about angels and Satan, about life and death, and all that is future and all that is past. "All scripture is given by inspiration of God, and is profitable for doctrine, for reproof, for correction, for instruction in righteousness: that the man of God may be perfect, thoroughly furnished unto all good works" (2 Tim. 3:16); "Thy word is a lamp unto my feet, and a light unto my path" (Ps. 119:105).

The Word of God is as a title deed to all that the Christian possesses *in Christ*. It is a covenant guaranty from God which is sealed in heaven. Assurance of the divine grace and blessing is never left to depend on the changeable feelings, or vain misunderstanding and imaginations of the human heart. "It is written." "These things have I written unto you that believe on the name of the Son of God; that ye may know that ye have eternal life, and that ye may believe on the name of the Son of God" (1 John 5:13).

Third. *Christ, the Sphere of the Believer's Safe-Keeping.*

As the First Adam transmitted what he was to those who were born after the flesh, so the Last Adam transmits what He is to those who are born after the Spirit. The Christian's standing is *in Christ,* and there will be no fall in the Last Adam. He is as secure as God can make him secure, for the preservation of the believer is not conditioned by the thought which he has about the matter; it is according to the purpose of God. As has been stated, all the eternal purposes of infinite grace are involved in the issue of the safe-keeping of each one who is *in Christ.* In like manner, the security of the Christian is not merely the preservation of the possessions which together total his own inheritance; the believer is a part of the divine inheritance. God has an inheritance in the Christian (Eph. 1:18). The real question becomes one, therefore, as to whether God is *able* to keep that which is His inheritance and whether He is *disposed* to keep. Against His power nothing can prevail, and He has paid the price—the blood of His own Son—to redeem this possession to Himself. Since He is free through the cross to do so, and His love is unending, it is inconceivable that He will not keep the one He has saved. He has sealed His inheritance unto the day of redemption.

An illustration of the safe-keeping which results from being *in Christ,* is seen in the panoply which

God has provided under which the believer may "stand" against the strategies and warfare of Satan. "Wherefore take unto you the whole armour of God, that ye may be able to withstand in the evil day, and having done all, to stand. Stand therefore, having your loins girt about with truth, and having on the breastplate of righteousness; and your feet shod with the preparation of the gospel of peace; above all, taking the shield of faith, wherewith ye shall be able to quench all the fiery darts of the wicked. And take the helmet of salvation, and the sword of the Spirit, which is the word of God" (Eph. 6:13-17).

The fact that Christ is the armour is a hidden beauty in this passage. He is the Truth, our Righteousness, our Peace, our Faith, our Salvation, and the Word of God. Christ encompasses the believer and insulates him from the power of every foe.

Fourth. *Christ, the Sphere of the Believer's Association.*

The believer's association extends to every relationship he sustains, and the character of these associations is molded in conformity to his position *in Christ.* Some of these relationships are:

1. *With God the Father.*

Through the death of Christ, and through the regenerating work of the Spirit, an individual who believes is made a son of God by receiving the divine nature and is made to stand before God forgiven, righteous, and justified forever. He has entered the family and household of God, and the Father's tender care, which is all that infinite grace can provide, is over him. The unsaved do not know God; He is not in all their thoughts. They may know *about* God; but this is far short of *knowing* God. Such knowledge is only gained by the personal introduction to the Father by the Son: "Neither knoweth any man the Father, save the Son, and he to whomsoever the Son will reveal him" (Mt. 11:27). And to *know* the Father signifies the possession of eternal life: "And this is life eternal, that they might know thee the only true God, and Jesus Christ, whom thou hast sent" (John 17:3).

God was not usually known as *Father* under the past dispensation. He was honored and trusted as a "covenant-keeping God." The Psalmist wrote: "Like as a father pitieth his children, so the LORD pitieth them that fear him" (Ps. 103:13).

2. *With Christ the Son.*

The extent of this relationship is limitless since it contains all that enters into the new sphere *in Christ.* It includes all that He is as Saviour and Lord; all that He is in partnership with the believer in service, in suffering, and in betrothal; and all that He is in the Christian's fellowship, "and truly our fellowship is with the Father, and with his Son Jesus Christ" (1 John 1:3). Christ is the object of ceaseless devotion and praise.

3. *With the Spirit of God.*

At this point, association is nothing less than identification itself in all matters of life, character, and service; for the believer is appointed to live only by the power of the indwelling Spirit. The association with the Spirit is immediate and intimate because He indwells every believer. The presence of the Spirit is not disclosed through human emotions and feelings; it is rather detected by the things which He does.

4. *With Satan and his emissaries.*

As has been stated, the believer is brought, through his new position *in Christ,* into a sphere wherein Satan's enmity is directed against him as it is directed against God. "For our wrestling is not against flesh and blood, but against the principalities, against the powers, against the world-rulers of this darkness, against the spiritual host of wickedness in the heavenly places" (Eph. 6:12. R. V.). The victory is provided only through the indwelling Spirit: Because greater is he that is in you, than he that is in the world" (1 John 4:4).

5. *With the angels.*

The angels are messengers or ministering spirits "sent forth to minister for them who shall be heirs of salvation" (Heb. 1:14). While their care attends the child of God, it has not pleased God to give the Christian fellowship with them. Their ministry as messengers is revealed throughout the Word of God.

6. *With the world.*

The Christian is not of this world. He has been translated into the kingdom of Christ. He is a citizen of heaven, and his only relation to this world is that of an ambassador and witness. He is in the enemy's land; for Satan is "the god of this world." The kingdoms of this world are given unto Satan under the permission and purpose of God (Lk. 4: 6). The Christian is related to the world and all that is in the world only as he is related to it *through Christ.* This relationship is three-fold:

a. *To the world system.*

This is the whole sphere of human life with its institutions, ideals, and projects. Concerning this world-system the believer is thus warned: "Love not the world, neither the things that are in the world. If any man love the world, the love of the Father is not in him. For all that is in the world, the lust of the flesh, and the lust of the eyes, and the pride of life, is not of the Father, but is of the world. And the world passeth away, and the lust thereof: but he that doeth the will of God abideth for ever" (1 John 2: 15-17); "And have no fellowship with the unfruitful works of darkness, but rather reprove them" (Eph. 5: 11); "Walk in wisdom toward them that are without, redeeming the time. Let your speech be always with grace, seasoned with salt, that ye may know how ye ought to answer every man" (Col. 4: 5, 6).

b. *To human governments.*

According to the Bible, these are under the direct authority of the Gentiles. The present is the times of the Gentiles (Lk. 21: 24). Human government is of God only to the extent of His permissive will and the realization of His purpose; but the citizen of

heaven is instructed to be in subjection to governments: "Let every soul be subject unto the higher
powers. For there is no power but of God: the
powers that be are ordained of God. Whosoever
therefore resisteth the power, resisteth the ordinance
of God: and they that resist shall receive to themselves damnation [judgment]. For rulers are not a
terror to good works, but to the evil. Wilt thou
then not be afraid of the power? do that which is
good, and thou shalt have praise of the same: for
he is the minister of God to thee for good. But if
thou do that which is evil, be afraid; for he beareth
not the sword in vain: for he is the minister of God,
a revenger to execute wrath upon him that doeth
evil. Wherefore ye must needs be subject, not only
for wrath, but also for conscience sake. For for this
cause pay ye tribute also: for they are God's ministers, attending continually upon this very thing.
Render therefore to all their dues: tribute to whom
tribute is due; custom to whom custom; fear to whom
fear; honour to whom honour" (Rom. 13: 1-7);
"Submit yourselves to every ordinance of man for
the Lord's sake: whether it be to the king, as
supreme; or unto governors, as unto them that are
sent by him for the punishment of evildoers, and
for the praise of them that do well. For so is the
will of God, that with well doing ye may put to
silence the ignorance of foolish men: as free, and not
using your liberty for a cloak of maliciousness, but
as the servants of God. Honour all men. Love the
brotherhood. Fear God. Honour the king" (1 Pet.
2: 13-17).

c. *To the unsaved individual.*

The consistent attitude of the Christian is the same as that of his Lord who died for lost men. As He is, so are we, and therefore we are to manifest His spirit in this world.

Of his own attitude toward lost men, the Apostle Paul wrote: "For the love of Christ constraineth us; because we thus judge, that if one died for all, then were all dead [all died in the Substitute] . . . Wherefore henceforth know we no man after the flesh: yea, though we have known Christ after the flesh, yet now henceforth know we him no more" (2 Cor. 5: 14-16). Having beheld Christ as God's Lamb which taketh away the sin of the world, and the One who died for *all,* and in whose death *all* have partaken, the Apostle says: "Henceforth know we no man after the flesh." The usual distinctions among men, of Jew and Gentile, rich and poor, bond and free, are submerged in the overwhelming estimation of that which is accomplished for all men through the death of Christ. The Apostle now recognizes them only as men for whom Christ has died. This conception of the estate of the unsaved is the normal one for all Christians, and it leads on to a reasonable service for Christ in soul-winning.

7. *With the whole body of Christ.*

The Epistles of the New Testament disclose the basis for a fellowship and kinship within the company of the redeemed which exists in no other association of people in this world, and this union calls for a corresponding manner of conduct from the

Christian toward fellow-believers. This relationship is seven-fold:

a. *A Christian's relation to other Christians in general.*

Love is revealed as the underlying principle of this relationship. It is embodied in the first commandment of Christ in the grace teachings of the upper room: "A new commandment I give unto you, That ye love one another; as I have loved you, that ye also love one another. By this shall all men know that ye are my disciples, if ye have love one to another" (John 13:34, 35). This same truth is set forth in many passages. "We know that we have passed from death unto life, because we love the brethren" (1 John 3:14); "And whether one member suffer, all the members suffer with it; or one member be honoured, all the members rejoice with it" (1 Cor. 12:26); "And walk in love, as Christ also hath loved us" (Eph. 5:2); "Beloved, let us love one another: for love is of God"; "Beloved, if God so loved us, we ought also to love one another" (1 John 4:7, 11); "Let brotherly love continue" (Heb. 13:1); "Let love be without dissimulation." This is one of the great passages on Christian love and care one for another. The whole context should be read (Rom. 12:9-16). "Put on therefore, as the elect of God, holy and beloved, bowels of mercies, kindness, humbleness of mind, meekness, longsuffering; forbearing one another, and forgiving one another, if any man have a quarrel against any: even as Christ forgave you, so also do ye" (Col. 3:12, 13). "Finally, be ye all of one mind, having compassion one of another, love as brethren, be pitiful, be courteous: not rendering evil for evil, or railing for railing: but contrariwise blessing; knowing that ye are thereunto called, that ye should inherit a blessing" (1 Pet. 3: 8, 9); "And above all things have fervent charity among yourselves: for charity shall cover the multitude of sins. Use hospitality one to another without grudging" (1 Pet. 4: 8, 9).

The Christian is called upon to *recognize the vital union* into which he has been brought by the baptism with the spirit: "I therefore, the prisoner of the Lord, beseech you that ye walk worthy of the vocation wherewith ye are called, with all lowliness and meekness, with longsuffering, forbearing one another in love; endeavoring to keep the unity of the Spirit in the bond of peace" (Eph. 4: 1-3).

Special emphasis is given as well to *Christian kindness*: "Let all bitterness, and wrath, and anger, and clamour, and evil speaking, be put away from you, with all malice: and be ye kind one to another, tenderhearted, forgiving one another, even as God for Christ's sake hath forgiven you" (Eph. 4: 31, 32); "That no man go beyond and defraud his brother in any matter: because that the Lord is the avenger of all such, as we also have forewarned you and testified;" "But as touching brotherly love ye need not that I write unto you: for ye yourselves are taught of God to love one another" (1 Thes. 4: 6, 9); "Wherefore comfort yourselves together, and edify one another, even as also ye do" (1 Thes. 5:11); "Speak not evil one of another, brethren" (Jas. 4: 11).

Christians are to *submit one to another* and in

honor prefer one another: "Submitting yourselves one to another in the fear of God" (Eph. 5:21); "Let nothing be done through strife or vainglory; but in lowliness of mind let each esteem others better than themselves. Look not every man on his own things, but every man also on the things of others" (Phil. 2:3, 4); "Likewise, ye younger, submit yourselves unto the elder. Yea, all of you be subject one to another, and be clothed with humility: for God resisteth the proud, and giveth grace to the humble" (1 Pet. 5:5).

The Christian's gifts are to be especially directed to the need of the children of God: "As we have therefore opportunity, let us do good unto all men, especially unto them who are of the household of faith" (Gal. 6:10); "But whoso hath this world's good, and seeth his brother have need, and shutteth up his bowels of compassion from him, how dwelleth the love of God in him?" (1 John 3:17).

Prayer is to be offered for all saints: "Praying always with all prayer and supplication in the Spirit, and watching thereunto with all perseverance and supplication for all saints" (Eph. 6:18); "Confess your faults one to another, and pray one for another, that ye may be healed" (Jas. 5:16).

b. *A Christian's relation to those who are in authority in the assembly of believers.*

On this important question the Word of God is explicit and comment is unnecessary: "Remember them which have the rule over you, who have spoken unto you the word of God: whose faith follow, considering the end of their conversation" (Heb. 13:7); "Obey

them that have the rule over you, and submit yourselves: for they watch for your souls, as they that
must give account, that they may do it with joy, and
not with grief: for that is unprofitable · for you"
(Heb. 13:17); "And we beseech you, brethren, to
know them which labour among you, and are over
you in the Lord, and admonish you; and to esteem
them very highly for their work's sake. And be at
peace among yourselves" (1 Thes. 5:12, 13). To
this body of truth should be added all of the pastoral
Epistles.

c. *The relation of Christian husbands and wives.*

The grace teaching on this aspect of Christian
relationship is also explicit: "Husbands, love your
wives, even as Christ also loved the church, and gave
himself for it;" "Wives, submit yourselves unto your
own husbands, as unto the Lord" (Eph. 5:22, 25.
Cf Eph. 5:21-33; Col. 3:18, 19; 1 Pet. 3:1-7).

d. *The relation of Christian parents and children.*

"And, ye fathers, provoke not your children to
wrath: but bring them up in the nurture and admon-
ition of the Lord;" "Children, obey your parents
in the Lord: for this is right" (Eph. 6:1, 4. Cf Eph.
6:1-4; Col. 3:20, 21). From this body of revelation
it will be seen that the children of Christian parents
are to be governed as *in the Lord*. One of the conditions which will characterize the last days of this
age will be the disobedience of children (2 Tim. 3:2).

e. *The relation of Christian masters and servants.*

"Servants, obey in all things your masters according to the flesh; not with eyeservice, as menpleasers;

but in singleness of heart, fearing God;" "Masters, give unto your servants that which is just and equal; knowing that ye also have a Master in heaven" (Col. 3:22 to 4:1. Cf Eph. 6:5-9).

f. *A Christian's obligation to an erring brother.*

"Brethren, if a man be overtaken in a fault, ye which are spiritual, restore such an one in the spirit of meekness; considering thyself, lest thou also be tempted" (Gal. 6:1); "Now we exhort you, brethren, warn them that are unruly, comfort the feebleminded, support the weak, be patient toward all men" (1 Thes. 5:14); "Now we command you, brethren, in the name of the Lord Jesus Christ, that ye withdraw yourselves from every brother that walketh disorderly, and not after the tradition which ye received of us"; "For we hear that there are some which walk among you disorderly, working not at all, but are busybodies . . . yet count him not as an enemy, but admonish him as a brother" (2 Thes. 3:6, 11-15).

A sharp distinction must be drawn at this point between a disorderly brother who is a busybody, shirking his honest toil, and careless in matters of Christian conduct, on the one hand, and a sincere believer who may disagree with another on a matter of interpretation, on the other hand. Endless confusion and disgraceful contention has followed the exercise of unwarranted freedom among sincere believers in separating from each other over minor questions of doctrine. Should one fail to hold the true doctrine of Christ (2 John 9-11), that one can have no rightful place in a Christian communion;

but men have divided over secondary issues and have gone so far as to *exclude* earnest Christians from their fellowship with whom perchance they disagree in a minor question of doctrine. Such separation is unscriptural, a violation of the priceless unity of the Spirit, and foreign to the order of grace. There is Scripture teaching concerning Christian discipline, but it does not necessarilly impose a penalty of separation. The brother who may have been overtaken in a fault is to be *restored,* and only by one who is himself *spiritual.* This he must do in the spirit of meekness considering his own utter weakness apart from the enabling power of God. No other may undertake this important service. If the erring brother proves to be persistent in his fault, it is required that he be debarred from the fellowship of believers until he has seen the error of his way. Equally sincere brethren must not break fellowship, however, over minor issues. Of those who are thus disposed, the Apostle writes: "Now I beseech you, brethren, mark them which cause divisions and offences contrary to the doctrine which ye have learned; and avoid them. For they that are such serve not our Lord Jesus Christ, but their own belly; and by good words and fair speeches deceive the hearts of the simple" (Rom. 16:17, 18).

g. *A Christian's obligations to a weak brother.*

The tender conscience of a weak brother must be considered. This important principle applies to very many questions of the day. In the Apostles' time there was a grave question concerning the eating of meat which had been offered to idols and was after-

wards placed in the public market for sale. There
were those who had only recently been saved and
rescued from the grip of the power of idol worship.
There were others who were so deeply prejudiced
by their former experiences with idols that, while
saved and free, they were not willing even to touch
anything connected with an idol. It would be
natural to say that the first class should know better
than to be drawn back to idols, and that the second
class should be made to give up their prejudice; but
this is not according to the "law of love." It is
written: "Him that is weak in the faith receive ye,
but not to doubtful disputations. For one believeth
that he may eat all things: another, who is weak,
eateth herbs. Let not him that eateth despise him
that eateth not; and let not him which eateth not
judge him that eateth: for God hath received him.
Who art thou that judgest another man's servant?
to his own master he standeth or falleth. Yea, he
shall be holden up: for God is able to make him
stand" (Rom. 14:1-4).

From this passage it is clear that instruction is also
given to the weaker brother to the intent that he shall
not "judge" the Christian who, through years of
Christian training and deeper understanding of the
liberty in grace, is free to do what he himself in his
limitations may not be able to do. There is hardly
a more important exhortation for Christians to-day
than this. The cure is clearly revealed: God reserves
the right to correct and direct the life of His own
child. Much hurtful criticism might be avoided if
Christians would only believe this and trust Him to
do with His own child what He purposes to do. God

is the master before whom alone the servant standeth
or falleth. The passage continues: "But if thy
brother be grieved with thy meat, now walkest thou
not charitably. Destroy not him with thy meat, for
whom Christ died. . . . For meat destroy not the
work of God. All things indeed are pure; but it is
evil for that man who eateth with offense [to his own
convictions]. It is good neither to eat flesh, nor to
drink wine, nor any thing whereby thy brother stum-
bleth, or is offended, or is made weak. Hast thou
faith? have it to thyself before God. Happy is he
that condemneth not himself in that thing which he
alloweth. And he that doubteth is damned [con-
demned] if he eat, because he eateth not of faith: for
whatsoever is not of faith is sin" (Rom. 14: 15-23).
"Bear ye one another's burdens, and so fulfil the law
of Christ" (Gal. 6: 2).

Due regard for the conscience and liberty of others
is two-fold: On the one hand, let the strong be chari-
table toward the weak. On the other hand, let the
weak desist from judgment of the strong. The result
will be a mutual fellowship and an exercise of all the
liberties of grace.

2. "I In You."

The believer's new sphere consists not only in his
place *in Christ* with its positions, possessions, safe-
keeping, and associations; it consists as well, in the
fact that Christ is *in* the believer.

The Scriptures teach that God the Father (Eph.
4: 6), that God the Son (Col. 1: 27), and that God
the Spirit (1 Cor. 6: 19) indwell every child of God.

No doubt the mystery of the unity of the Godhead is involved in this revelation; for it is also said that the Christian has partaken of the divine nature, and this divine nature is not identified as being one only of the three Persons of the Trinity. The divine nature is evidently the indwelling presence of God—Father, Son, and Spirit. There is a body of truth which teaches that God, in the unity of the three Persons, dwells in the heart of the child of God. Likewise there is an even greater body of Scripture which emphasizes the indwelling of the believer by the *individual* Persons of the Godhead. When the full unity of God is in view, it is usually spoken of as the indwelling Christ. As indwelling the Christian, the Spirit of God is once spoken of as "the Spirit of Christ" (Rom. 8:9).

It may be concluded, therefore, that the phrase *I in you* is to be received as referring to the whole divine Person—Father, Son, and Spirit. The result of this indwelling of Christ is three-fold: (1) A new divine life, (2) A new enabling power, and (3) A new "hope of glory."

First. *A New Divine Life.*

The branch is in the vine and the vine by its life and vitality is in the branch. Thus the believer is *in Christ* and Christ is *in* the believer. The new imparted life is *Christ,* and is therefore eternal because He is eternal. When only the question of an unbroken *manifestation* of that new life is under consideration, it is said to depend on *abiding* in Christ as the sole condition. The believer's place, or position, *in Christ* is neither attained, nor maintained, through abiding in Him. That position is instantly wrought by the power of God through grace for every one who believes. Nor is the possession of the divine life, which is the indwelling Christ, secured by abiding in Him; it is the "gift of God." However, the normal manifestation of that life does depend on abiding in Him. Abiding is simply the right adjustment between the Christian and his Lord. "If ye keep my commandments, ye shall abide in my love; even as I have kept my Father's commandments, and abide in his love" (John 15:10). How important, then, it is that the Christian should understand precisely what is included and required in the commandments of Christ! As pointed out before, the commandments of Christ are only His grace teachings; this term being not once employed by Christ before He began in the upper room to unfold the believer's life and walk in grace.

Eternal, divine life, therefore, is Christ indwelling the believer by His Spirit and that life is the present possession of all who believe. The victories, joys, and fruits of that life depend upon abiding in Him which abiding is accomplished only by doing His will.

Second. *A New Enabling Power.*

The theme of the enabling power of God, being one of the most vital in the divine plan of grace, though before mentioned, should at this point be reviewed in its two-fold aspect:

1. *Christian character.*

Under the law relationship between God and man, character was the product of the energy and struggle of the flesh. This, too, is the conception of human character which is held by the world, and, alas, through false teaching, it is the only one in the minds of many Christians. It is commonly preached that the sum-total of an individual's acts will determine his habits, the sum-total of his habits will determine his character, and the sum-total of his character will determine his destiny. Whatever may have been true under the law, this doctrine is foreign to grace. Destiny is not now determined by self-promoted character; it depends only on the faith which receives the saving grace of God. Heaven's glory will not be a display of human character; it is to be the unveiling of the riches of grace in Christ Jesus. Nor is Christian character a product of the flesh; it is "the fruit of the Spirit." The divine record of all that enters into true Christian character is stated thus: "But the fruit of the Spirit is love, joy, peace, longsuffering, gentleness, goodness, faith, meekness, temperance" (self-control, Gal. 5:22, 23).

These graces are elements of divine character which are never found unless divinely wrought. They are "the fruit of the Spirit." They are never gained by struggle, long or short; they are the immediate experience of every believer who comes into right adjustment with the Spirit. Therefore the way to a victorious life is not by self-development; it is through a "walk in the Spirit." In the context in which the above passage appears, the Apostle also states: "This I say then, Walk in the Spirit [by means of the Spirit], and ye shall not fulfil the lust of the flesh" (5:16). The believer's responsibility is not the *walk*; it is rather that of yieldedness to the Spirit who promotes the walk. When thus yielded, the result is instant and perfect: "Ye shall not fulfil the lust of the flesh." So long as the walk is continued by the power of the Spirit, this spiritual life will be experienced. Should the adjustment to the Spirit cease, the walk must cease, and the flesh will again be manifested.

The New Testament term, "the flesh," indicates the sum-total of what the natural man is—body, soul and spirit. Within this whole, and as a part of it, is the fallen Adamic nature—*sin*. Three means for the control of the sin-nature are taught—two of which are the product of human reason and one the revealed provision of God:

a. *Is the sin-nature controlled by eradication?*

Though this theory is advanced by certain schools of thought it lacks the support of even one passage of Scripture. It is accepted because it seems reasonable, the thought being that if the source of sin is checked, would not the flow cease? Doubtless it would; but God has revealed no such program.

If eradication of the sin-nature were accomplished, there would be no physical death; for physical death is the result of that nature (Rom. 5:12-21); parents who had experienced eradication would, of necessity, generate unfallen children. But if eradication were secured, there would still be the conflict with the world, the flesh (apart from the sin-nature), and the devil; for eradication of these is obviously unscriptural and is not included in the theory itself. As God purposes to deal with the world, the flesh, and the devil, thus He proposes to deal with the sin-nature which is a part of the flesh. The full deliverance is by the overcoming power of the Spirit through the work of Christ on the cross. The work of Christ on the cross secured the judgment of the old nature (Rom. 6:6); but it also secured the judgment of the world (Gal. 6:14), the flesh (Gal. 5:24), and the devil (Col. 2:15). The work of Christ is a divine judgment which has made it righteously possible for God to control the world, the flesh and the devil as they may affect the believer. Within the flesh, and as a part of it, is the sin-nature. This nature is no more subject to eradication than is the world, the flesh, or the devil. The divine plan for the deliverance of the believer from the power of the sin-nature is exactly the same as for the deliverance from the other opposing principles. It is by the overcoming power of the Spirit made possible through the death of Christ.

This provision brings the child of God into moment-by-moment dependence upon his Lord. It drives him to the most intimate relationship with God. Eradication, if it were true, would tend to wean the Christian from Christ in the measure in which it would fit him to get on alone. In the midst of the description of the divine ideal for a spiritual walk, it is said that the victory is due to the fact that the Spirit is lusting against the flesh, therefore, when walking by means of the Spirit, "ye cannot do the things that ye otherwise would" (5:17). It is evident from this passage wherein the highest ideal of life is presented that the flesh is contemplated as being present, but it is under the control of the Spirit.

b. *Is the sin-nature controlled by rules?*

It is proposed by others that the flesh shall be controlled by rules and regulations. The seeming sanction of the Scriptures for this theory is gained by turning to the law; for under the law, the flesh was to be governed by rules. The law-history of 1500 years, however, is sufficient evidence of the failure of this method; yet it seems impossible for many to be delivered from the belief that a spiritual life may be gained by the keeping of rules. It is supposed that the divine ideal has been realized when people have been induced to attempt to regulate their lives by rules.

c. *Is the sin-nature controlled by the Spirit?*

According to the Scriptures, such is the divine plan for the control of the flesh in the believer's life under grace. It provides *all* that God desires or requires in any life, and brings the saved one into the closest fellowship with God, and into constant dependence upon the Spirit. It is the only victory possible for the Christian to experience; for it only is according to the purpose and Word of God.

If the quality of the believer's daily life is to be improved, what steps are to be taken? Will carnality and coldness of heart be corrected by enforcing rules of conduct? When a carnal Christian does not wish to do the will of God, will God be satisfied if that Christian merely complies externally with the law of God? The answer is obvious. God looks on the heart. In the provisions of grace, God proposes to change the desires of the heart and to empower unto the full realization of these God-wrought desires. The law could work no change in the heart, nor can the attempt to keep rules; but the Spirit can change the desires. The law could give no enabling power; but the Spirit can. Therefore it is said: "But if ye be led of the Spirit, ye are not under the law" (Gal. 5:18); and against the "fruit of the Spirit," "there is no law" (Gal. 5:23); again, "For sin shall not have dominion over you: for ye are not under the law, but under grace" (Rom. 6:14).

2. *Christian conduct.*

The manner of the Christian's life, including every activity of the child of God, is described in the Scriptures by the words *walk* and *conversation.* This aspect of the truth is to be distinguished from the believer's character. The *walk* refers to that which is outward; while *character*—"the fruit of the Spirit" —is inward. In point of importance, character is supreme; for out of the abundance of the heart the mouth speaketh. Under grace, God proposes by the Spirit first to create the heavenly motives and desires, and then, by the same Spirit, to empower the life unto the full realization of those desires. While these heavenly desires are said to be "the fruit of the Spirit," the resulting activities are said to be the exercise of a "gift" through the Spirit. A "gift," like the "fruit" of the Spirit, is never a product of the flesh nor any ability within the flesh. The Spirit may choose to use the native ability, but a "gift" is the direct undertaking of the Spirit in and through the human instrument. It is the Spirit doing a work and using the one in whom He dwells to do it. Thus both Christian character and Christian conduct are dependent on the enabling ministration of the Spirit. This divine provision is not merely for crisis-moments in the experience of the Christian; it is for *every* moment, whether it be one of activity or one of rest.

The divine standards for the believer's character and conduct are superhuman. This is reasonable since he is a citizen of heaven. The superhuman manner of life becoming to a heavenly citizen is to be lived by the enabling, supernatural power of the Spirit. The Spirit has taken up His abode in the heart in order that He may undertake this for the child of God, and if He does not accomplish His work, it is because He is hindered by the carnality of an unyielded life. The problem of improvement in the conduct of a Christian is never solved by the application of laws, nor by exhorting and stimulating the flesh; it is only solved by adjustment to the Spirit. When Spirit-filled, the child of God is both *moved* to glorify God in every moment of life, and is *enabled to realize that heavenly ideal.*

There is much said in the Scriptures about the Christian life being a "warfare," a "fight," and a "race." The Christian is to be watchful, steadfast, and unmovable. He is not exhorted to attempt to do what the Spirit alone can do; he is rather to *maintain* the attitude of co-operation with, and yieldedness to, and dependence on, the Spirit.

The grace-manner of life in the Spirit will be lived according to the grace teachings. These teachings, or principles of life, are written both to *prepare* the Christian for an intelligent walk in the Spirit, and to furnish a norm by which he may *compare* his daily life with the divine ideal. The grace teachings are not *laws;* they are *suggestions.* They are not *demands*; they are *beseechings.* They are not followed in order to gain acceptance or favor; they are acknowledged and followed in the glad assurance of present acceptance and completeness in Christ through grace.

There are three laws, or principles, which characterize the teachings of grace concerning the manner of the daily life of the believer:

a. *The perfect law of liberty.*

The child of God is *free.* He has been delivered from every aspect of the law—as a rule of life, as an obligation to make himself acceptable to God, and as a dependence on the impotent flesh. Likewise, he has been delivered from ideals and conventionalities of the world. He is as free in himself as though he had already passed on into heaven. He has been brought into the priceless liberty of grace. Against the spoiling of this liberty the Christian is to contend: "Stand fast therefore in the liberty wherewith Christ hath made us free, and be not entangled again with the yoke of bondage" (Gal. 5:1). The actual experience of contending for the preservation of liberty which is *in Christ Jesus* is foreign to the great mass of nominal Christians. Pressing in on every hand are the false teachings of a law-ridden church, the fleshly ideals of the world and its god, the natural rationalism of the human mind, and the ever-present tendency to depend on self. Against all this, the fact of true liberty in Christ is little known. It is therefore important that the scope and character of Christian liberty be defined, and, in so doing, no aspect of liberty is in view other than the liberty which belongs to the child of God under grace.

The word *liberty* is defined thus: "The state of being exempt from the dominion of others, or from restricting circumstances." It is freedom to do according to one's own preference and choice. It is emancipation. The thought of necessity and servitude is of the law. Grace glories in liberty and freedom.

Is it not imperative that the children of God should be placed within the bounds of reasonable law? *Absolutely No!* The Christian's liberty to do precisely as he chooses is as limitless and perfect as any other aspect of grace. But God has provided a sufficient safeguard which consists in the fact that the divine ideal is first wrought in the heart: "For it is God which worketh in you both to will and to do of his good pleasure" (Phil. 2:13).

In this one passage, the whole divine scheme for the believer's life under grace is crystalized. God can propose *absolute* liberty to the one in whom He is so working that the innermost choice is only that which He wills for him. Having molded the desires of the heart, He can give His child unbounded freedom. There is no other freedom in the world but this. By the inwrought "fruit of the Spirit," God Himself has determined the desires of the heart. The outworking of those desires will be according to His own energizing power.

Thus the character and the daily life of the Christian is wrought on the basis of pure grace. As God

saves and keeps in grace apart from every human assistance and merit, so, in like manner, He proposes to
produce the character and conduct of His child apart
from every assistance or intrusion of the flesh. "Are
ye so foolish? having begun in the Spirit, are ye now
made perfect by the flesh?" (Gal. 3:3). In harmony
with the whole program of divine grace, no other manner of life could be imposed on the believer than the
one in which God alone undertakes and accomplishes.
To be true to His own purposes in grace, He must
not only create the motive and choice of the heart
but He must provide the sufficient power for its execution.

Should it be objected that this is an idealism which
is effective only with a limited company of believers
who are so yielded to God as to be Spirit-filled, and
that the great mass of carnal Christians must be held
by rules, the reply would be that carnal Christians
are no more subject to law than are the spiritual
Christians. God does not countenance the attitude
of the carnal Christian to the extent of providing a
rule of government for him. As He holds only one
issue before the unsaved—the acceptance of Christ as
Saviour—likewise, He holds only one issue before the
carnal Christian. That issue is not, "Will you live
in a way which is in harmony with your carnality?"
It is, rather, "Yield yourselves unto God, as those
that are alive from the dead, and your members as
instruments of righteousness unto God" (Rom. 6:13).

The carnal Christian is *abnormal*. His *position* is
perfect *in Christ*, but in *character* and *conduct* he
violates the most precious principles and provisions
of grace. The divine ideal for the believer's life un-

der grace remains unchangeable. When God is molding the desires of the heart, there is *liberty*. When He is empowering the life, there is *victory*.

Thus it may be seen that grace is not a way of *escaping* obedience to God; it is the only possible way in which true obedience can be secured. The Spirit-filled believer is never abandoned to self-will; he is "inlawed to Christ." God in grace does not lower standards; He proposes and gloriously realizes the very character and conduct of heaven.

b. *The law of expediency.*

Because of the Christian's position and circumstances in the world, the law of personal liberty in Christ is subject to the law of expediency. That which is expedient is to be chosen for two reasons which are stated in the Scriptures: "All things are lawful unto me, but all things are not expedient: all things are lawful for me, but I will not be brought under the power of any"; "All things are lawful for me, but all things are not expedient: all things are lawful for me, but all things edify not" (1 Cor. 6:12; 10:23). Thus it is seen that the law of expediency contemplates the danger to the believer's own life in the matter of personal *habits* or *injury*, and the responsibility to others in the matter of *edification*. Much that he is free to do, so far as his relation to God is concerned, he is not free to do when contemplating his own personal good and the good of others. His manner of life must be adapted to the ignorance and prejudice of men to whom he is a witness for his Lord and whom he would seek to lead to Christ or to build up in the faith. Any sacrifice of personal liberty will be made willingly if Christ thereby may be made known. When considering the law of expediency, one does not ask, "What *harm* is there in this, or that?" He rather seeks to know what is the *good*. In all your precious liberty, "see then that ye walk circumspectly" (Eph. 5:15).

c. *The law of love.*

Again the liberty of the Christian will be qualified by the love which he has for others. The sympathy of the unsaved must be gained and the conscience of the weaker brother must be considered: "But meat commendeth us not to God: for neither, if we eat, are we the better; neither, if we eat not, are we the worse. But take heed lest by any means this liberty of yours become a stumbling block to them that are weak. . . . Wherefore, if meat make my brother to offend, I will eat no flesh while the world standeth, lest I make my brother to offend" (1 Cor. 8:8-13). Liberty is easily set aside by those who would be "all things to all men that by all means" they might save some. The supreme example of the sacrifical principle of grace was manifested by Christ in His death: "He saved others; himself he cannot save" (Mk. 15:31).

Third. *Christ in You the Hope of Glory.*

The word *mystery* as used in the New Testament refers to a sacred secret, or something which was not revealed in the ages past, but is revealed in the present time. The body of truth which has been unfolded in the revelation contained in the mysteries is the present plan and purpose of grace. Among these mysteries are two which are primary and around these the other mysteries are gathered.

1. *Christ the manifestation of God and of the Church.*

That portion of this truth which directly concerns and involves the child of God is regarding Christ as the Head of the Church which is His body, and the believers as "members in particular." This figure speaks of identity. Being *in Christ,* the member of His body partakes of all that the Head has ever been, all that He is now, and all that He will ever be. So, also, being *in Christ,* the member of His body partakes of all that Christ has ever done, of all that He is doing, and all that He will ever do. No human mind is able to grasp this revelation. Its inexhaustible riches will occupy the heart throughout the ages to come.

In the letter to the Colossians the Apostle Paul, by the Spirit, unfolds the glory of Christ. He presents Christ as the manifestation of God, the One in whom all divine purposes center, and the One in whom, by the mystery of unity, the saved one is forever complete. He writes of the "mystery of God" which is Christ (2:2). From all Scripture it may be discovered that Christ is both the manifestation of God and the manifestation of the saints who are *in Him.* What God is, may be seen in Christ. So, likewise, what the saved one is may be seen in Christ. The Son of God is not only the Mediator between God and man and the Saviour of the lost; He is the manifestation of all that God is, and, at the same time, the manifestation of all that the believer is *in Him.* Christ has brought

God to man, and He has brought man to God. **Man** now sees God *in Christ,* and God now sees saved men *in Christ.*

To the Christian, Christ is not only a position; He is also a possession. Through the marvels of divine grace, in the reckoning of God, whatever Christ is, the Christian is *in Christ,*—"Ye in me."

2. *The indwelling Christ.*

Accordingly, the second primary sacred secret is that of the indwelling Christ,—"I in you."

Turning again to the Colossian Epistle, we read: "To whom God would make known what is the riches of the glory of this mystery among the Gentiles; which is Christ in you, the hope of glory" (1:27).

Being *in Christ,* is a position which can have no corresponding experience. This is not true of the mystery of the indwelling Christ. His presence may be discerned and thus become an assurance and guaranty of every position and possession *in Christ.* The believer's heavenly glories will be unveiled when the Lord returns to receive His own: "For ye are dead [ye died], and your life is hid with Christ in God. When Christ, who is our life, shall appear, then shall ye also appear with him in glory" (Col. 3:3, 4). Not only is Christ Himself the "hope of glory," but, according to His own promise (John 14:1-3), that moment in which He will appear is a "blessed hope." The presence of "Christ in you" is the imperishable "hope of glory."

"Amen. Even so, come, Lord Jesus."

Both for want of space and that the thread of truth might not be broken, there has been but little mention in this section of the truth that these great features and properties of grace, which grow out of the fact that Christ is now the sphere of the believer's life, are not found, even to the slightest degree, in either the law of Moses or the kingdom teachings. These wonderful accomplishments in grace are what differentiate Christianity from Judaism. One is of the old creation with its earthly purpose and promise; the other is of the new creation with its heavenly glories. The believer could not be under law; he is "inlawed to Christ." He has been saved out of the world and is no longer a partaker of its past, its present, or its future. Its past is a record of sin and death; its present is a record of confusion under the permitted rule of "the god of this world"; and the future will be a record of judgment. Law is adapted to the earth. It is the divine method of dealing with the people of the earth whether it be in the age which is past, or in the age which is to come.

The child of God has been delivered from every aspect of the law. The code of rules contained in the law has been superseded by the injunctions and beseechings of grace. The legal necessity of becoming accepted of God by human merit, has been superseded by the divine accomplishment through grace wherein the Christian is already accepted and safe in Christ forever. And possessing the presence of God through the indwelling Spirit, the child of God is saved from that struggle and defeat of the flesh which characterized the law and because of which defeat, the law became a curse and an instrument of death.

In place of the law there is grace.

In place of condemnation there is salvation.

In place of death there is life.

In place of ruin in Adam there is resurrection in Christ.

In place of bondage there is liberty.

In place of defeat there is victory.

In place of hell there is heaven.

"But the God of all grace, who hath called us unto his eternal glory by Christ Jesus, after that ye have suffered a while, make you perfect, establish, strengthen, settle you. To him be glory and dominion for ever and ever. Amen."

CHAPTER V

CONCLUSION AND APPEAL

G RACE, more than any other single word, is the expression of the sum-total of all that enters into Christianity. The various divine undertakings in grace have been stated in these pages and it has been seen that, through the work of Christ on the cross and through the divine purposes and decrees for this dispensation, it is through grace that hell-deserving sinners are saved, it is through grace that they are preserved and are to be presented like Christ in glory, and it is "under grace" that the saved one now lives. Being under grace, he is "dead" to the law, and "delivered" from the law, whether the law is conceived of as being a rule of life, an obligation to establish merit before God, or a reliance upon the energy of the flesh.

On the other hand, the Christian is in no wise an *outlaw*. Since he is *in Christ* as the new sphere of both his standing and his state, he is now *inlawed* to Christ and is therefore under the governing principles of grace. These principles provide both an explicit and complete rule of conduct which is superhuman, and the enabling power of the indwelling Spirit which is supernatural. This manner of life which is to be lived in the power of the Spirit is addressed to, and designed for, the people of the new creation *in Christ*.

These teachings of grace may be defined as, that superhuman rule of life which grows out of acceptance with God and which is first wrought in the heart and then achieved by the enabling power of the Spirit. Grace makes all conformity to the will of God to be *voluntary*. Christian conduct and service must arise from *within* and be the expression of a free choice. Only such action is acceptable to God since it alone is in harmony with the new facts of relationship under grace. By faith in Christ the believer is instantly made *complete* in Him and the possessor of every spiritual blessing, the Spirit is given to indwell him, and he is "made accepted" in the Beloved. The Christian's life must be keyed to these new facts, and when this new relationship under grace is really comprehended, it is seen that there remains no ground for legality in any form whatsoever.

The people who are now saved by grace are of a new order of beings. They are a new *creation*. The people of the old creation are ruined by sin; the people of the new creation are renewed by the Spirit. The people of the old creation are wholly lost; the people of the new creation are perfectly saved. The people of the old creation are doomed forever; the people of the new creation are entirely safe *in Christ Jesus*. The people of the old creation have always failed to realize the holy will of God in their daily lives; the people of the new creation may now live well-pleasing to God by the new provisions in grace. They may know unbroken victory even on the plane of the high ideals and standards of heaven.

A clear understanding of the doctrines of grace will result in a discrimination between the transforming accomplishments of divine power through grace on the one hand, and the corresponding consistent manner of life which grows out of the salvation on the other hand. The relative importance of these two aspects of grace is also revealed.

Failure on the part of religious leaders to recognize the all important, supernatural salvation which is in Christ for all who *believe*, is largely responsible for the present tendency to treat Christianity as though it is merely an ethical system, and as though its standards of living were designed of God to be applied to a Christ-rejecting world. The unregenerate can hardly be expected to see more in Christianity than its ethical teachings, but the people of God should be led on to the full knowledge of the great realities in grace.

For those who attempt to explain the truth of God to others, there is need of a constant consideration of the measureless responsibility which accompanies any presentation of the Gospel. No amount of attention or painstaking study will be too great for the adequate preparation of a Gospel messenger. In the light of eternal issues it would be better that a tongue should be stilled in death rather than to voice misstatements concerning the way of salvation through Christ. Dealing with the destiny of men is a responsibility as limitless as eternity to which they hasten. The law of the state demands that a medical doctor who proposes to deal with the temporal, physical ills of man shall be fully educated for his task, subject to the closest examination by the government, and shall be held under severe legal penalty for any malpractice. All this is most reasonable and commendable; but how much greater is the responsibility of the person who traffics in those issues which determine the destiny of the soul! The state could not assume to educate, examine, and, in turn, punish the failure of those who assume to preach the Gospel to dying men. No human authority is capable of such action and no human sentence would be a proper penalty for the damage done through such failure. God alone must be the judge.

Three passages when taken together state the divine appeal and warning: "And hath given to us the ministry of reconciliation"; therefore, "Study to shew thyself approved unto God, a workman that needeth not to be ashamed, rightly dividing the word of truth"; for, "Though we, or an angel from heaven, preach any other gospel unto you than that which we have preached unto you, let him be accursed. As we said before, so say I now again, If any man preach any other gospel unto you than that ye have received, let him be accursed" (2 Cor. 5:18; 2 Tim. 2:15; Gal. 1:8, 9). The order and force of this truth needs no comment.

It is deplorable that Christian sentiment is not aroused to greater appreciation of the responsibility which is assumed by those who dare to preach, or to direct the steps of the lost. Good intentions and zeal cannot be substituted for the accurate knowledge of the exact facts which enter into the divine way of salvation by grace alone. The commission is given to every Christian and with it both the appeal for painstaking study, and the warning as to the terrible consequences for the misstatement of the Gospel.

Pause, reader, and consider! Are you attempting to explain the Gospel to others without the exact knowledge of your theme? Would you choose to take a remedy which had been compounded by a blind druggist? Are you persisting in error because of indolence, carelessness, or mere theological prejudice? Failure to state accurately the Gospel of saving grace may result in the damnation of the misguided, and the meriting, at least, of the anathema of God on the part of the blind guide. After due consideration, no sane person will treat these facts lightly.

Again, the daily life and service of the one who is alive unto God must be recognized as assuming infinite proportions when its issues are seen. Nothing short of that manner of life which is normal under grace glorifies God. Nothing short of this will be fruit-bearing with its eternal rewards. Nothing short of this will result in that personal experience of overflowing love, joy, and peace, without which the empty heart remains as a living witness *against* the truth of God. The importance of a daily life lived in the full measure of divine blessing provided under grace is likewise beyond human estimation.

"Ye therefore, beloved, seeing ye know these things before, beware lest ye also, being led away with the error of the wicked, fall from your own steadfastness. But grow in grace, and in the knowledge of our Lord and Saviour Jesus Christ. To him be glory now and for ever. Amen."

THE END

INDEX OF SUBJECTS

Index

Index

INDEX OF SCRIPTURE
TEXTS

Index   369

Index